aDefHELPDESK 4

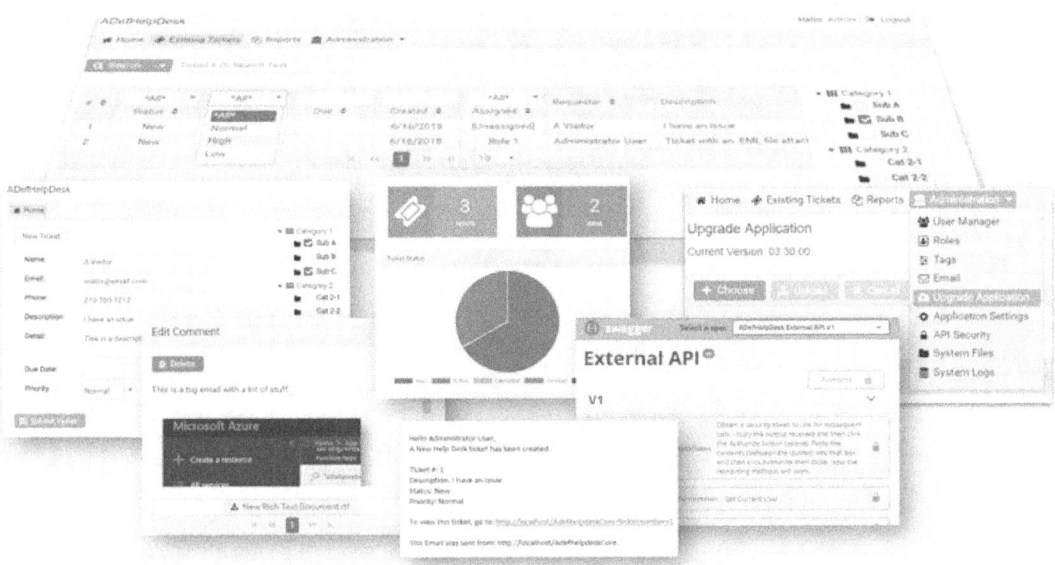

How to install, operate, and extend this popular help desk ticketing open source .Net Core Angular application

Michael Washington

www.ADefHelpDesk.com

ADefHelpDesk 4

ADefHelpDesk 4

How to install, operate, and extend this popular help desk ticketing open source .Net Core Angular application

Copyright 2019
Published By
ADefHelpDesk
http://www.ADefHelpDesk.com

Copyright

Copyright © 2019 by Michael Washington.

Cover and internal design © Michael Washington.

All rights reserved. No part of this book may be reproduced in any form or by any electronic or mechanical means including information storage and retrieval systems – except in the case of brief quotations in articles or reviews – without the permission in writing from its publisher, ADefHelpDesk.com.

All brand names and product names used in this book are trademarks, registered trademarks, or trade names of their respective holders. We are not associated with any product or vendor in this book.

Proofreading by Peter J. Francis,
hgpublishing@gmail.com
www.hgpublishing.com

Table of Contents

Michael Washington 1
Copyright 3
Table of Contents 4
Dedication 9
Preface 10
    Requirements 10
Chapter 1: Why I created ADefHelpDesk 11
    The Best Help Desk Program Possible 11
    A Help Desk Handles Issues 11
    Customizing the Help Desk Ticket 12
    ADefHelpDesk provides these solutions: 13
Chapter 2: Installing and Upgrading 14
    Windows and Windows Server 14
        Requirements: 14
        Set-Up (Configure Windows IIS Server and .Net Core 2.1+): 14
        Set Up SQL Server 14
        Windows IIS Web Server Set-up 16
        Deploy The Code 22
        Install Wizard 23
    Microsoft Azure 30
        Requirements: 30
        Set Up Azure SQL Database 30
        Deploy The Code 41

- Set Up Azure Storage 52
- Upgrading 55
- Chapter 3: Using ADefHelpDesk 61
  - Creating and Updating Account and Password 61
    - Account Registration 62
    - Logging In 67
    - Updating Passwords and Account Information 68
    - Logging Out 70
  - Creating a Help Desk Ticket 70
    - Confirmation Emails 76
    - Attaching Files 78
  - Search Existing Tickets 79
    - Clearing The Search 81
    - Paging Options 82
    - Selecting A Help Desk Ticket 83
  - Updating Existing Tickets 84
    - Ticket Editing By Ticket Requestors 85
    - Editing Tickets By Administrators 90
    - Add and Edit Comments 93
    - Add and Edit Work Items 95
    - Edit Tags 97
    - View Logs 98
- Chapter 4: Administration 99
  - Creating a Ticket for a User 99
  - Assigning Tickets to Groups 103

ADefHelpDesk 4

      Creating Roles 104

      Assigning Users To Groups... 107

      Assigning Help Desk Tickets To Roles... 111

   Reports..112

Chapter 5: Administration Settings 115

   Application Settings 115

      File System Settings 117

      User Registration Settings 118

   User Manager 118

      Role Management 122

   Roles 124

   Tags 127

      Creating Tags... 128

      Editing Tags / Reordering Tags... 129

      Deleting Tags... 130

   Email Settings.. 131

      SMTP Authentication 133

      Send Test Email Button 133

   Upgrade Application 134

   API Security(Swagger Rest API).. 134

      Using The Swagger End Point 139

      Consuming The Swagger API Definition For Custom Applications 147

   Systems Files 149

      Updating Templates 151

   System Logs 152

      Type of Logs.. 152

  Paging Options 153
Chapter 6: Integrations 154
 Creating a .Net Core Web Application to Create a Ticket 154
  Create The Application..158
  Load Application Settings 161
  Get The JSON Web Token (JWT) (Authentication Token).........166
  Retrieve The Current User..176
  Create A Help Desk Ticket...182
  DTOStatus.cs...185
  DTOTask.cs 185
  DTOTaskDetail.cs 186
  Upload A File 197
  Advantages Of A REST API 201
 Creating an Azure Function to Retrieve Emails and Create Tickets 202
  Create The Application..206
  Add MailKit...213
  Add The Model Code 214
  DTOApiToken...215
  DTOStatus 216
  DTOTask 217
  DTOTaskDetail 218
  Add The Extension Code..218
  Get The Authentication Token 221
  Create The Help Desk Ticket 223
  The Main Code 227

    Run The Project 230
  Creating a Bot to Search Help Desk Tickets 234
    Requirements 236
    Create The Application 240
    Connect Using The Bot Framework Emulator 242
    Add The NuGet Package 246
    Add The Models 248
    CustomSettings.cs 249
    DTOApiToken.cs 249
    DTOSearchParameters.cs 250
    DTOTask.cs 251
    DTOTaskDetail.cs 252
    DTOTaskList.cs 252
    Add and Load Settings 253
    Create The Bot Flow 256
    Create The Bot Code 261
    Add The ADefHelpDesk Methods 264
    Create the MainDialog 268

Chapter 7: Technical 273
  Class Diagram 273
  Data Dictionary 273
  Creating An Install or Upgrade Package 285
    To Make an "Upgrade" Package: 286
About the Author 288

Dedication

As always, for Valerie and Zachary.

Preface

Requirements

To install **ADefHelpDesk**, the following are required:

- Microsoft Windows 7 (or higher) or Microsoft Widows Server 2008 R2 (or higher)
- SQL Server 2012 (or higher): https://www.microsoft.com/en-us/sql-server/sql-server-downloads
- Recommended environment for running **ADefHelpDesk** is **Microsoft Azure**

Chapter 1: Why I created ADefHelpDesk

I had a need for a Help Desk / Support Desk / Ticket Tracker.

I decided to create one.

I decided that a Help Desk module should be the best Support Desk program possible and, just as importantly, not be anything else. A Help Desk program should be easy to configure and easy to use because people may have to use the program all day every working day.

ADefHelpDesk implements all the standard features of a conventional Help Desk program and introduces unlimited nested Tags and easy-to-use search to provide for most customization needs.

In addition, **ADefHelpDesk** features a full REST-based API that exposes all the functionality to allow you to incorporate it with any external application.

The Best Help Desk Program Possible

A Help Desk should allow you to handle issues that you need to resolve. That's it. Yes, it could do "other things" but those "other things" start to stray into other areas such as CRM (customer relationship management). CRM tracks your associations with current and prospective customers. "Prospective customers" means a customer who may not necessarily want to have any interaction with you. A Help Desk is only for people who do want you to do something, and they may not even be customers.

A Help Desk Handles Issues

Let's call a Help Desk issue a Ticket. This is the life of a Ticket:

- **Take a New Ticket** - This can be a visitor entering a new Ticket on the website or a Support Desk employee entering a Ticket while on the phone with a Requestor.
- **Route Ticket** -A Ticket needs to be assigned to someone. With **ADefHelpDesk,** a Ticket is always assigned to a group. One or more people can be members of a group.
- **Work on Ticket** - When a Ticket is assigned to a group, it is important to capture what work was done. You also want to capture communication with the Requestor.
- **Resolve the Ticket** – How do you know when the work is complete? Is the Status set to Closed or Resolved? Do you enter a date in the Completed Date field? **ADefHelpDesk** lets you decide. The program does not dictate how you should behave.

Customizing the Help Desk Ticket

A Help Desk Ticket that needs to accomplish the tasks outlined above usually requires the following fields: Status, Requestor, Assigned Group, and Comments (with file attachments).

In addition, the following fields are standard on most Help Desk applications: Priority, Due Date, Estimated Hours, Start Date, and Complete Date.

The question that arises is, "How do we capture important custom information such as cost center and billing type?" Most Help Desk applications allow you to define custom fields that will appear on the Help Desk Ticket. The problems that this can cause are:

- The Help Desk becomes difficult to configure. What if you don't set it up right?
- If options are added and later removed, how will you find Tickets in the system?
- The screen becomes large, and users frequently have to scroll the page just to look at a Ticket.

ADefHelpDesk provides these solutions:

- **Nested Categories** – Unlimited levels of nested categories allow for hundreds of categories to be easily grouped and understood. With **ADefHelpDesk,** a Ticket can be tagged with an unlimited number of categories that are determined by the Administrator. Go ahead and create a category and then move it to another position. The Tickets don't lose their association. If you delete a category, you can still find the Tickets with the full-text search.
- **Full-Text Search** – If you enter "Cost Center: 1245" you will be able to find all Tickets with that entered in any description field.

What I set out to accomplish was to create a program that you can just install and enter Tickets in, without any configuration. The other features, such as nested tags, unlimited file attachments, unlimited assignment groups, and more, can be discovered by you as you need them.

ADefHelpDesk 4

Chapter 2: Installing and Upgrading

- Recommended environment for **ADefHelpDesk** is **Microsoft Azure**.
- You can upgrade any version of **ADefHelpDesk** *prior* to version **03.00.00** by pointing to the previous database connection during the installation process (in the **Installation Wizard**).

Windows and Windows Server

Requirements:

To install **ADefHelpDesk**, the following are required:

- Microsoft Windows 7 (or higher) or Microsoft Widows Server 2008 R2 (or higher)
- SQL Server 2012 (or higher): https://www.microsoft.com/en-us/sql-server/sql-server-downloads

Set-Up (Configure Windows IIS Server and .Net Core 2.1+):

- **IIS configuration:** https://docs.microsoft.com/en-us/aspnet/core/host-and-deploy/iis/?view=aspnetcore-2.1#iis-configuration
- **Install the .NET Core Hosting Bundle:** https://docs.microsoft.com/en-us/aspnet/core/host-and-deploy/iis/?view=aspnetcore-2.1#install-the-net-core-hosting-bundle

Set Up SQL Server

Open **Microsoft SQL Server Management Studio** and connect to **SQL Server** (2008 or higher).

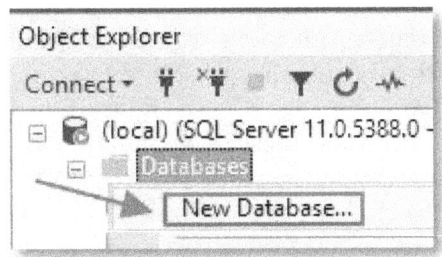

In **SQL Server,** create a **new database**.

For help creating a new database see: https://docs.microsoft.com/en-us/sql/relational-databases/databases/create-a-database?view=sql-server-2017

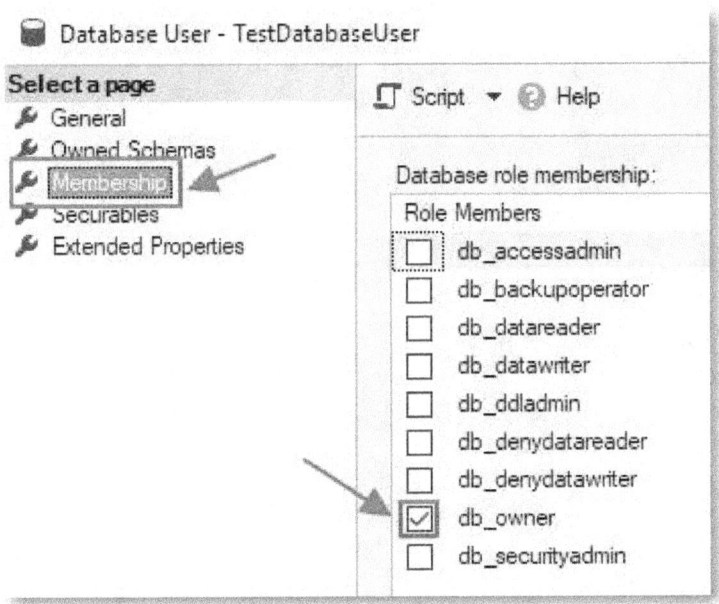

Create a **new user** or assign an **existing user** to the database and provide them with **db_owner** permission to the database.

ADefHelpDesk 4

For help assigning a user to a database see: https://docs.microsoft.com/en-us/sql/relational-databases/security/authentication-access/create-a-database-user?view=sql-server-2017

Important: Note the **username** and **password** of the account you created and the **location** of the **database server** and the **name** of the **database** you created. You will need this information in the set-up wizard in later steps.

Windows IIS Web Server Set-up

In Windows **open IIS Manager**.

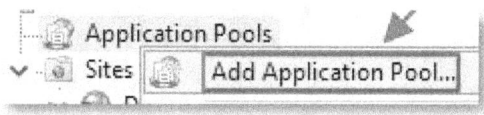

Select the **Application Pools** node.

Right-click on it and select **Add Application Pool**.

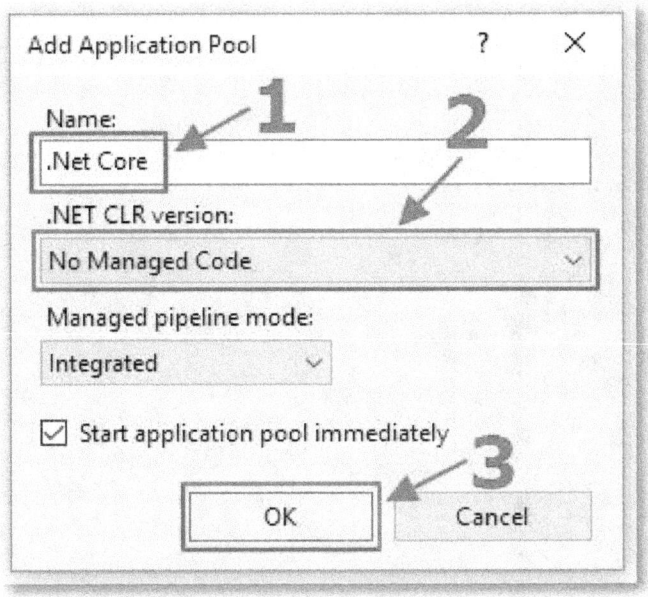

Create an **Application Pool** that has **No Managed Code** selected as the **.NET CLR version**.

ADefHelpDesk 4

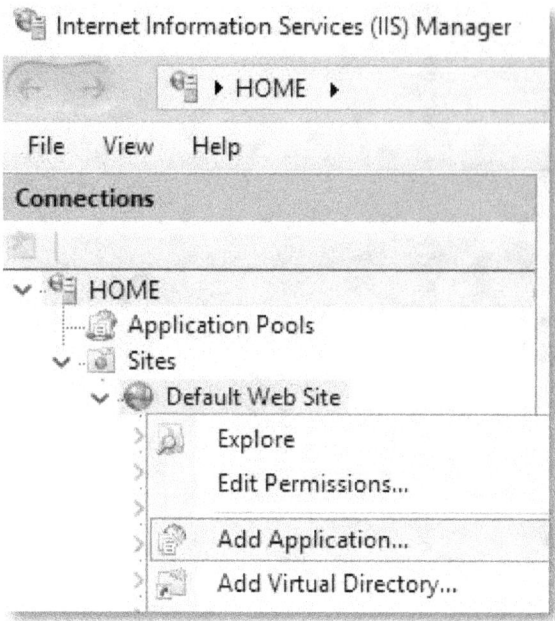

Create a new website.

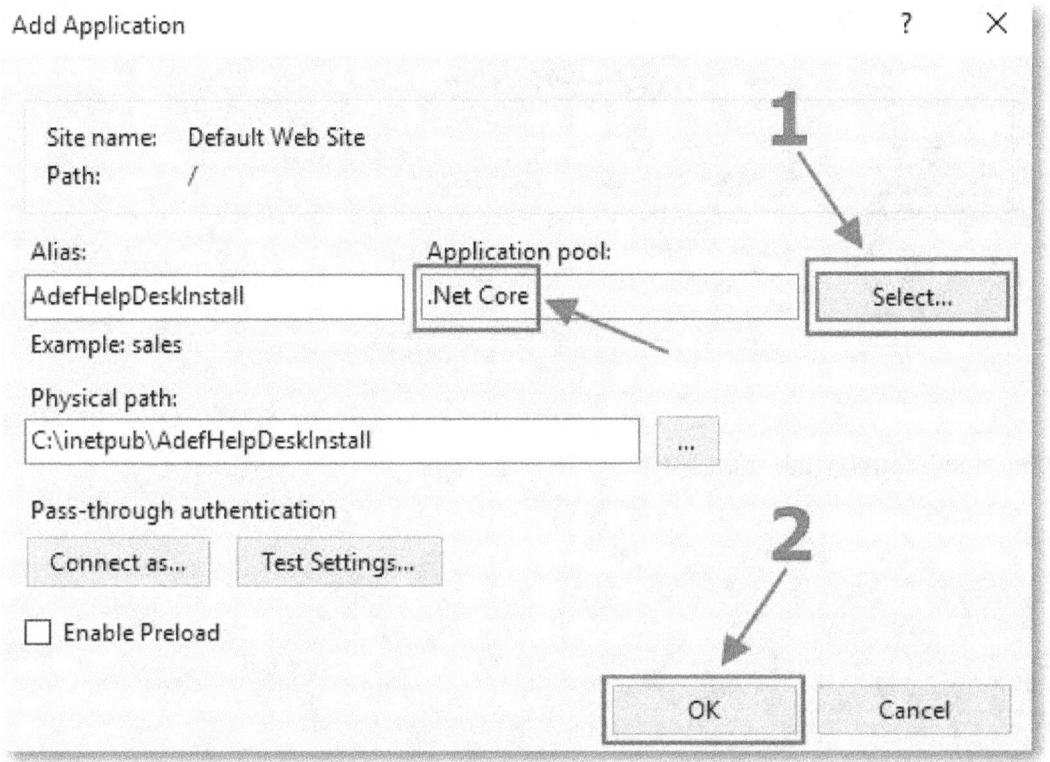

Ensure that you select the application pool you created for the **Application pool**.

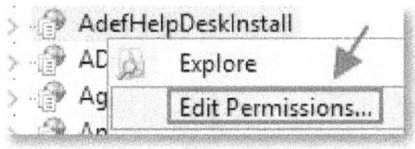

Right-click on the web application in **IIS** and select **Edit Permissions**.

ADefHelpDesk 4

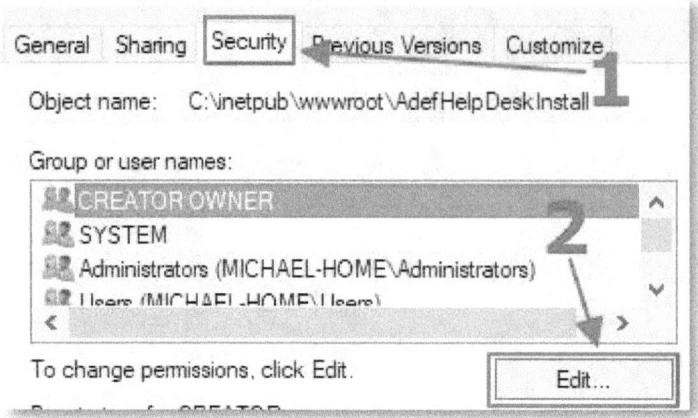

Select the **Security** tab then **Edit**.

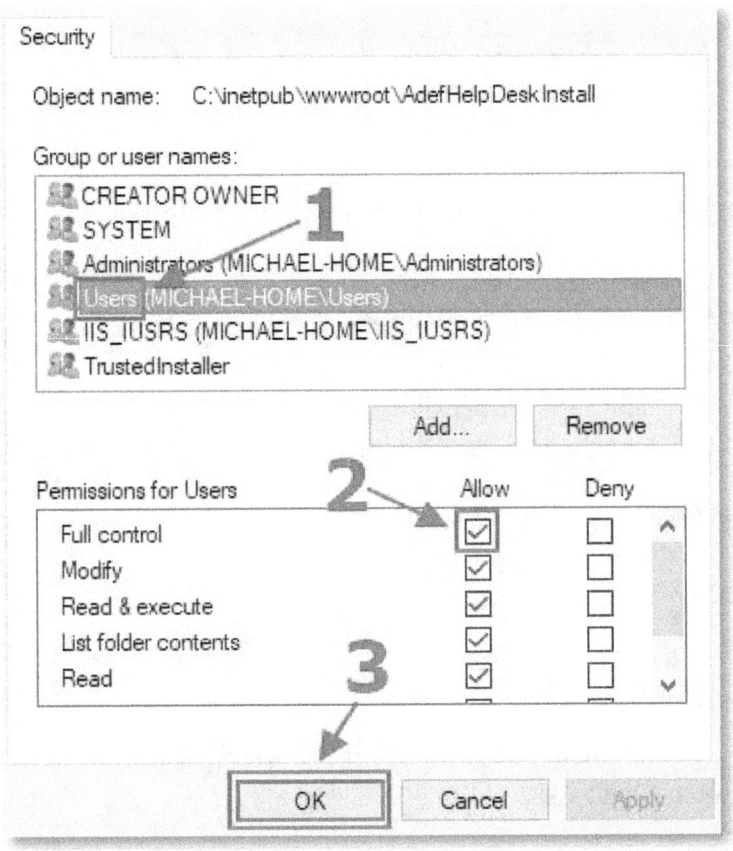

Select the **Users**, then **Full control**, then click **OK**.

Click **OK** to close the previous dialog box.

For help creating a **.Net Core IIS website** see: https://docs.microsoft.com/en-us/aspnet/core/host-and-deploy/iis/?view=aspnetcore-2.1#create-the-iis-site

ADefHelpDesk 4

Deploy The Code

Download the installation *_InstallPackage.zip* file from the **ADefHelpDesk** downloads page (http://ADefHelpDesk.com/Download.aspx).

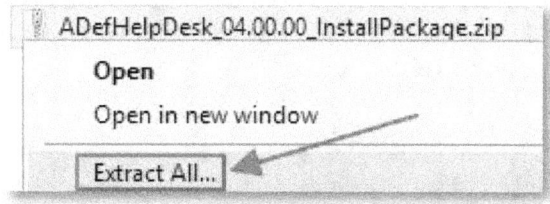

Unzip the **ADefHelpDesk installation** .zip file.

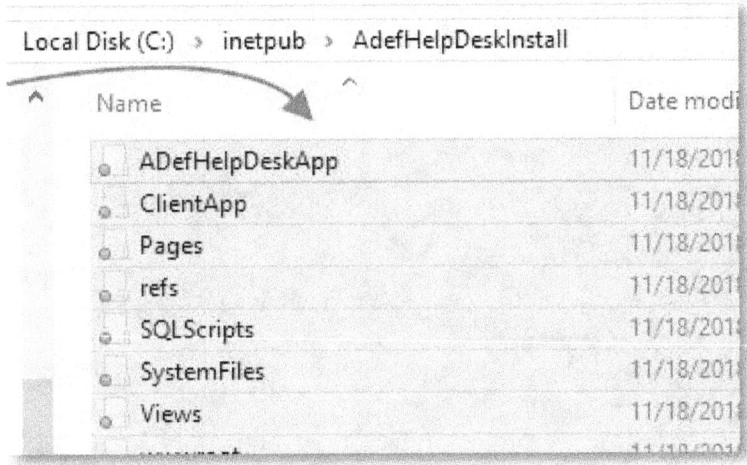

Copy all the files to the location of the **Physical path** of the web site you created in **IIS**.

Install Wizard

Navigate to the website in your web browser…

Note: For the best installation experience, use the **Google Chrome** web browser.

ADefHelpDesk 4

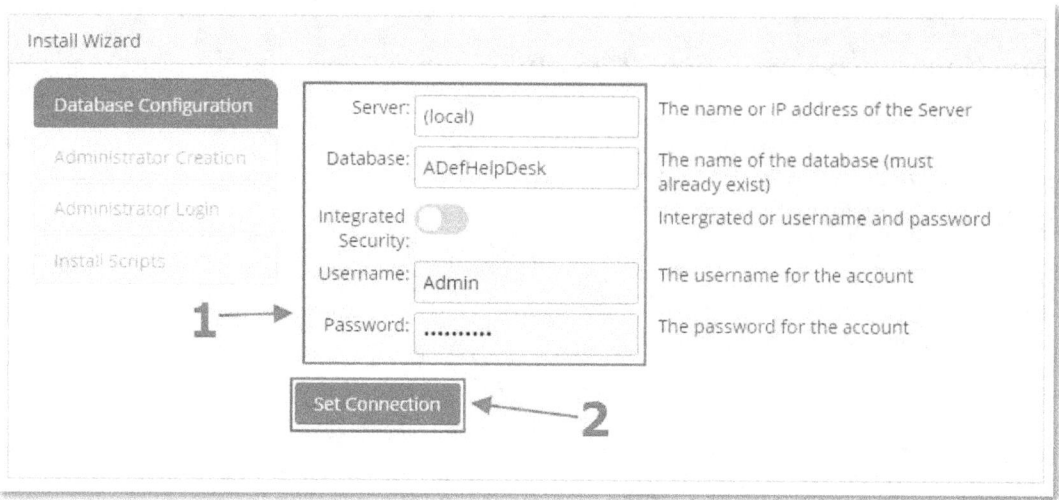

You will see the **Installation Wizard**.

Fill in the information to connect to the database and click the **Set Connection** button.

If you get an error instead, see this page for help to enable the logs to diagnose the error: https://docs.microsoft.com/en-us/aspnet/core/host-and-deploy/iis/troubleshoot?view=aspnetcore-2.1#aspnet-core-module-stdout-log. The problem is usually a *permissions* problem.

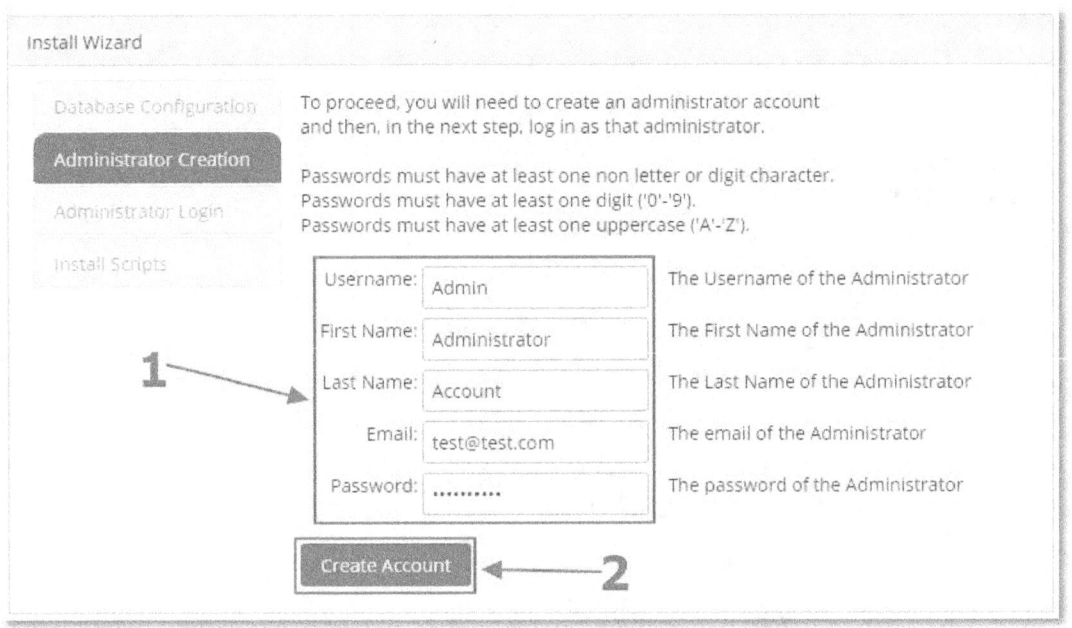

Enter the information for an **Administrator account** that you want the application to create for you.

Note: Ensure the **Password** entered is a strong password (a popup box will display to indicate when the password is considered strong).

Click the **Create Account** button.

ADefHelpDesk 4

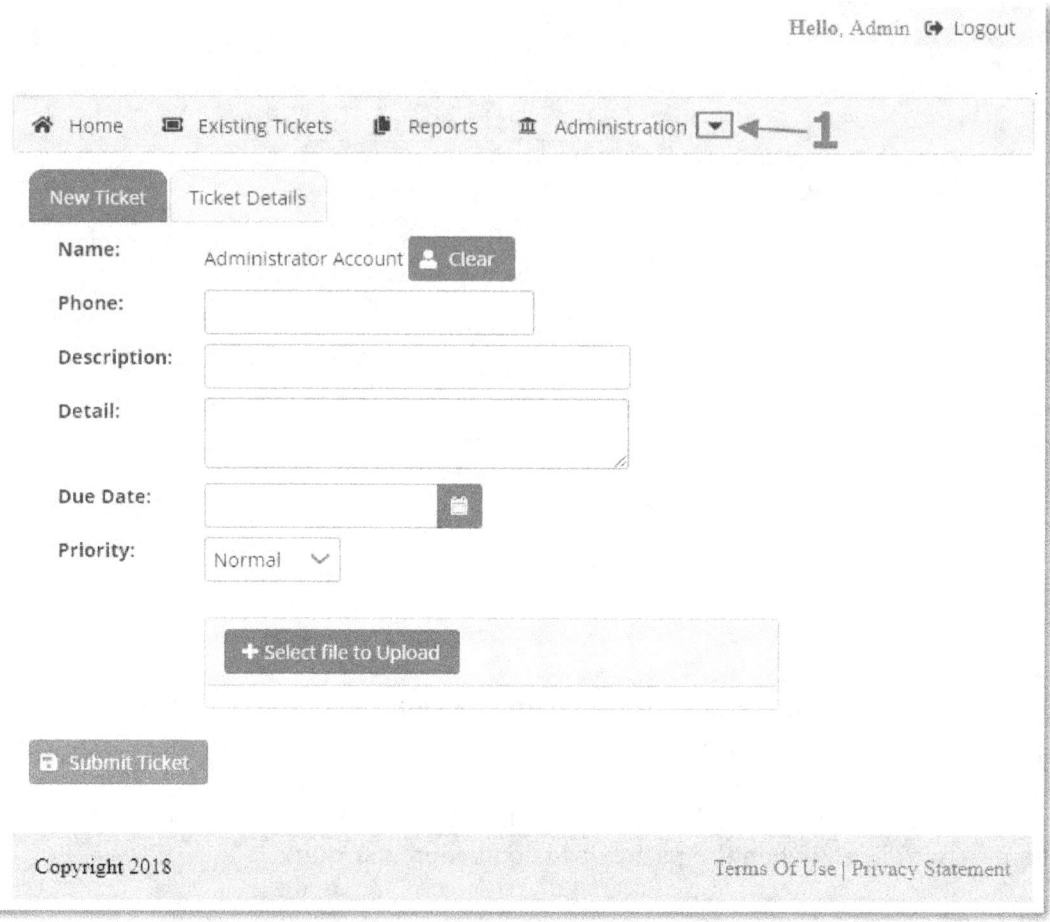

After it is set up you will be automatically logged in as the **Super User**.

Click the **Administration** link.

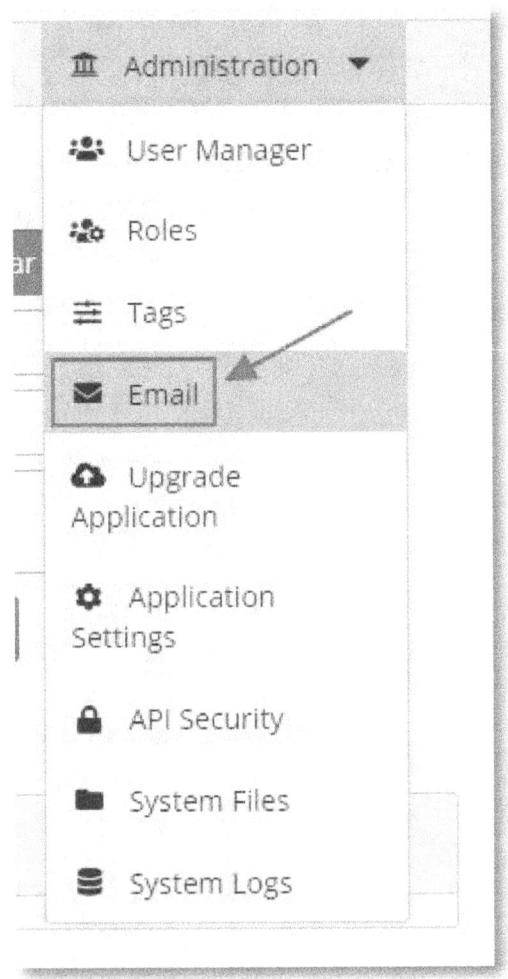

In **Administration**, click **Email**

ADefHelpDesk 4

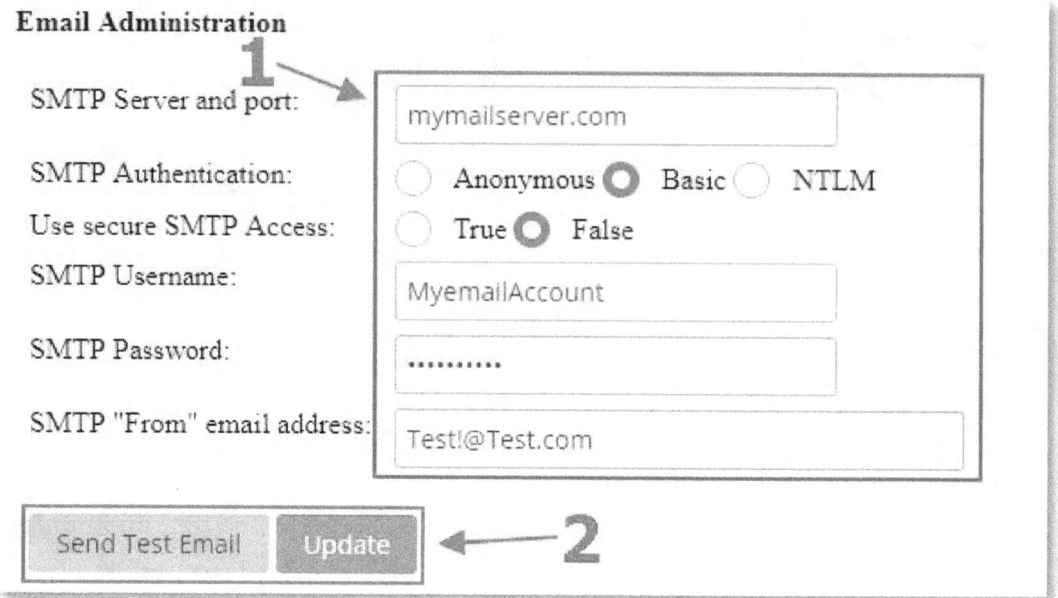

Set-up the email settings.

To test the settings, click **Send Test Email**.

When complete, click the **Update** button to save the settings.

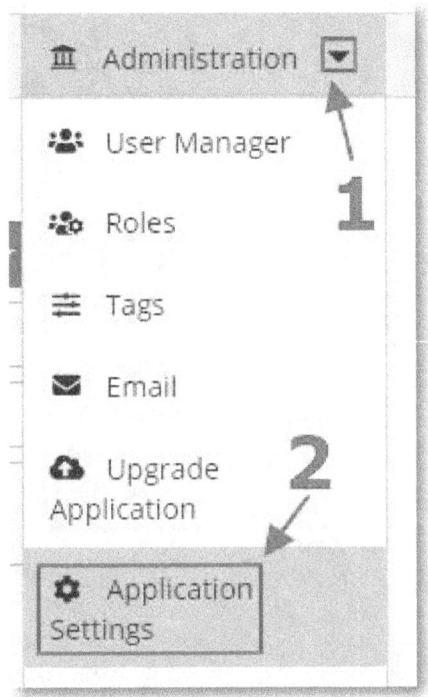

Select **Administration** then **Application Settings**.

ADefHelpDesk 4

Application Settings

Application Name:	ADefHelpDesk
File Storage Type:	File System
File Upload Path:	C:\inetpub\wwwroot\AdefHelpDeskInstall\w
File Upload Permission:	Administrator
Allow User Registration:	True
Verified Registration:	True
Application GUID:	1BC36123-8E54-475B-AD0D-8F810B9C83C8

Set the **file upload** and **user registration** options and click the **Save** button.

ADefHelpDesk is now set-up

Microsoft Azure

Requirements:

- A **Microsoft Azure Account** (you can create one at this link: https://azure.microsoft.com/en-us/free/

Set Up Azure SQL Database

Log into the **Microsoft Azure** portal at: https://portal.azure.com

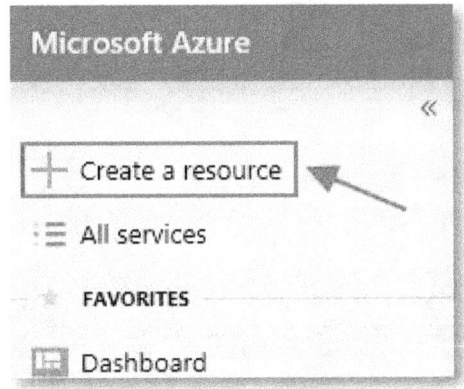

Click **Create a resource**.

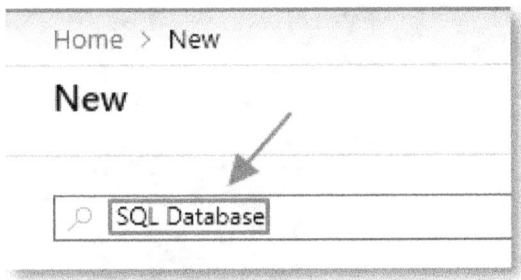

Enter **SQL Database** and press the **Enter** key to initiate a search.

ADefHelpDesk 4

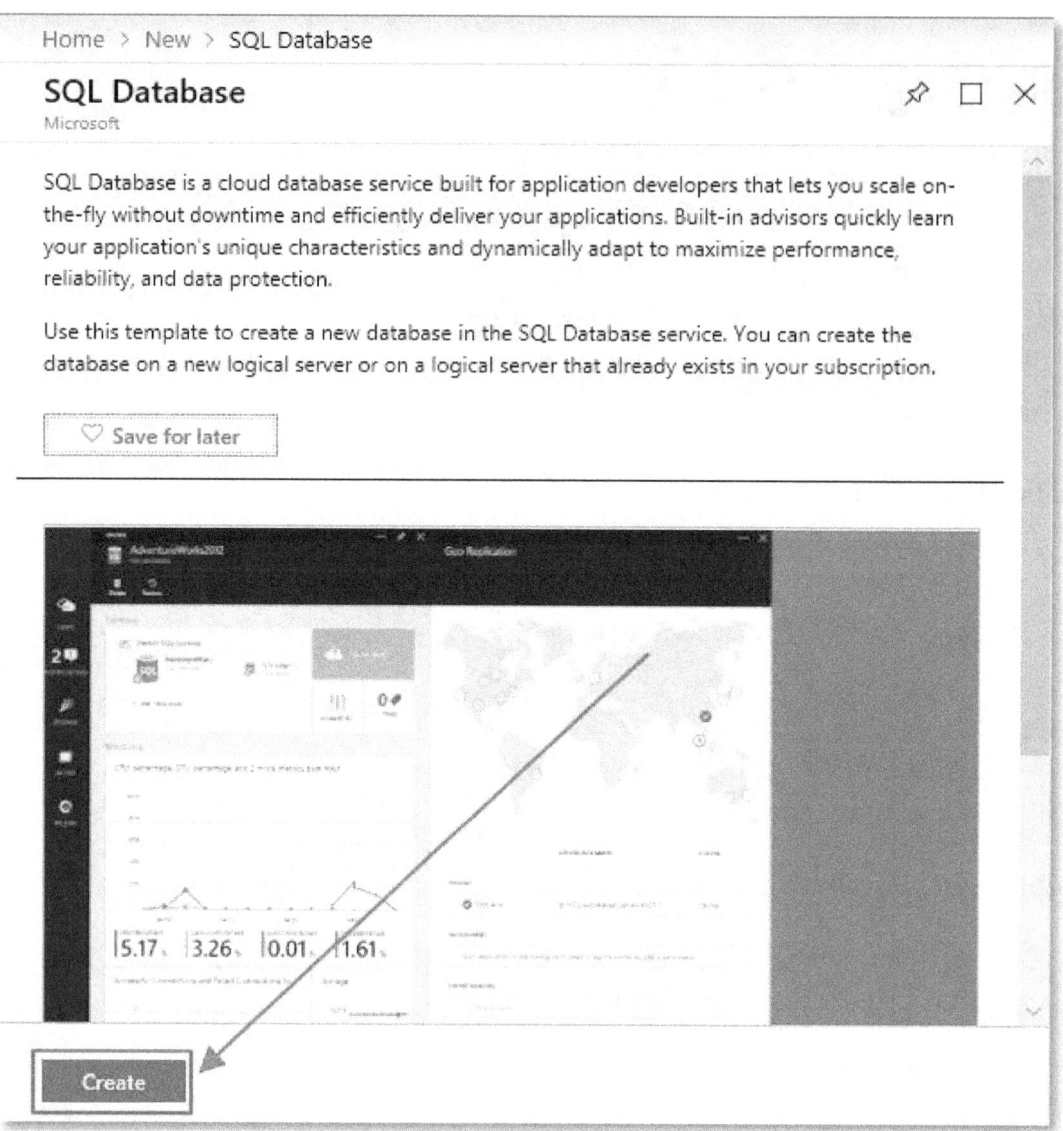

Click the **Create** button.

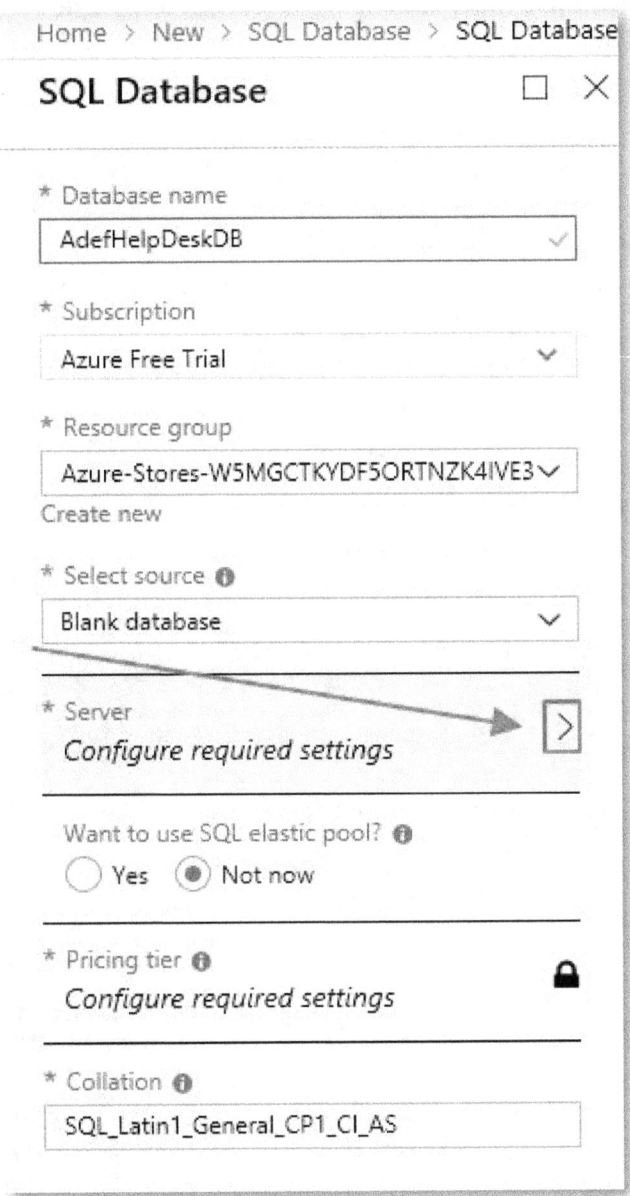

Fill in the required fields and click the arrow next to **Server**.

ADefHelpDesk 4

Note: You will need to note the **Database name** to use in the **ADefHelpDesk Installation Wizard** in the later steps.

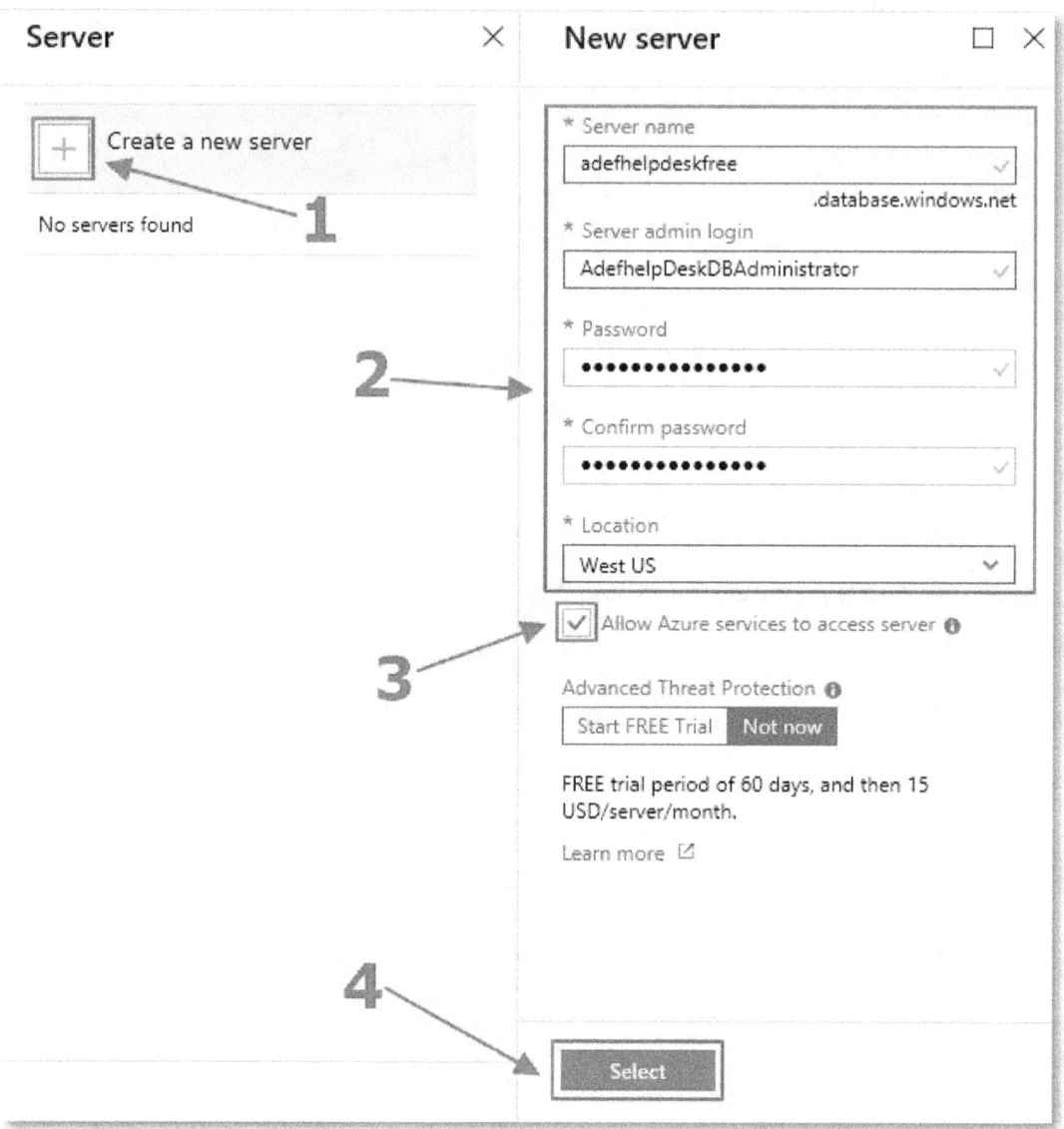

If you have an existing **Azure SQL Server** to host the database, you can select it at this point.

Otherwise, fill in the information and click the **Select** button.

Note: You will need to note the server name (including the **.database.windows.net** part), the **username,** and the **password** to use in the **ADefHelpDesk Installation Wizard** in the later steps.

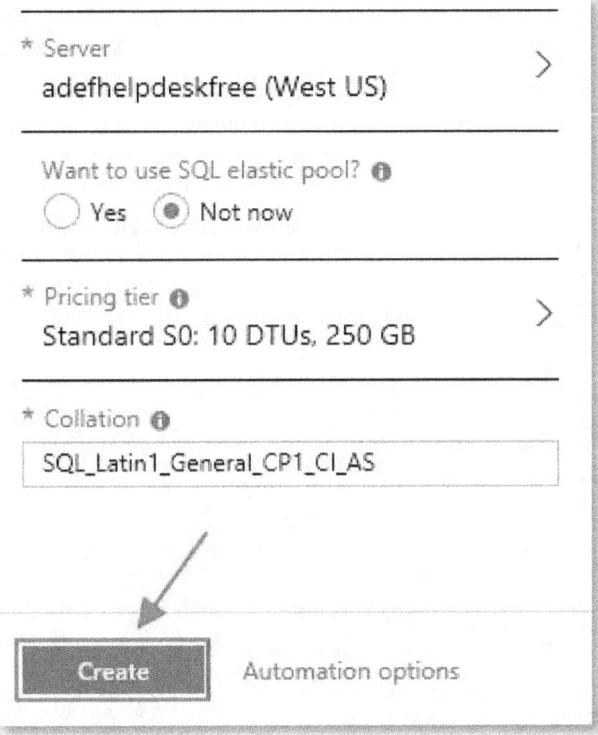

This will return you to the main **SQL Server** blade.

Click the **Create** button.

Set Up The Azure Website

ADefHelpDesk 4

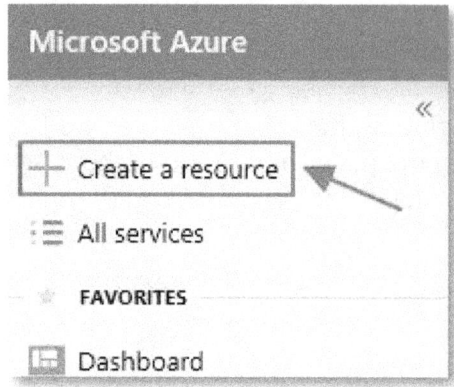

Select **Create a resource**.

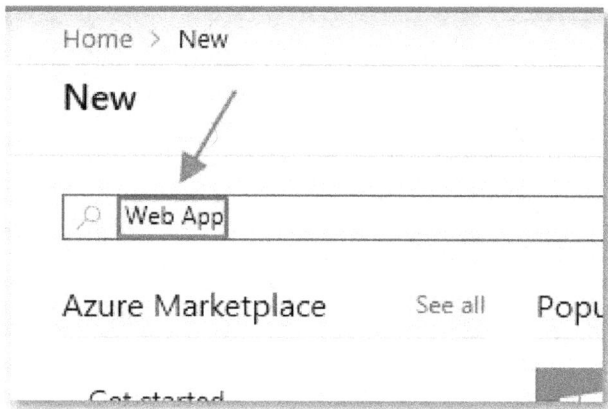

Enter **Web App** and press the **Enter** key to initiate a search.

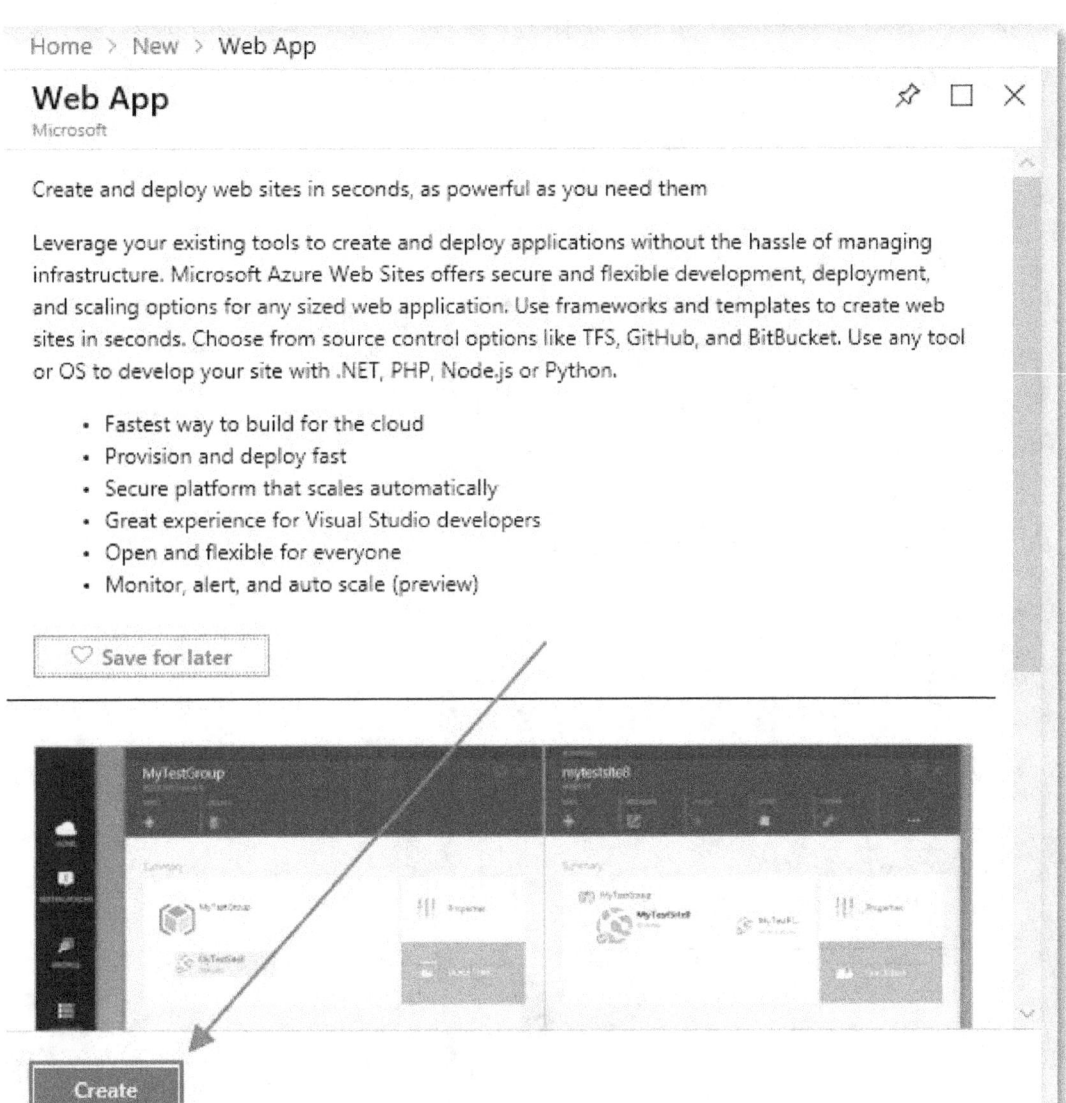

Click the **Create** button.

ADefHelpDesk 4

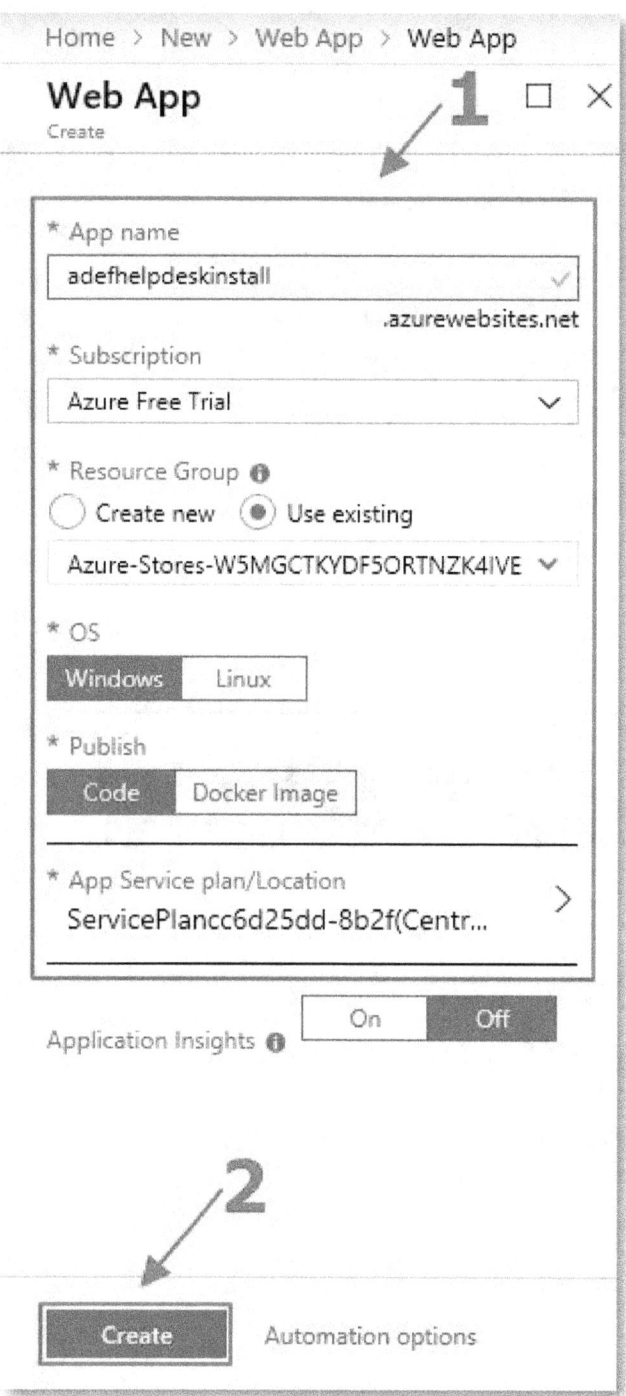

Fill in the required fields and click the **Create** button.

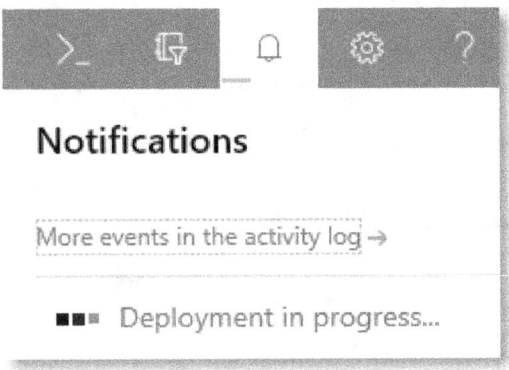

It may take some time for **Azure** to create and deploy the **Web App**.

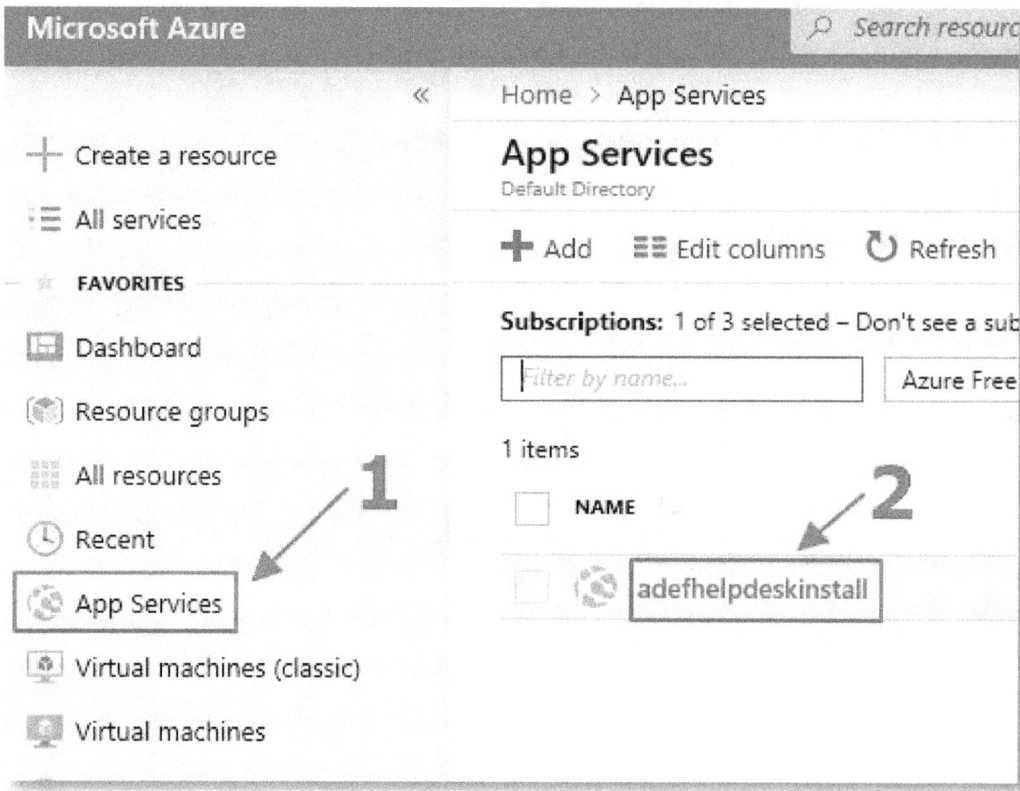

When it is ready, it will display in the **App Services** section in the **Azure Portal**.

Click on the name of your App Serviceto select it.

Deploy The Code

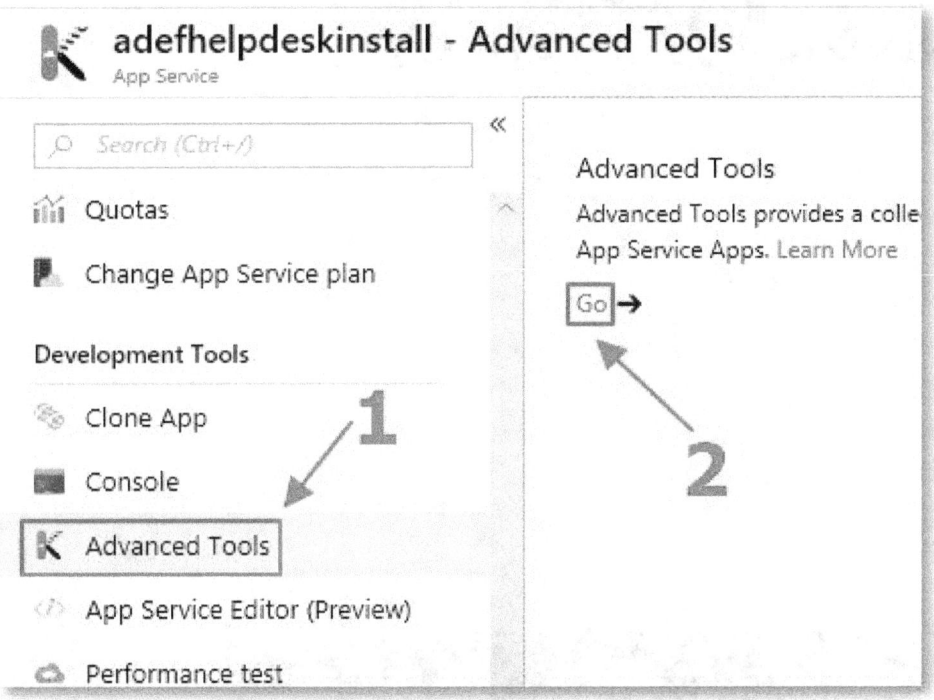

In the **Development Tools** section, select **Advanced Tools**, then select **Go**.

ADefHelpDesk 4

When the **Kudu** window opens, from the **Debug console** menu, select **CMD**.

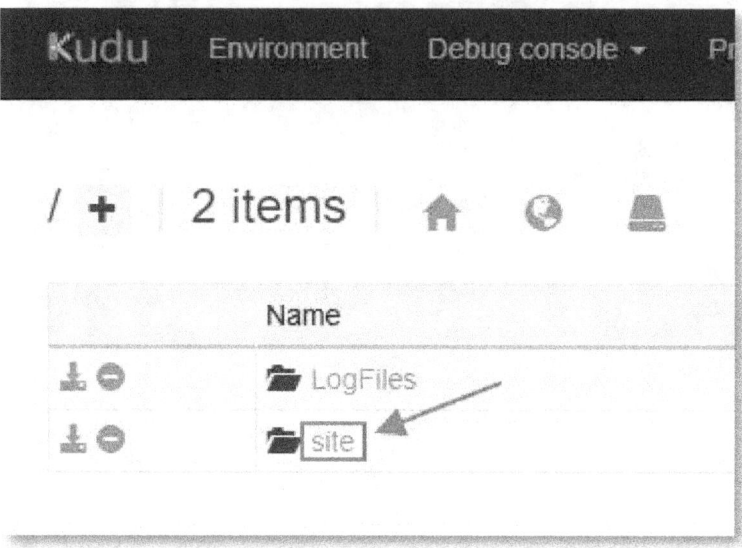

Select **site**.

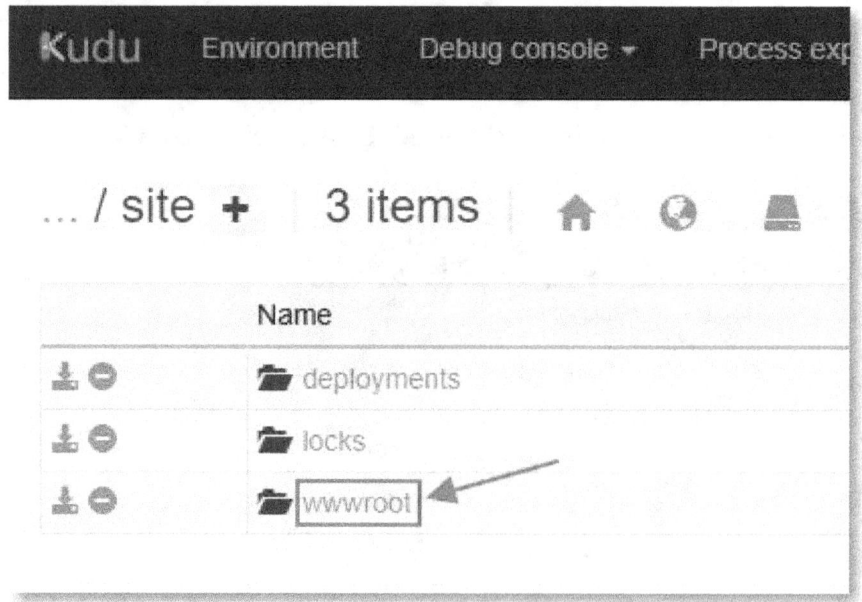

Then select **wwwroot**.

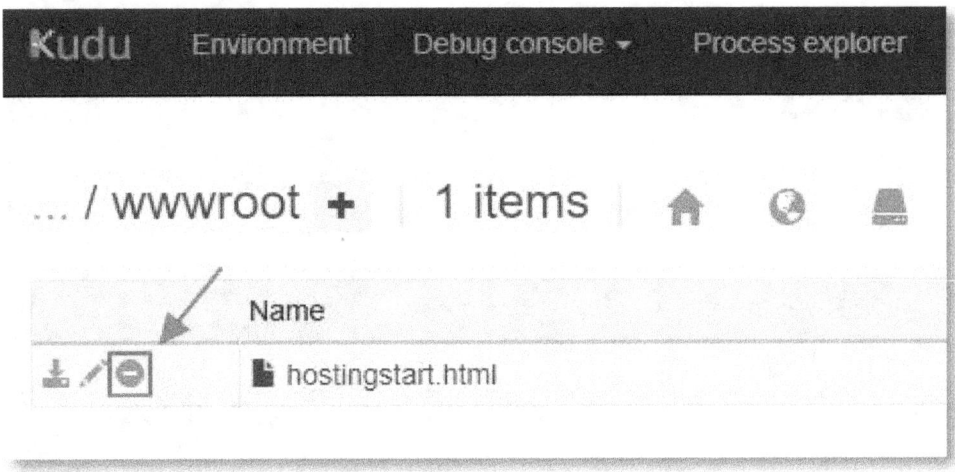

In the **wwwroot** folder, click the **delete** button to **delete** any files already there.

ADefHelpDesk 4

Download the installation **_InstallPackage.zip** file from the **ADefHelpDesk** downloads page (http://ADefHelpDesk.com/Download.aspx).

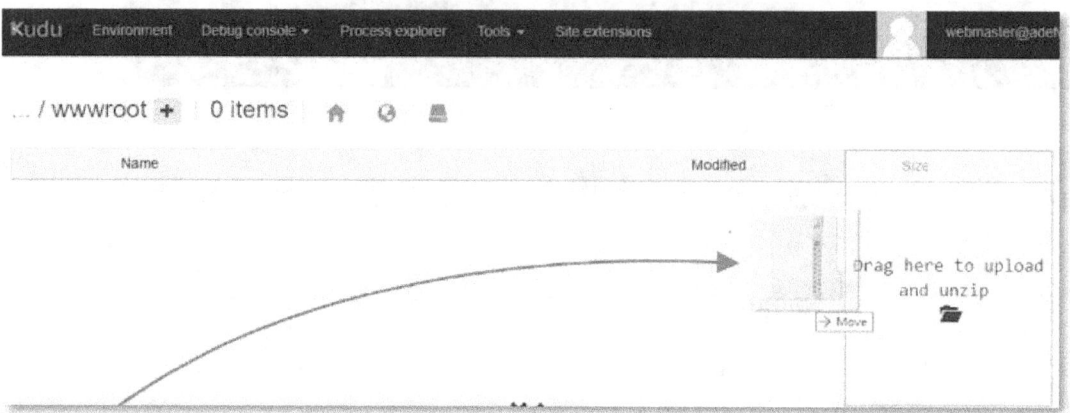

Drag that file onto the **web browser window** until you see the box that says: **Drag here to upload and unzip**.

Release your finger on your mouse to drop the **.zip** file in that box.

The file will be **uploaded** and **unzipped**.

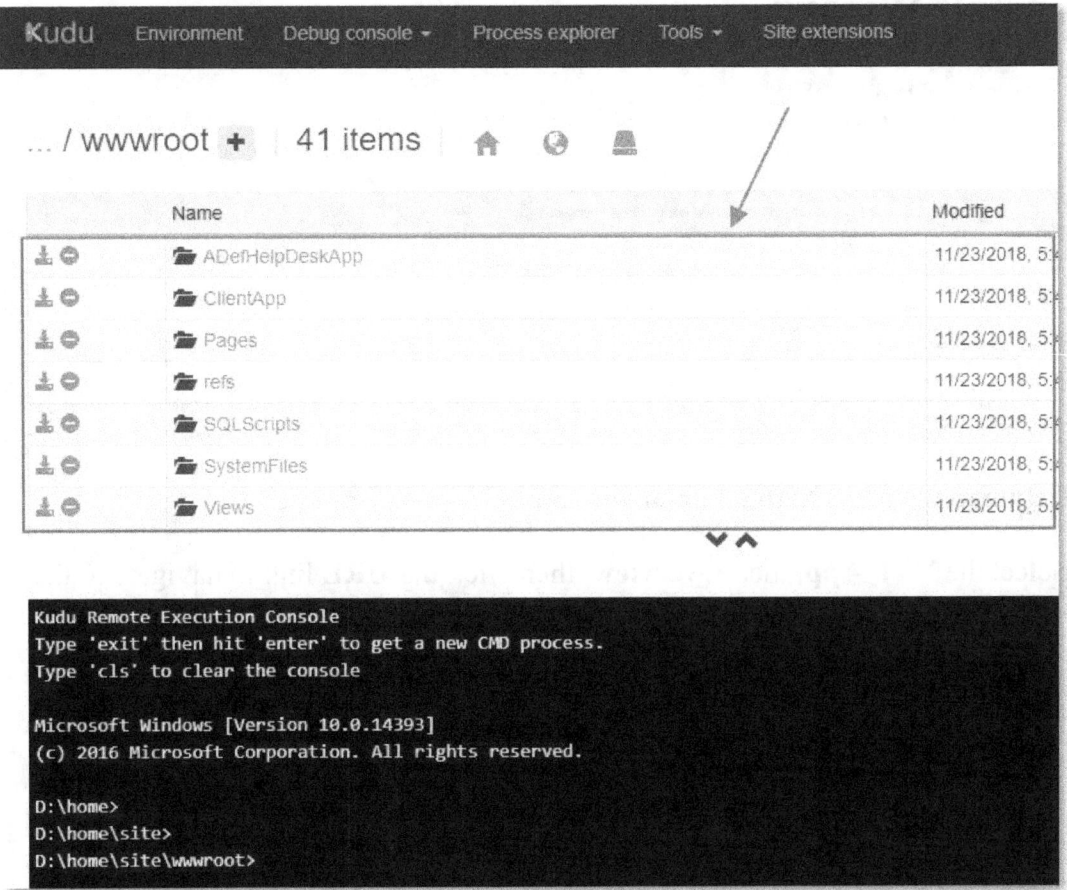

When the process is complete, the pages will display.

Note: If you have any issues, you can also deploy the files to the **wwwroot** directory using other methods such as **FTP**.

ADefHelpDesk 4

Install Wizard

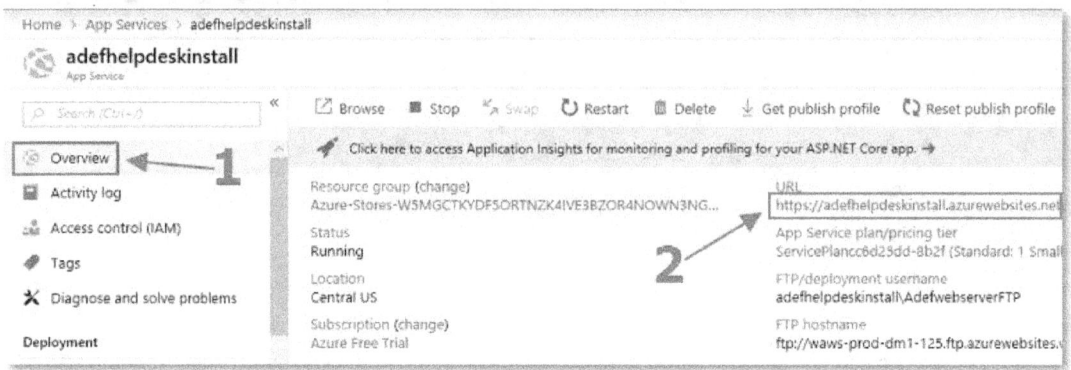

Return to the main **Azure Portal** window.

Select the **Web App**, then **Overview**, then click the **URL** link to navigate to the website.

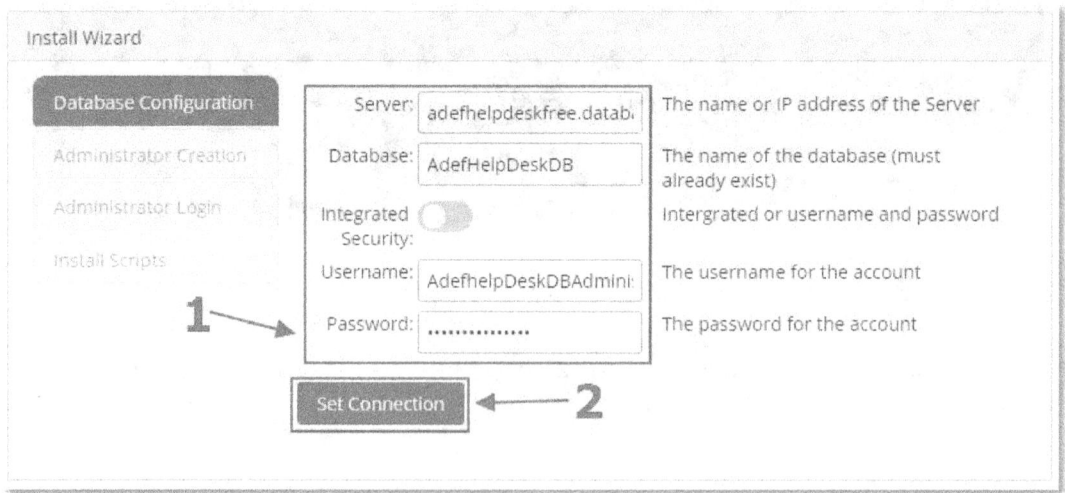

You will see the **Installation Wizard**.

Enter the values you noted from the earlier steps and click the **Set Connection** button.

Note:

- For the best installation experience, use the **Google Chrome** web browser.
- If you see another screen that appears for a long time, the files are still loading. Wait for the **Installation Wizard** to show before proceeding.

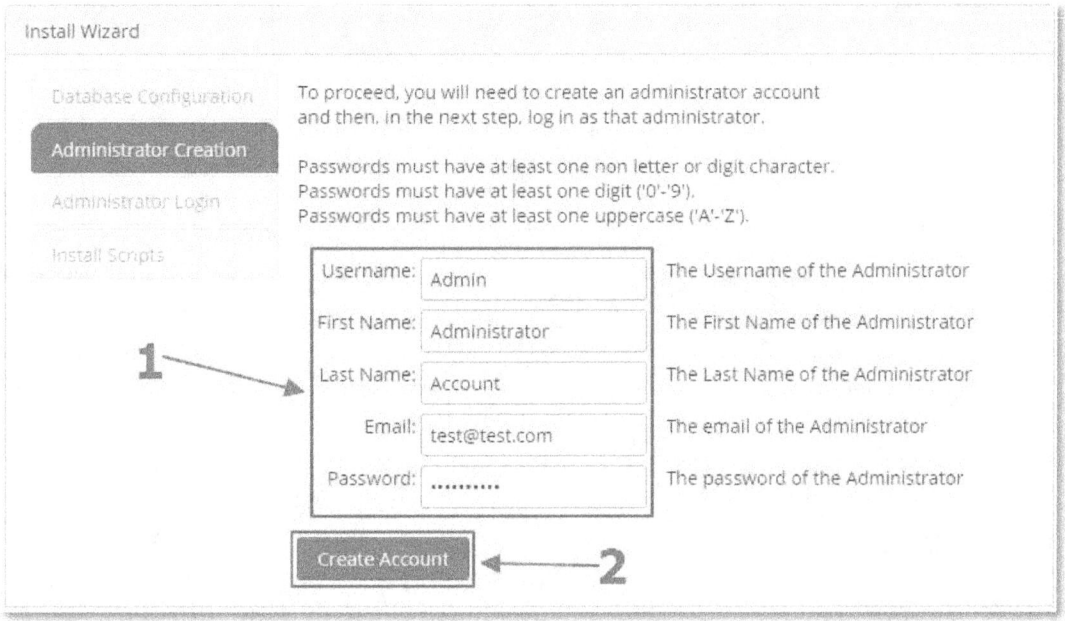

Enter the information for an **Administrator account** that you want the application to create for you.

Note: Ensure the **Password** entered is a strong password (a popup box will display to indicate when the password is considered strong).

Click the **Create Account** button.

ADefHelpDesk 4

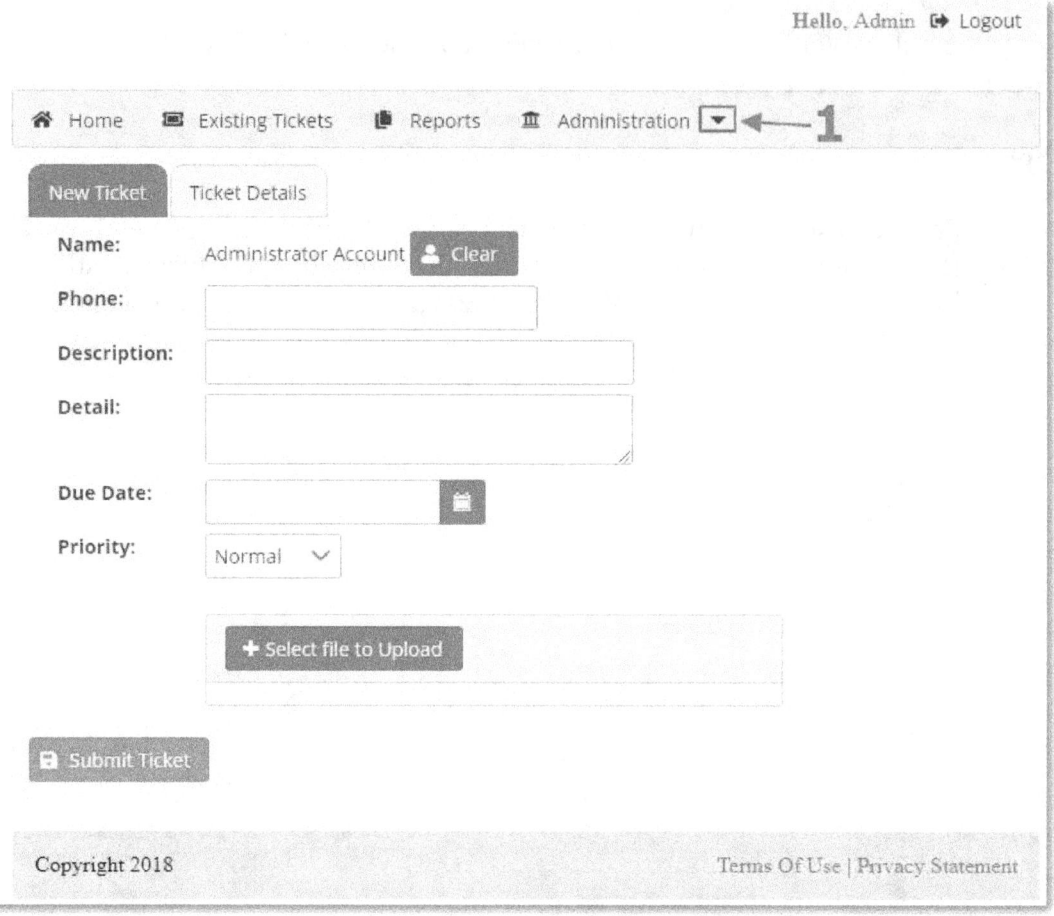

After it is set up, you will be automatically logged in as the **Super User**.

Click the **Administration** link.

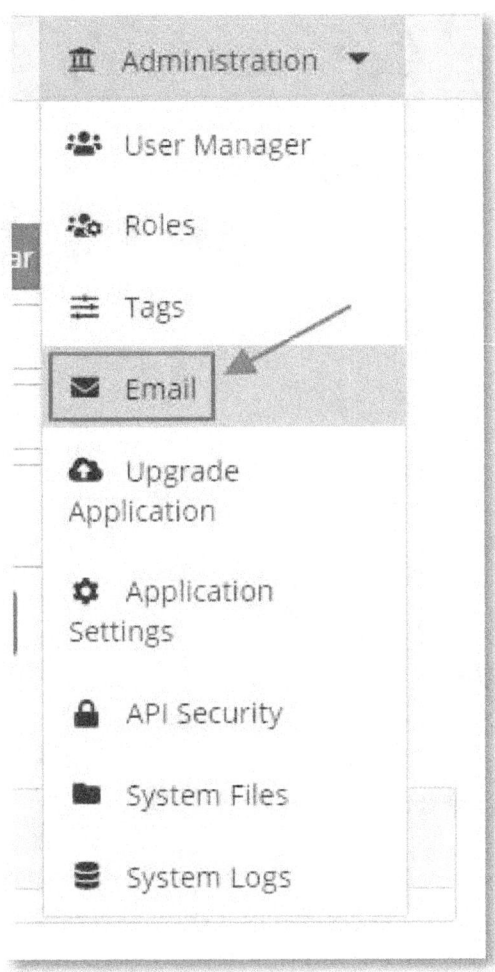

In **Administration**, click **Email**

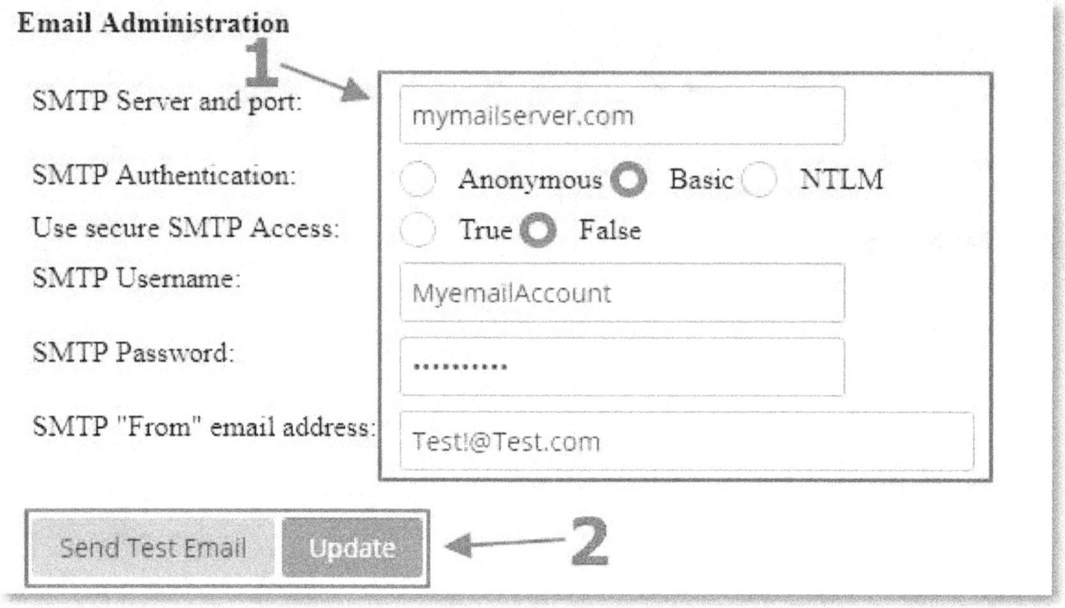

ADefHelpDesk 4

Email Administration

SMTP Server and port:	mymailserver.com
SMTP Authentication:	○ Anonymous ● Basic ○ NTLM
Use secure SMTP Access:	○ True ● False
SMTP Username:	MyemailAccount
SMTP Password:	....
SMTP "From" email address:	Test!@Test.com

[Send Test Email] [Update]

Set-up the email settings.

To test the settings, click **Send Test Email**.

When complete, click the **Update** button to save the settings.

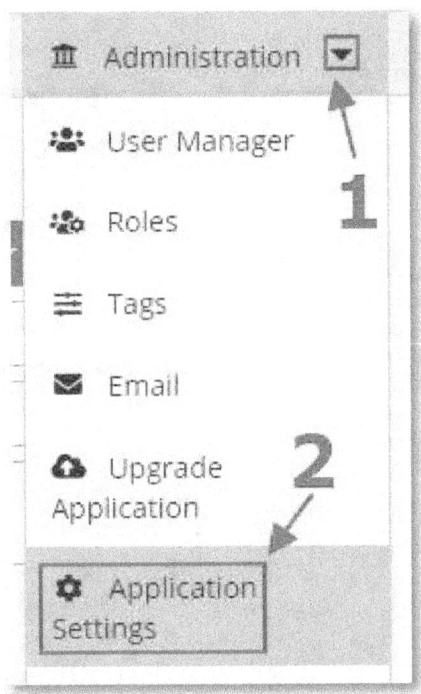

Select **Administration** then **Application Settings**.

ADefHelpDesk 4

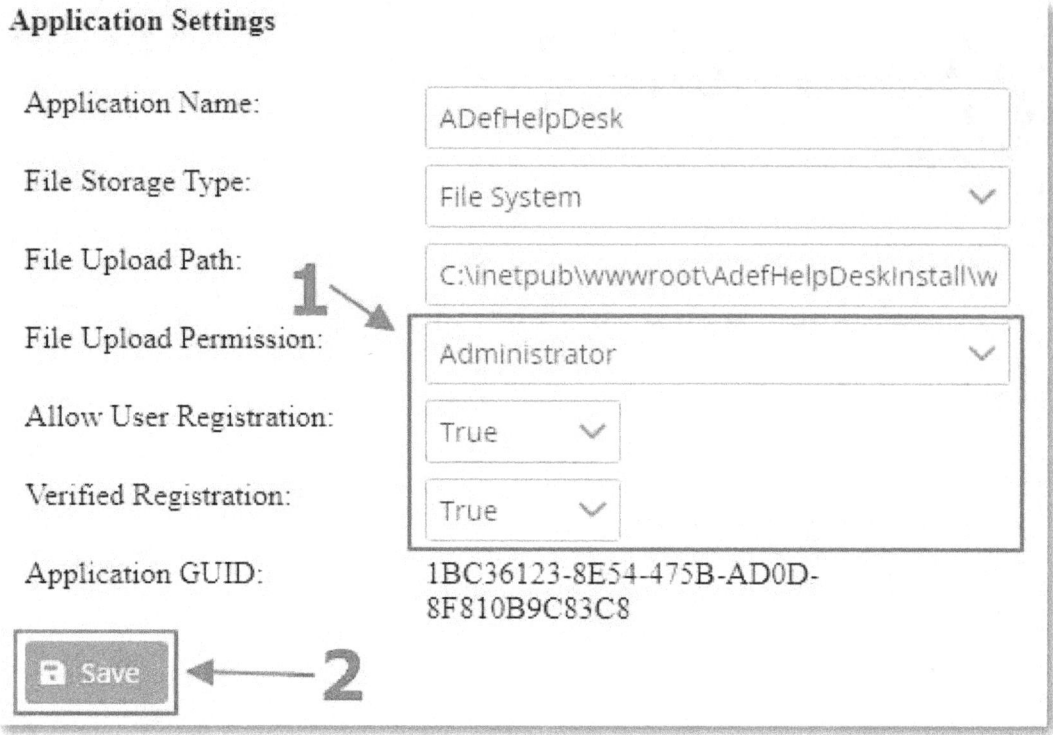

Set the **file upload** and **user registration** options and click the **Save** button.

Set Up Azure Storage

When **ADefHelpDesk** is running as a cloud hosted web application, it must use **Azure Storage** for the storage of files attached to help desk tickets.

See the following link for information on setting up an **Azure Storage Account**: https://docs.microsoft.com/en-us/azure/storage/common/storage-quickstart-create-account

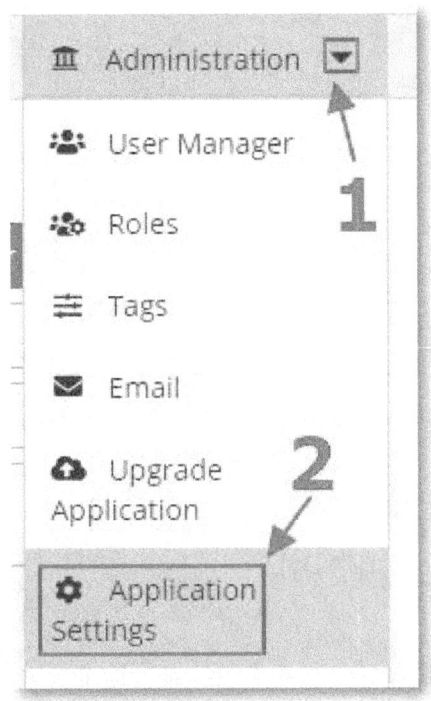

Select **Administration** then **Application Settings**.

ADefHelpDesk 4

Application Settings

Application Name:	ADefHelpDesk
File Storage Type:	Azure Storage
Azure Storage Connection:	DefaultEndpointsProtocol=https;AccountNa
File Upload Permission:	Administrator
Allow User Registration:	True
Verified Registration:	True
Application GUID:	1BC36123-8E54-475B-AD0D-8F810B9C83C8

[**Save**]

Set the **File Storage Type** to **Azure Storage**, enter the connection string to the **Azure** storage account in **Azure Storage Connection,** and click the **Save** button.

Note: See the following link for information on how to determine what the **Azure** storage connection string is: https://docs.microsoft.com/en-us/azure/storage/common/storage-configure-connection-string#create-a-connection-string-for-an-azure-storage-account

Note: In the Azure portal, you can go to **Settings** then **Access keys** in your storage account's menu blade to see connection strings. You can use either the primary or secondary access keys.

ADefHelpDesk is now set-up

Upgrading

Download the upgrade file from the **ADefHelpDesk** downloads page (http://ADefHelpDesk.com/Download.aspx).

- **Important:** The .zip file must have *_UpgradePackage.zip* in the name! Do not try to upgrade an **ADefHelpDesk** version *greater* than version **03.00.00** with a *_InstallPackage.zip* file!
- **Important:** You must back up the SQL database file, and the *entire* directory containing the files before performing an upgrade.
- **Note:** To upgrade any version of **ADefHelpDesk** *prior* to version **03.00.00**, create a new installation using the *_InstallPackage.zip* package, and during the installation, point the database connection to the *database* of any previous version of the stand-alone ADefHelpDesk. This newly installed version will run using that upgraded database.

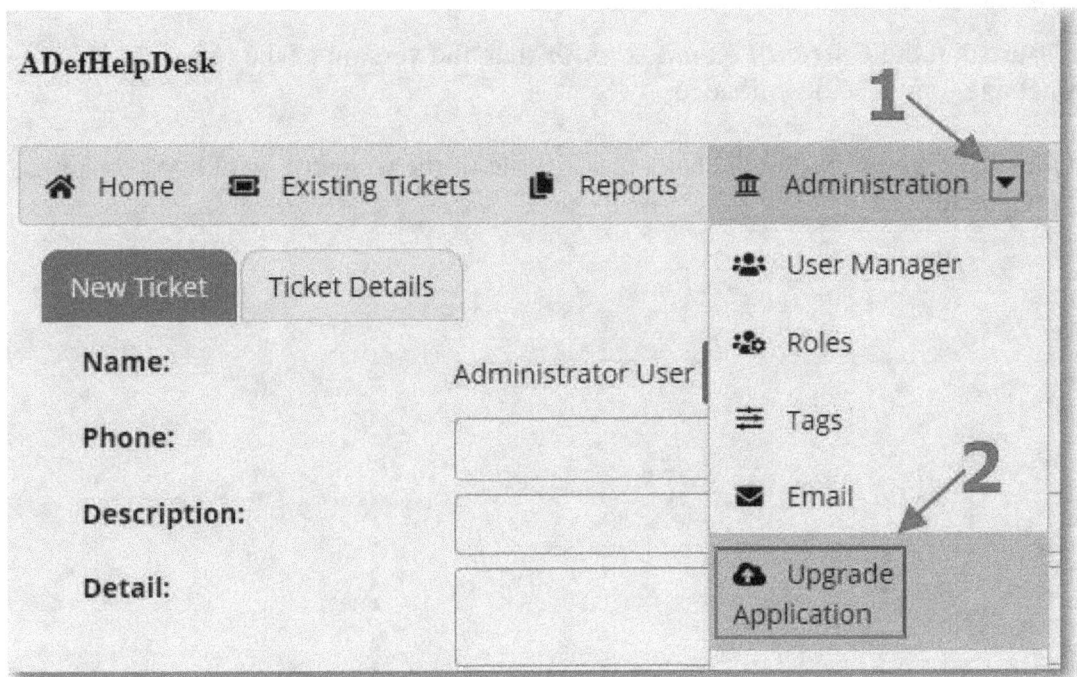

ADefHelpDesk 4

Log in as a user who is marked, in the **User Manager**, as **Is SuperUser**.

From the menu bar, select **Administration** then **Upgrade Application**.

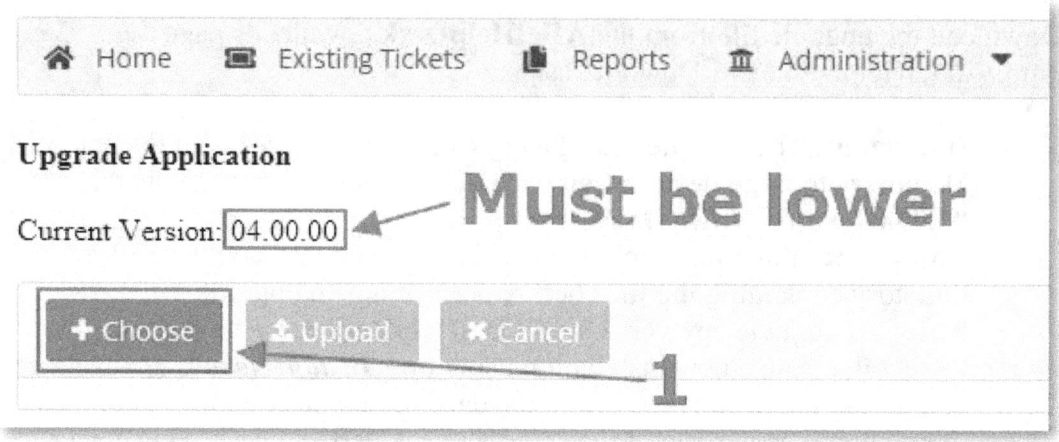

The Upgrade Application page will display.

Ensure that the *Current Version* is *lower* than the version of the **upgrade package** you have downloaded.

Click the **Choose** button to select the **.zip** file of the **upgrade package** you have downloaded.

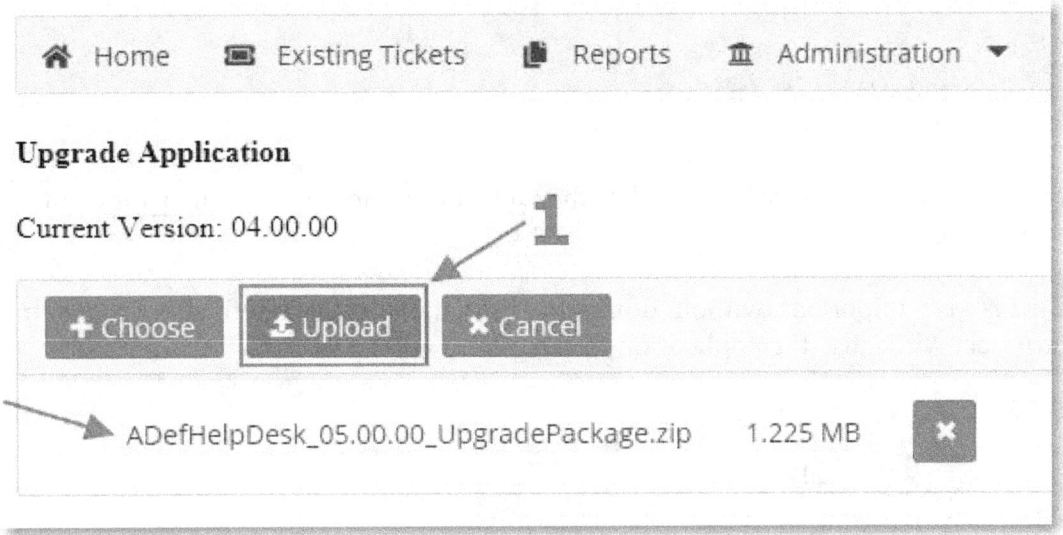

The name of the selected file will display in the upload control.

Click the **Upload** button to start the upgrade.

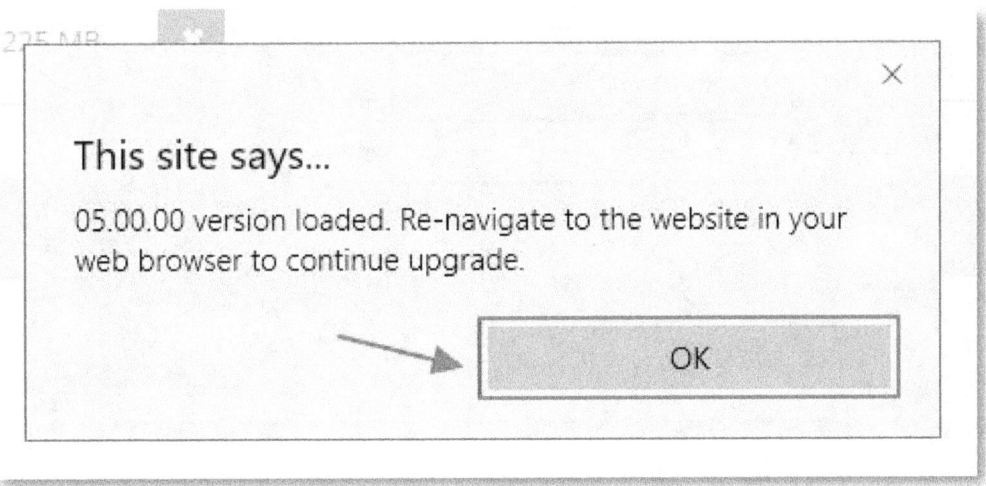

After the files are uploaded, a confirmation message box will appear.

ADefHelpDesk 4

Click **OK**.

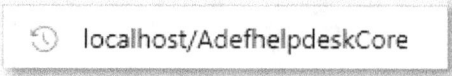

In your web browser, manually alter the web address to return to the **root** of the application.

This is very important; without doing this first, the next step (refreshing the web browser) will cause the application to *hang*.

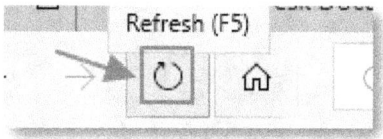

Refresh your web browser.

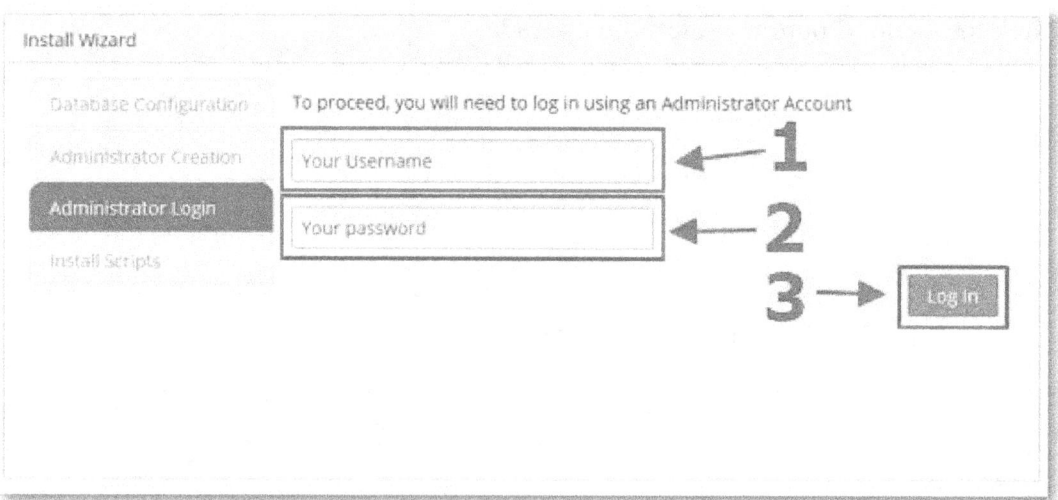

The **Install Wizard** will show.

Enter the **username** and **password** of the user you used to upload the **upgrade package** (or any user marked **Is SuperUser**), and click **Log In**.

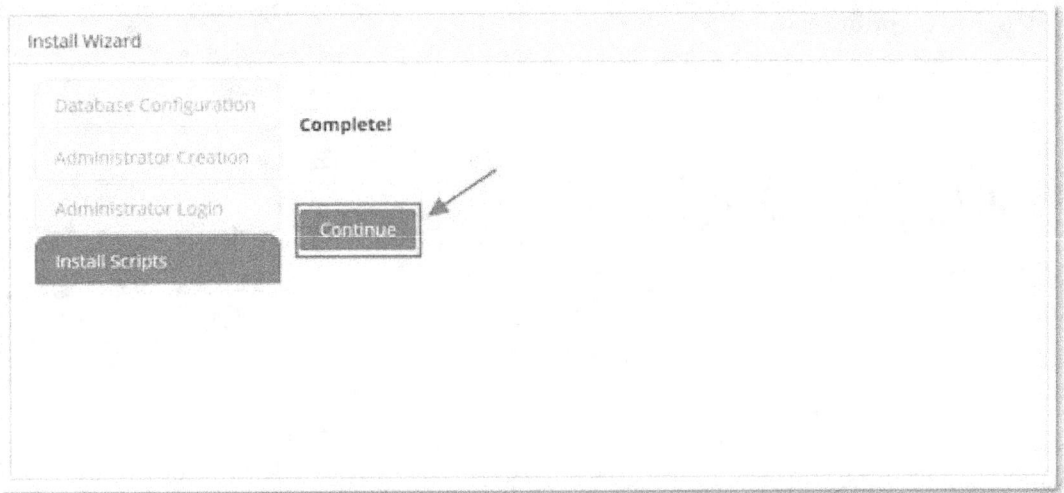

The upgrade will complete.

Click **Continue**.

ADefHelpDesk 4

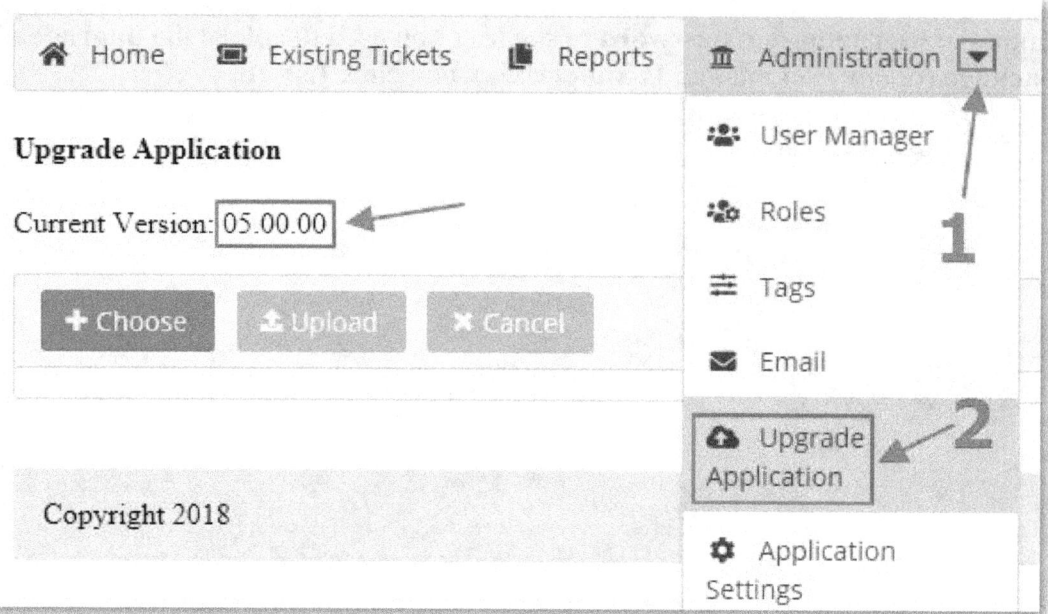

From the main menu, you can select **Administration**, then **Upgrade Application** to verify the updated application version.

Chapter 3: Using ADefHelpDesk

Creating and Updating Account and Password

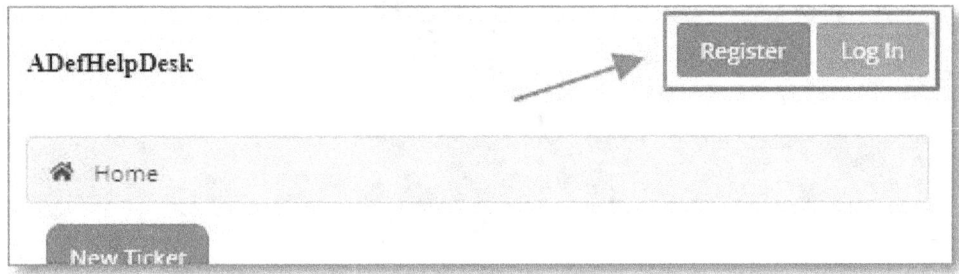

If the ability to create an account has been enabled by the **Administrator** (by setting **Allow User Registration** to **True** in the **Administration/Application Settings** section) when a **User** is not logged in, they will see a **Register** button and a **Log In** button. Otherwise, a **Log In** button will always show.

Note: An **Administrator** (any **User** who has the **Is SuperUser** box checked in **Administration/User Manager**) can always create an account for a **User** in **Administration/User Manager**.

ADefHelpDesk 4

Account Registration

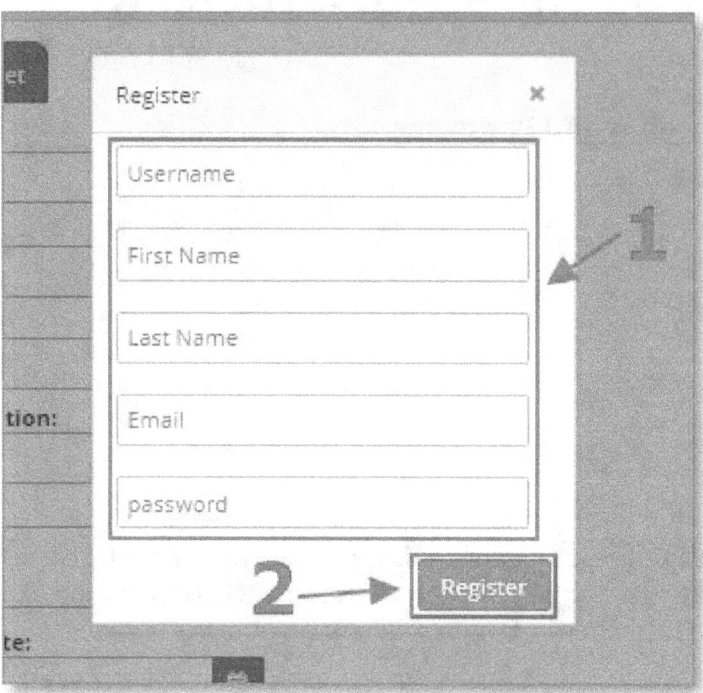

If **Registration** is available, when a **User** clicks the **Register** button, they will see the **Register** form.

All fields except **First Name** and **Last Name** are required. After filling in all the required fields, the **User** clicks the **Register** button to proceed with the account creation.

If the **User** chooses an **Email** address that is used by another **User**, they will see a warning popup. They will have to close the popup and change the **Email** to proceed with the registration.

ADefHelpDesk 4

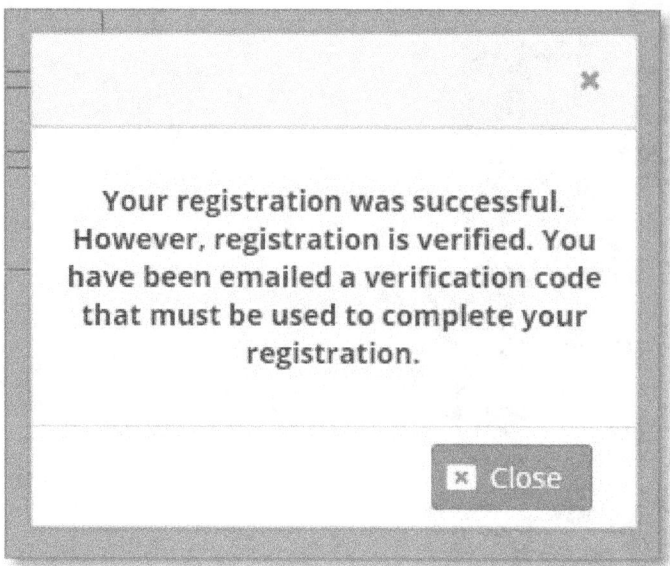

After completing registration, if **Verified Registration** has been enabled by the **Administrator** (by setting both **Allow User Registration** to **True**, and **Verified Registration** to **True** in the **Administration/Application Settings** section), the **User** will see a confirmation screen informing them that they need to check their **Email**, to receive the **Verification Code**, which they will need to use to complete their registration.

Note: The **Email** is sent to the **Email** address they entered for their **User** account.

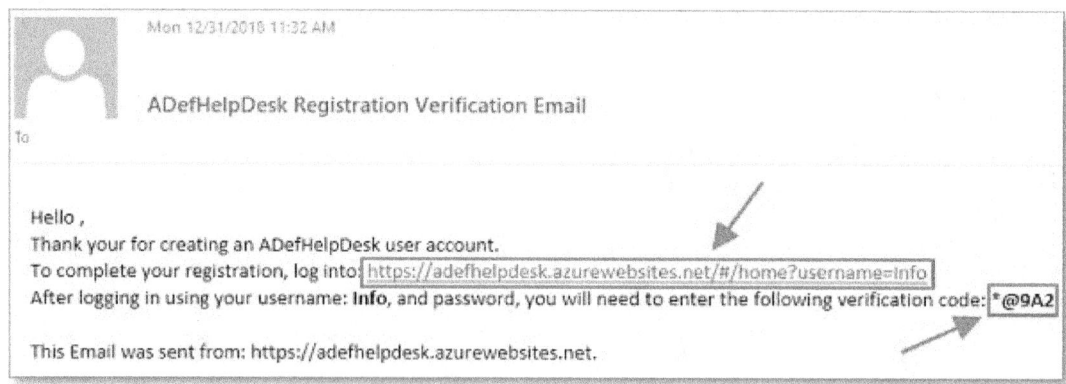

When the **User** checks their **Email**, they will see the **website address** to navigate to, and the **Verification Code** needed to complete their registration.

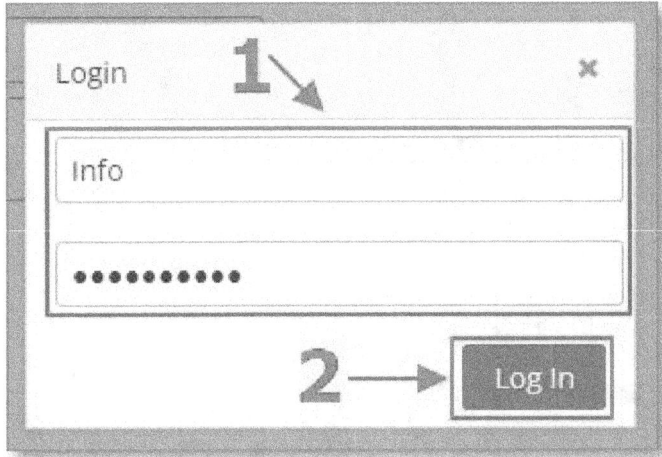

After navigating to the website address located in the **Email**, the **User** will be presented with a **Login** box.

The **User** will enter their **Username** and **Password** (that they indicated on the **Registration** form) and click **Log In**.

ADefHelpDesk 4

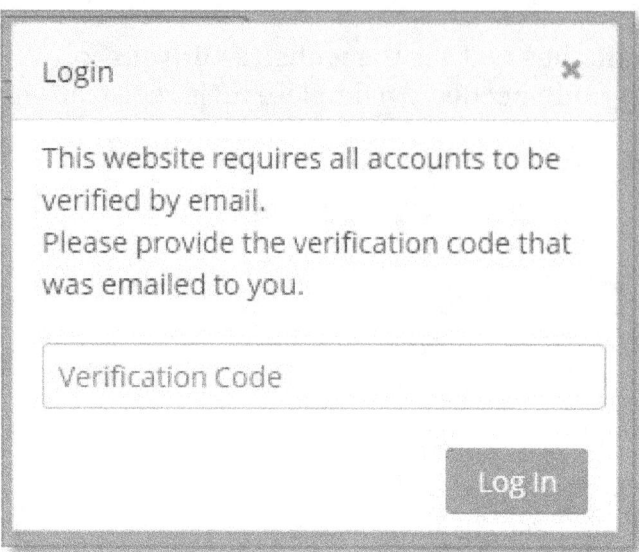

They will be presented with a box asking for the **Verification Code** (from the **Email**) to be entered.

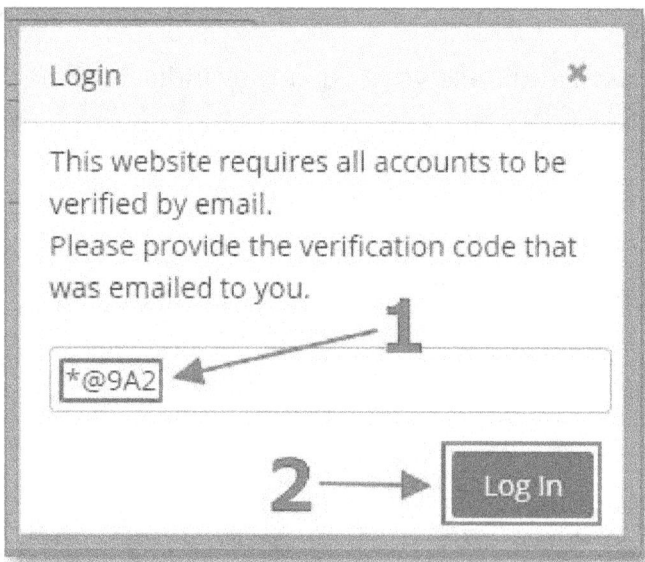

The **User** will enter the **Verification Code** and click the **Log In** button.

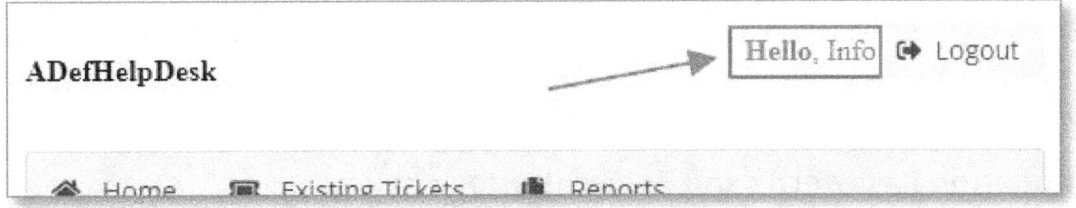

The **User** will be **logged in**.

Logging In

Any time a **User** is not logged in, they will see the **Log In** button.

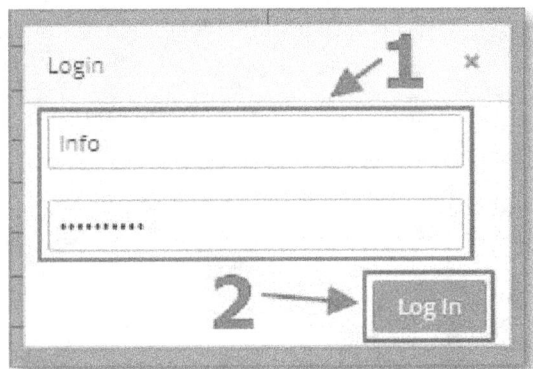

Clicking the **Log In** button will display the **Login** dialog.

ADefHelpDesk 4

To complete the **log in** process, the **User** enters their **user name** in the top box, and their **password** in the bottom box, and clicks the **Log In** button.

Updating Passwords and Account Information

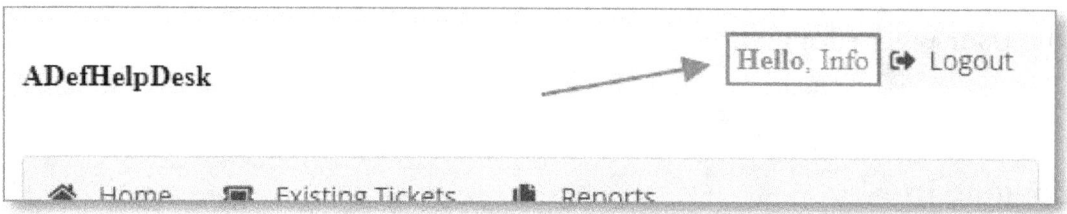

A logged in **User** can click on their **user name** at any time to update their **password** and **account information**.

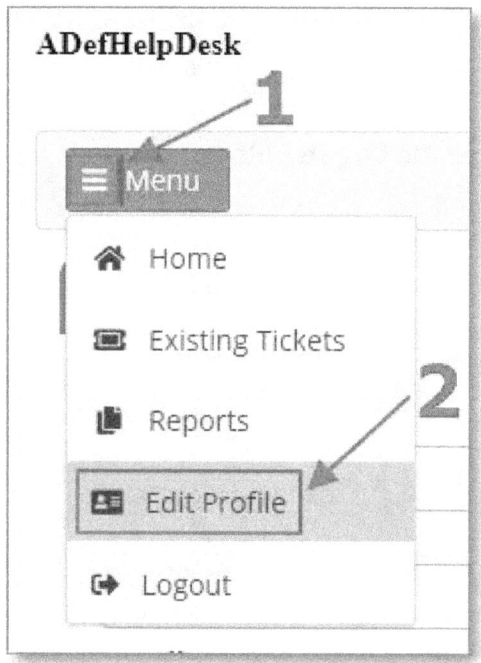

However, if the web browser is in the *minimized* mode, the *hamburger menu button* will display. Clicking this button will display the menu. To edit their profile information, the **User** will need to select the **Edit Profile** option.

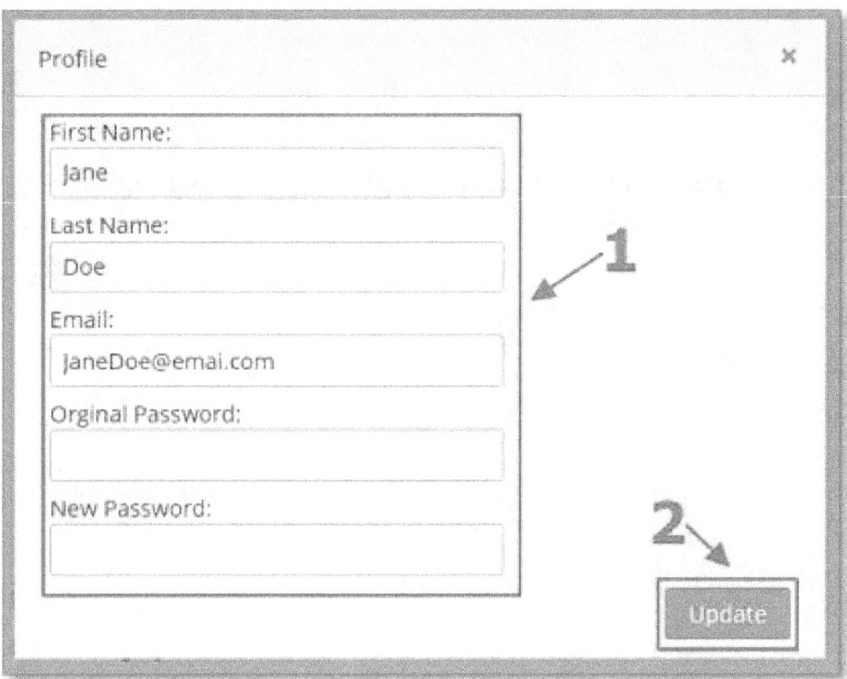

The **User** will be presented with the **Profile** dialog.

- The profile information can be updated by entering or changing the information in the text boxes on the form and *saved* by clicking the **Update** button
- To change their password, the **User** must enter their **current** password in the **Original Password** box, their **new** password in the **New Password** box, and click the **Update** button.
- If the **User** does not enter anything in the **Original Password** box *and* the **New Password** box, and clicks the **Update** button, the password will not be changed, but, all other profile information will be updated.

ADefHelpDesk 4

Logging Out

At any time, a logged in **User** can log out of the application by clicking the **Logout** button.

Creating a Help Desk Ticket

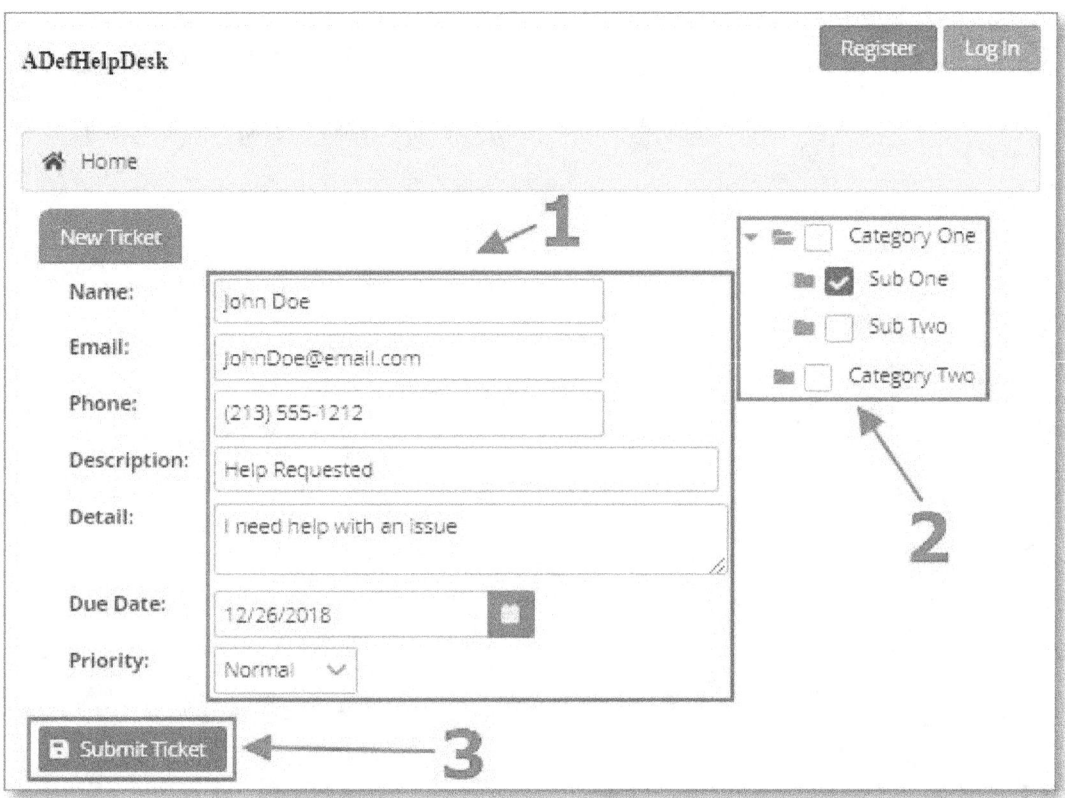

If a **User** does not have an account (or the ability to create an account has been disabled by the **Administrator**) or has decided to not log in, a **Help Desk Ticket** can be created by filling out the information and clicking the **Submit Ticket** button.

Note:

- **Name**, **Email**, and **Description** are *required*. All other fields are *optional* and can be left blank.

ADefHelpDesk 4

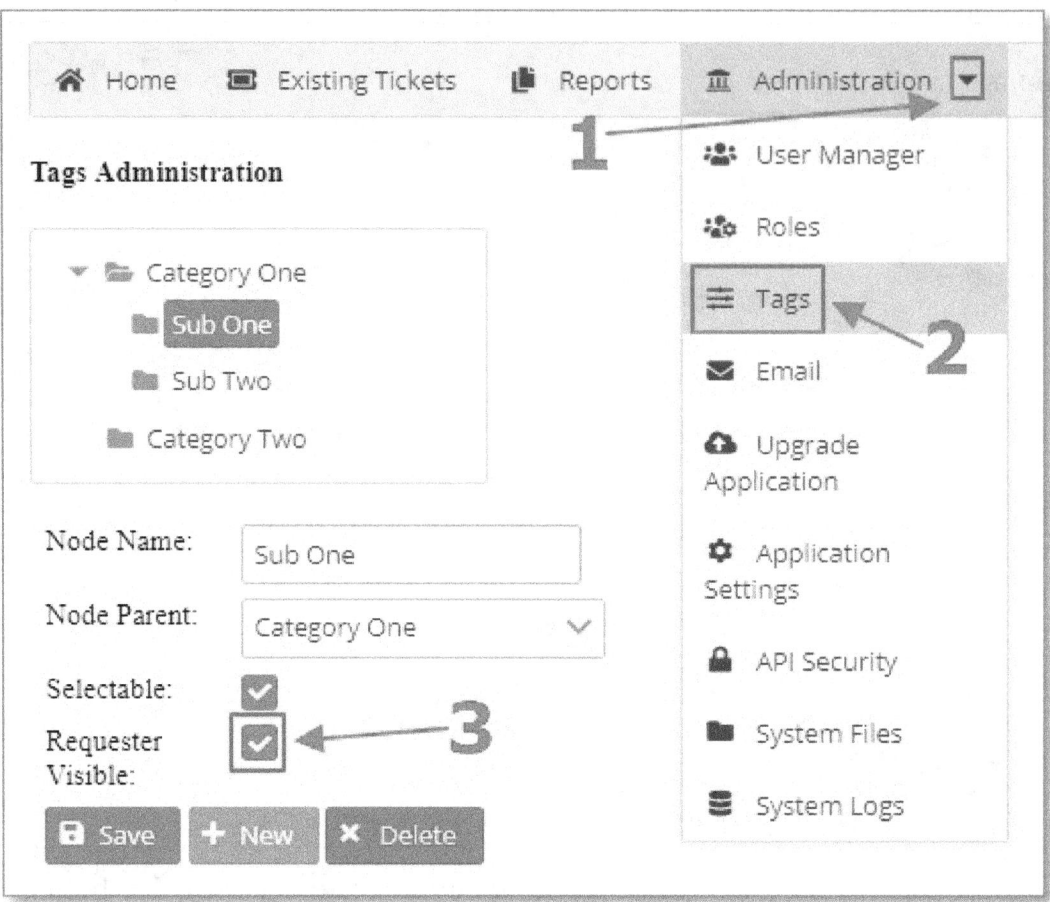

- The **Tags**, displayed as a nested tree, with options that can be checked, will only display if the **Administrator** has created **Tags** in the **Administration/Tags** section, and has set one or more **Tags** to be **Requester Visible**, either as a root **Tag**, or as a child of a **Tag** that is also set as **Requester Visible**.

If a **User** does have an account, they can log in, before creating a **Help Desk Ticket**, by clicking the **Log In** button.

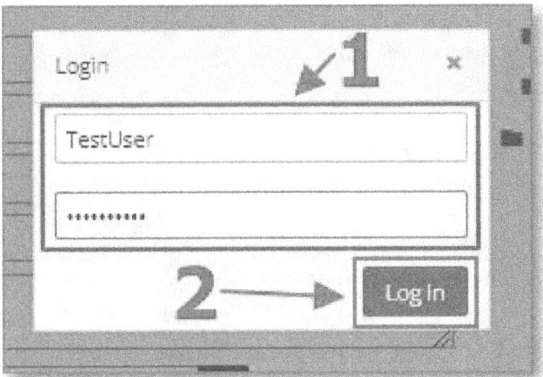

The **User** enters their **User Name** in the top box, their **Password** in the lower box, and then clicks the **Log In** button.

ADefHelpDesk 4

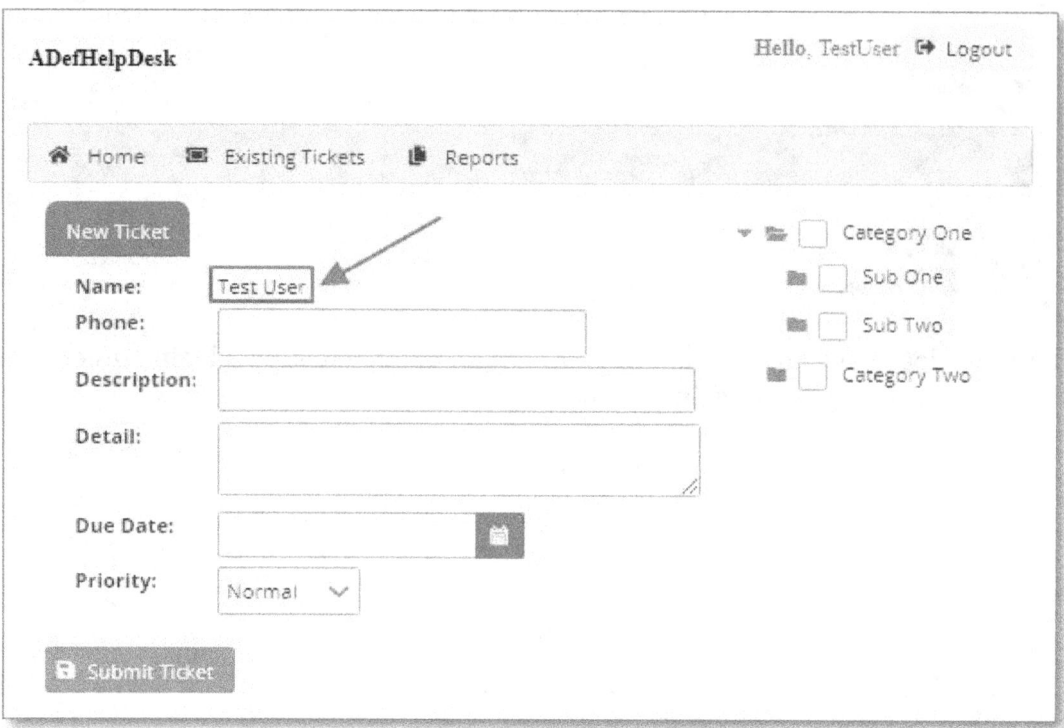

When a logged in **User** views the **Help Desk Ticket** form, their **Name** will be already set. Also, their **Email** address is attached to their **User Account**, so it does not need to be entered.

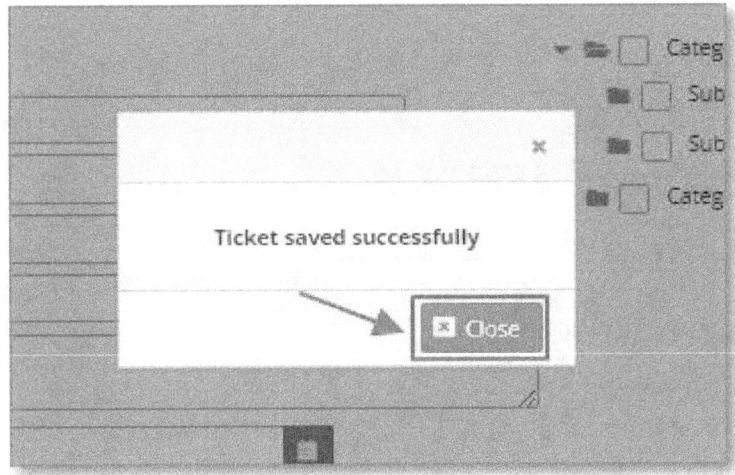

After the **Help Desk Ticket** is *submitted*, a **confirmation box** will appear.

Click the **Close** button will dismiss it.

ADefHelpDesk 4

Confirmation Emails

Sat 12/29/2018 12:24 PM

A New Help Desk ticket has been created (#47)

To   John Doe

Hello John Doe,
A New Help Desk ticket has been created for you.

Ticket #: 47
Description: Help Requested
Status: New
Priority: Normal

To view this ticket, go to: http://localhost/AdefhelpdeskCore?ticketnumber=47&code=0ZOJCVS7LX

This Email was sent from: http://localhost/AdefhelpdeskCore.

If **Email** has been configured by the **Administrator** (in **Administration/Email**), an **Email** will be sent to the address entered in the **Email** field (if the **Help Desk Ticket** was created by a user who was not logged in) or to the **Email** that is set for the **User Account** of the logged in **User**.

If the **Help Desk Ticket** was created by a **User** who was not logged in, the **Email** will contain a link (with a random code for security) that will allow the user to view and update the **Help Desk Ticket**.

If the **Help Desk Ticket** was created by a **User** who was logged in, the **Email** will also contain a link that will allow the user to view and update the **Help Desk Ticket**; however, when using that link, the **User** will be required to *log in* first.

All users who have the **Is SuperUser** box checked (in **Administration/User Manager**) will also receive an **Email** notifying them that a new **Help Desk Ticket** has been created, with a link to the **Help Desk Ticket**.

ADefHelpDesk 4

Attaching Files

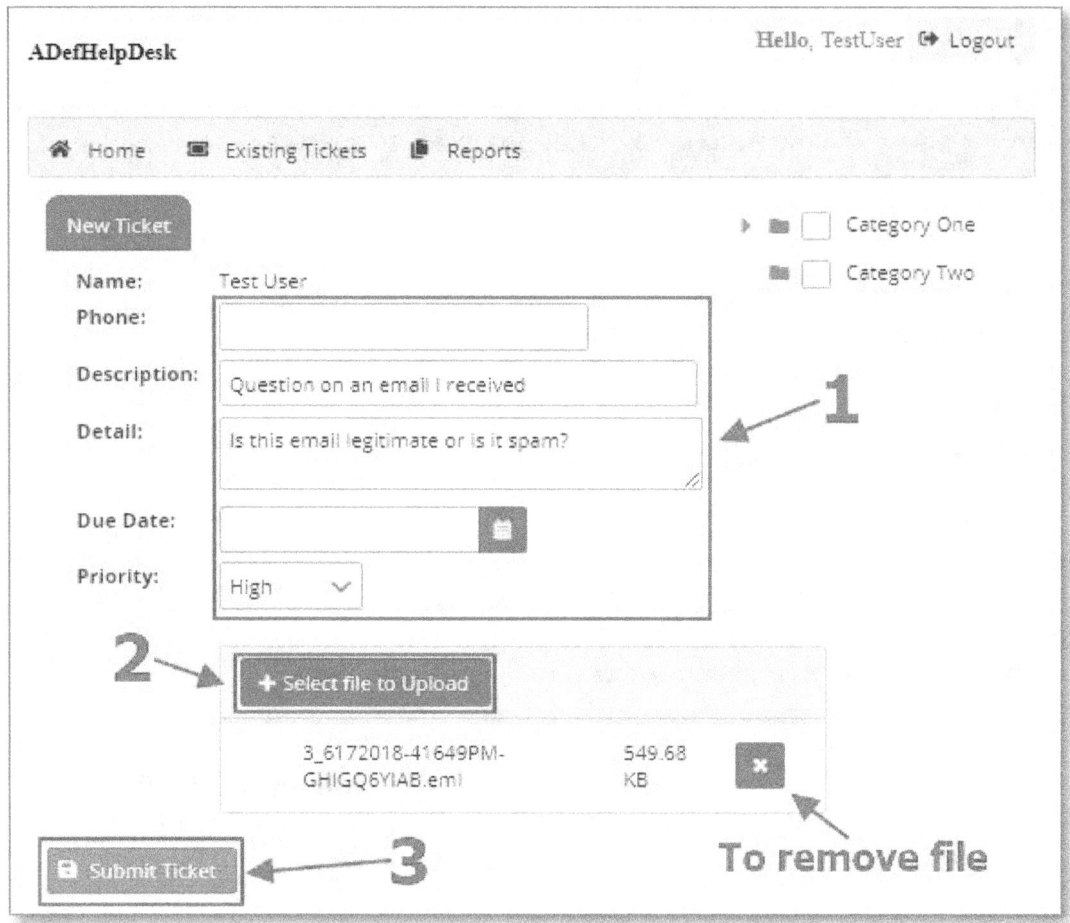

If the **Administrator** has enabled *file uploading* by setting the **File Upload Permission** to **ALL** in **Administration/Application Settings**, a **Select file to Upload** button will appear.

Clicking this button will allow the **User** to upload a single file to attach to the **Help Desk Ticket**.

Note: If a file attachment is an **.EML (Email)** file, and in one of the supported *MIME* formats, **ADefHelpDesk** will display the **Email** and any attachments in the **Email** in the online web interface when viewing the **Help Desk Ticket** in the **Existing Tickets** section of **ADefHelpDesk** (otherwise, it will display a link for the original email to be downloaded).

Search Existing Tickets

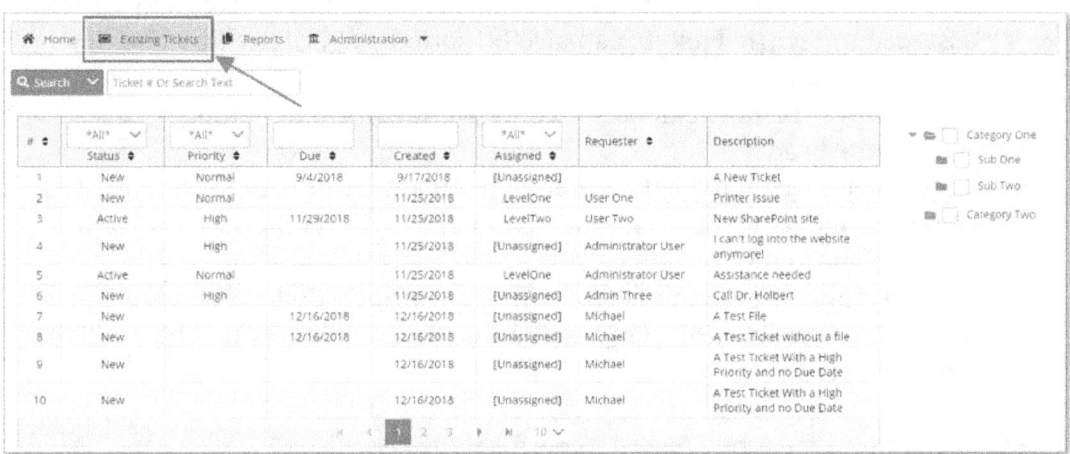

All logged in **Users** are able to access the **Existing Tickets** screen by clicking the **Existing Tickets** tab. **Users** will only have the ability to search for **Tickets** they are authorized to see. The rules to determine *ticket visibility* are:

- The **User** is the **Ticket Requestor**
- The **User** is in the group the **Ticket** is assigned to (an **Administrator** can assign a user to a *role* in **Administration/User Manager**)
- The **User** is an **Administrator** (any **User** who has the **Is SuperUser** box checked in **Administration/User Manager**)

All **Users** are able to *search* using the following search criteria:

- <u>**Status**</u> - *All, New, Active, On Hold, Resolved, Cancelled*. **Tickets** can also be sorted by **Status** by clicking on the **Status** header.

- **Priority** - *All, Normal, Low, High*. **Tickets** can also be sorted by **Priority** by clicking on the **Priority** header.
- **Due** - Entering a date will display **Tickets** that are **Due** on the date entered or greater. **Tickets** can also be sorted by **Due date** by clicking on the **Due** header.
- **Created** - Entering a date will display **Tickets** that are **Created** on the date entered or greater. **Tickets** can also be sorted by **Created date** by clicking on the **Created** header.
- **Assigned** - *All*, (and a list of all possible roles that have ever had a **Ticket** assigned to them). **Tickets** can also be sorted by **Assigned** by clicking on the **Assigned** header.
- **Requestor** - **Tickets** can be sorted by **Requestor** by clicking on the **Requestor** header.
- **Ticket # Or Search Text** - Entering a **Ticket** number or search text will retrieve **Tickets** that contain the text in either the **Ticket Description** or **Ticket Comment**s.
- **Search Tags** - Checking a **Tag** will only retrieve **Tickets** that have that **Tag**. Checking multiple **Tags** will only retrieve **Tickets** that have *all* the **Tags** selected.

The **Search** button must be pressed to perform the *search*.

Clearing The Search

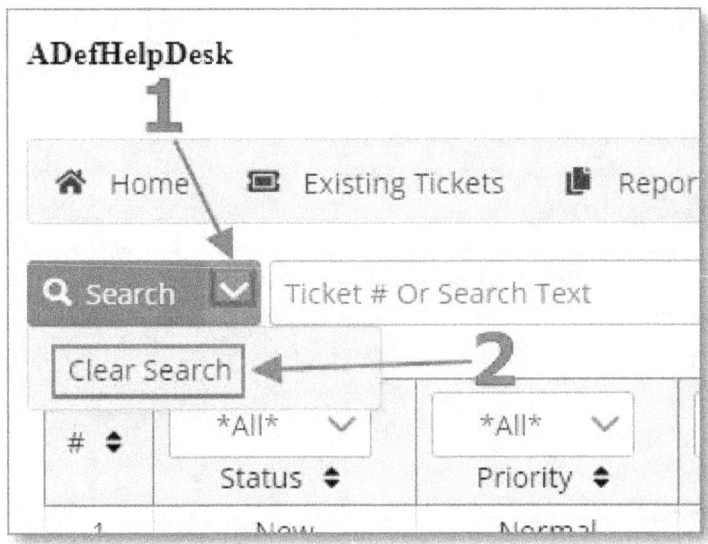

The **ADefHelpDesk** application will remember the last executed search and refresh it when the **User** returns to the **Existing Tickets** screen. To clear the search, select the downward pointing arrow next to the **Search** button and select **Clear Search**.

ADefHelpDesk 4

Paging Options

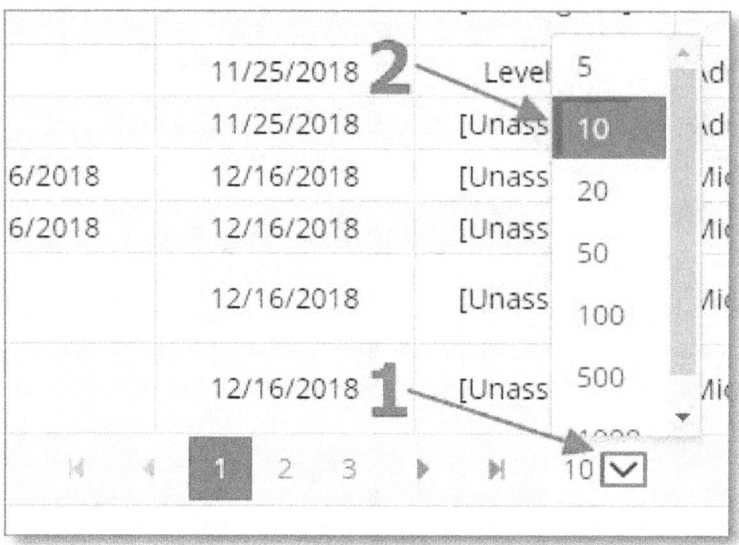

The **User** can navigate through the *search results* using the pager control at the bottom of the *search results* grid. The number of records displayed on each page can be changed by clicking the downward arrow next to the *current records per page* setting and selecting a different number.

Selecting A Help Desk Ticket

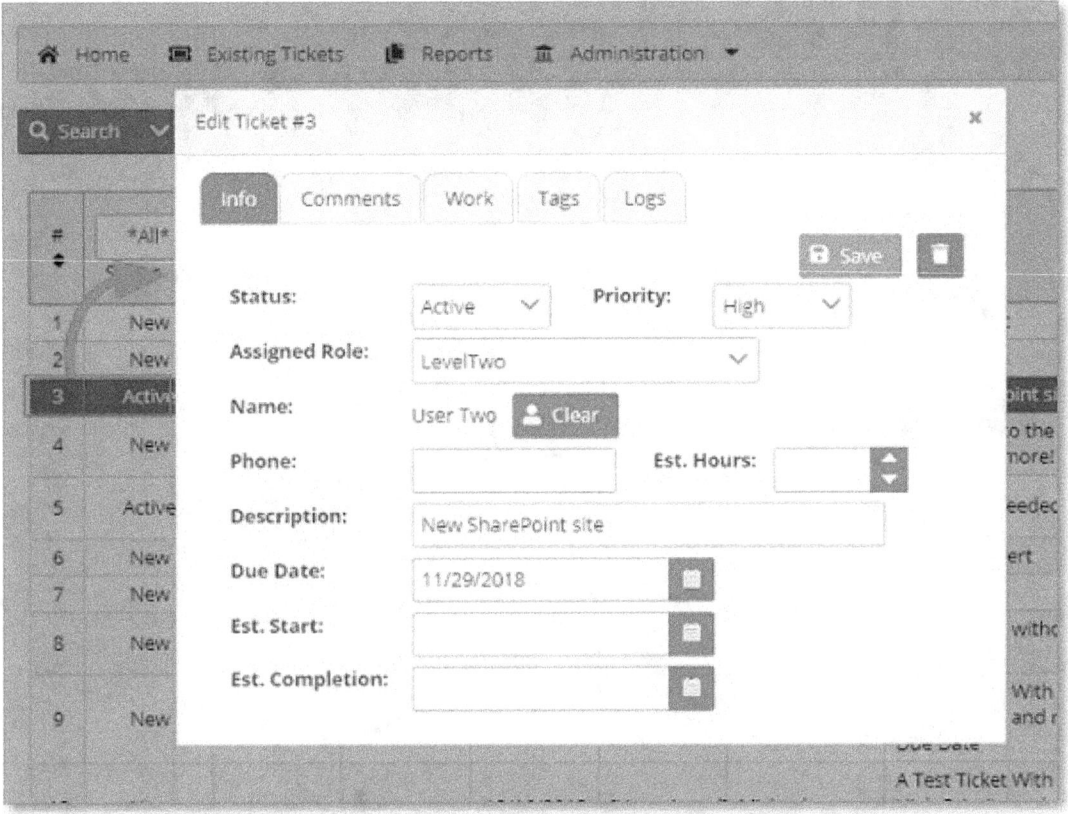

Clicking a row in the *search results grid* will open that **Help Desk Ticket** to be viewed and edited.

ADefHelpDesk 4

Updating Existing Tickets

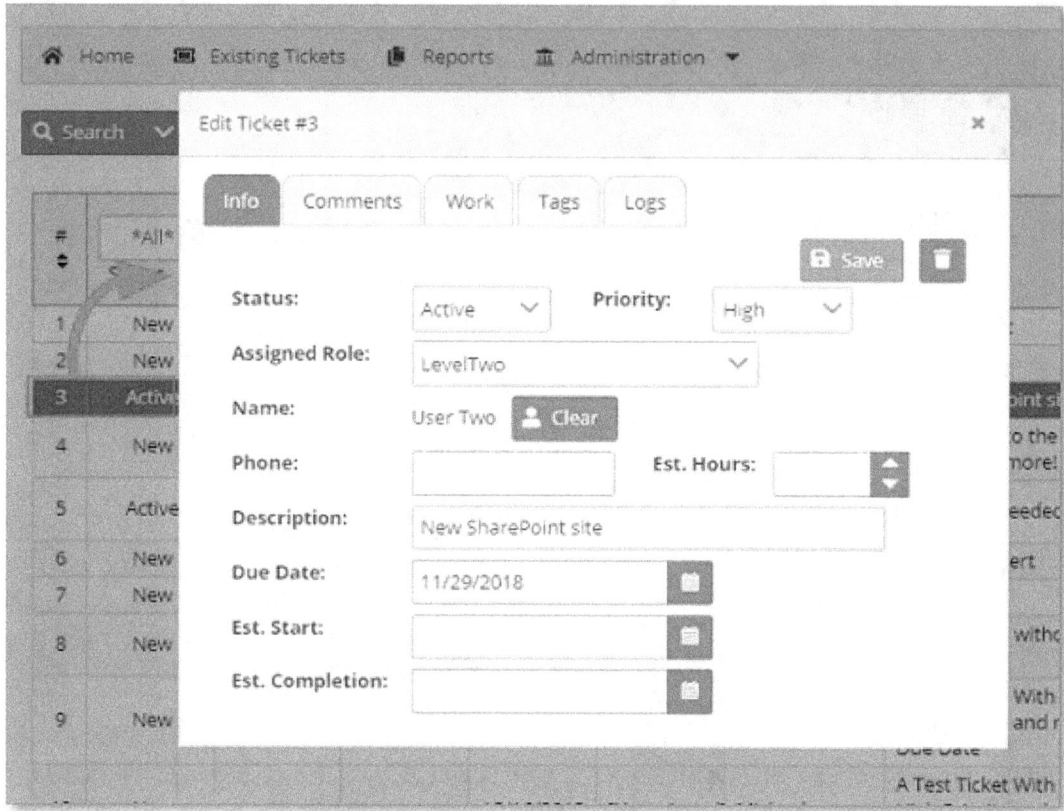

For logged in **Users**, on the **Existing Tickets** screen, clicking a row in the *search results grid* will open that **Help Desk Ticket** to be viewed and edited.

Note:

- Only **Users** who are **Administrators** (any **User** who has the **Is SuperUser** box checked in **Administration/User Manager**) or who are members of the **Role** assigned to the **Help Desk Ticket** are able to edit the details of a **Ticket** (**Note:** An **Administrator can** assign a **User** to a *role* in **Administration/User Manager**).

- **Non-Administrator Users** who are only the **Ticket Requestor** have the ability to view the details of their **Tickets**, but they do not have the ability to change any values except to add a new **Comment**.

Ticket Editing By Ticket Requestors

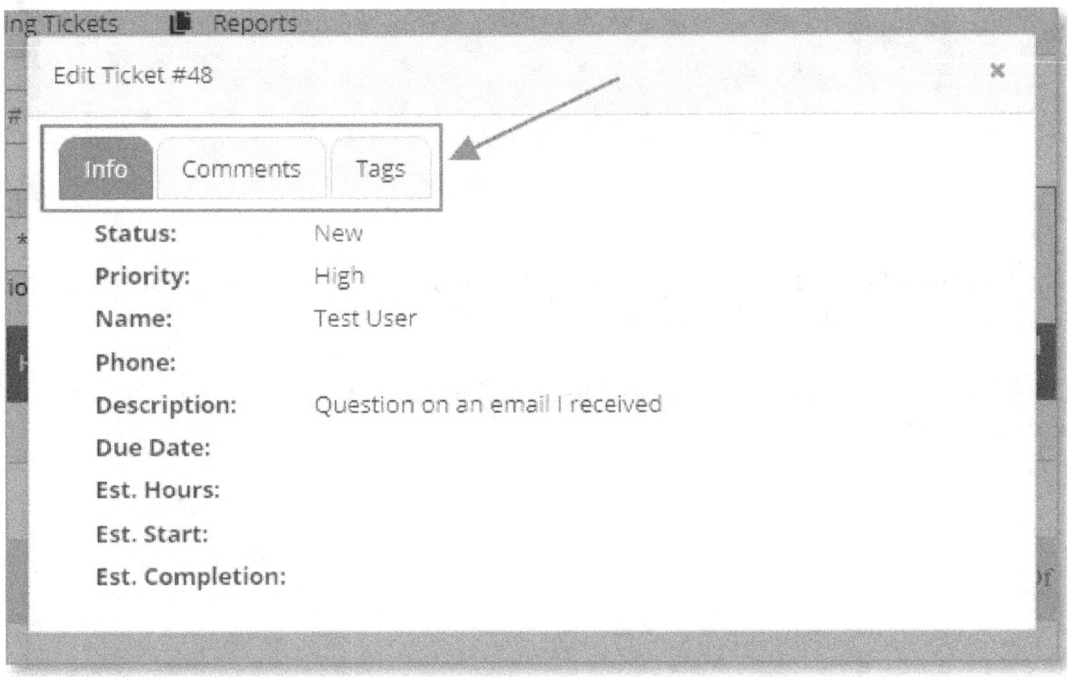

Users who are **Ticket Requestors** (not **Administrators**) will only have the ability to view the **Info**, **Comments**, and **Tags** screens.

They will have the ability to *view* the information on the **Info** screen but not *edit* it.

ADefHelpDesk 4

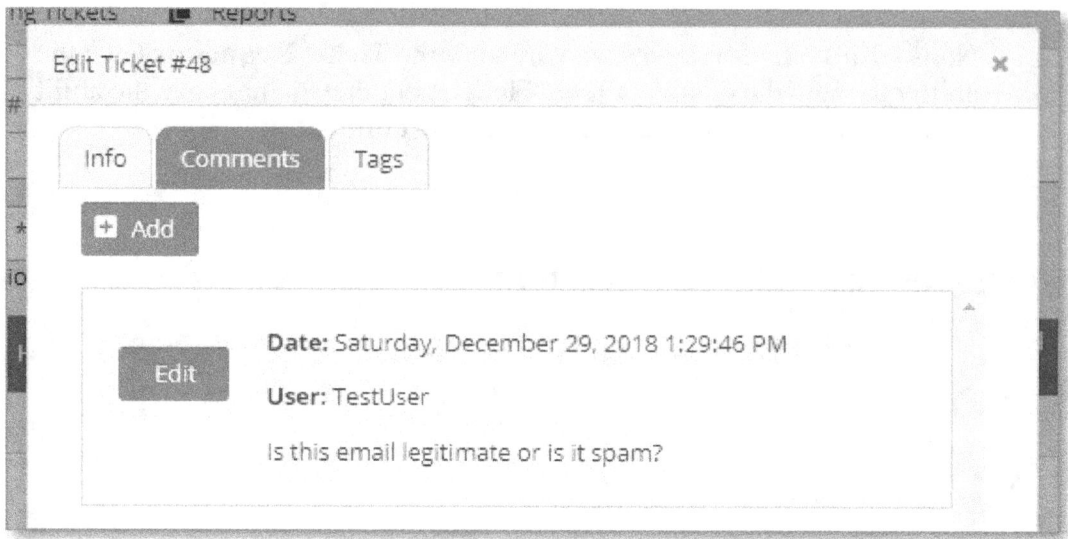

The **Comments** screen will only show comments that have the **Requester Visible** flag checked (by an **Administrator**).

Clicking the **Edit** button next to an existing **Comment** will display the **Comment** in *view only* mode.

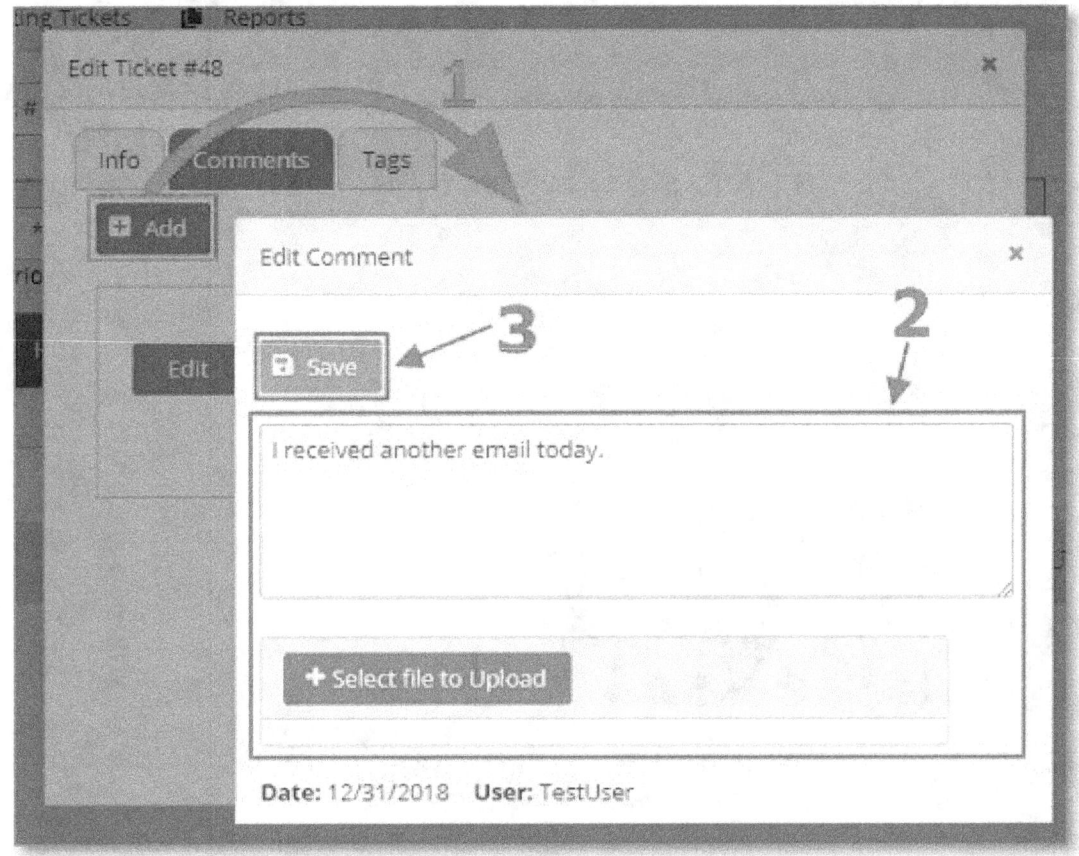

Clicking the **Add** button on the **Comments** screen will allow a new **Comment** to be added.

If the **Administrator** has enabled *file uploading* (by setting the **File Upload Permission** to **ALL** in **Administration/Application Settings**), a **Select file to Upload** button will appear.

Clicking this button will allow the **User** to upload a single file to attach to the **Comment**.

Clicking the **Save** button will save the **Comment**.

ADefHelpDesk 4

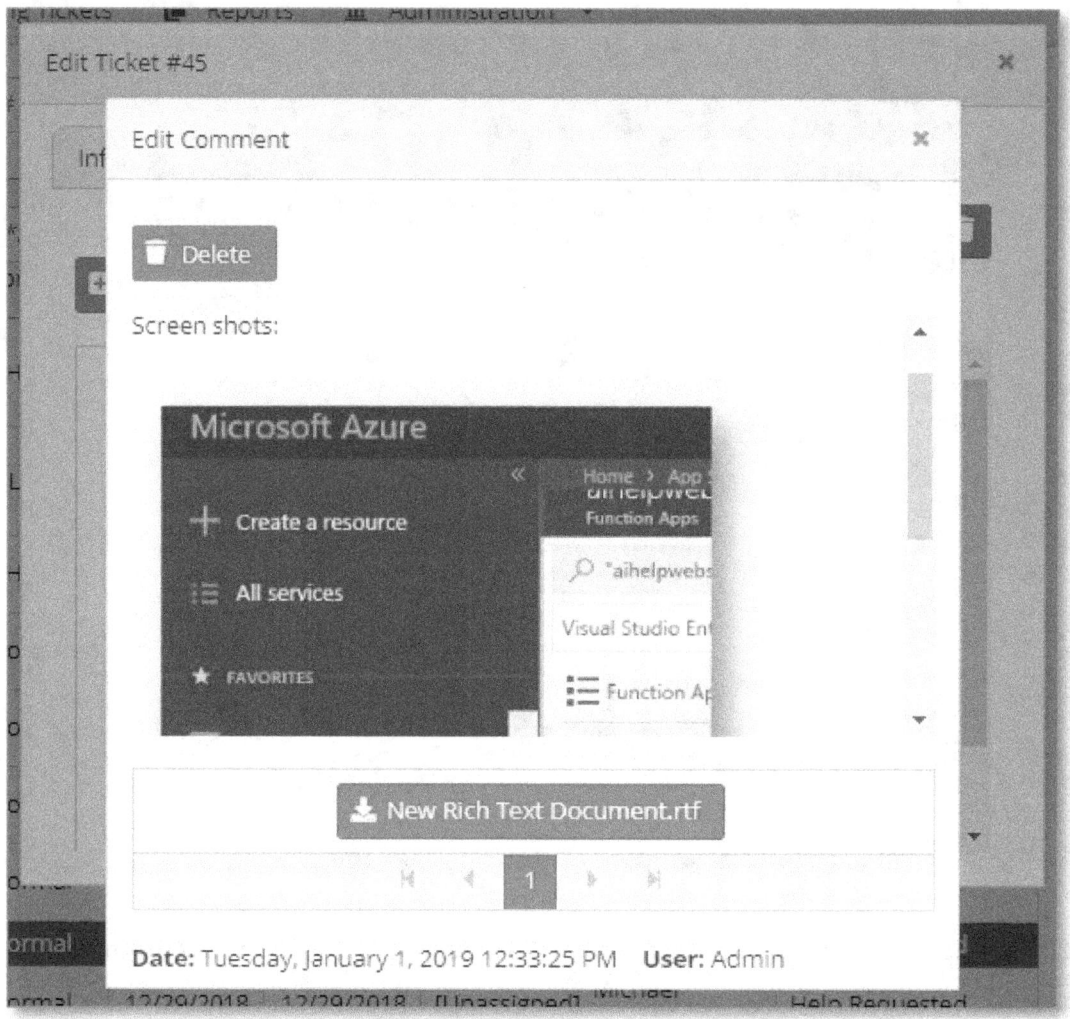

If the file attachment is an **.EML (Email)** file and in one of the supported *MIME* formats, after saving the **Comment** and then re-opening the **Comment**, **ADefHelpDesk** will display the **Email** contents in the **Edit Comment** screen and a link to download any attachments in the **Email**. Otherwise, it will display a link for the original email to be downloaded.

Mon 12/31/2018 5:54 PM

A Help Desk ticket assigned to your Role has been updated (#48)

To   Administrator User

Hello Administrator User,
A Help Desk ticket assigned to your Role: SuperUsers has been updated.

Ticket #: 48 (Comment #: 45)
Description: Question on an email I received
Status: New
Priority: High
Date: Monday, December 31, 2018 5:54:22 PM

Details: I received another email today.

To view this ticket, go to: http://localhost/AdefhelpdeskCore/#/home?ticketnumber=48

This Email was sent from: http://localhost/AdefhelpdeskCore.

Users in *role* that a **Ticket** is assigned to will receive an **Email** when a **Comment** is added by the **Ticket Requestor** (or another **Administrator**).

ADefHelpDesk 4

Editing Tickets By Administrators

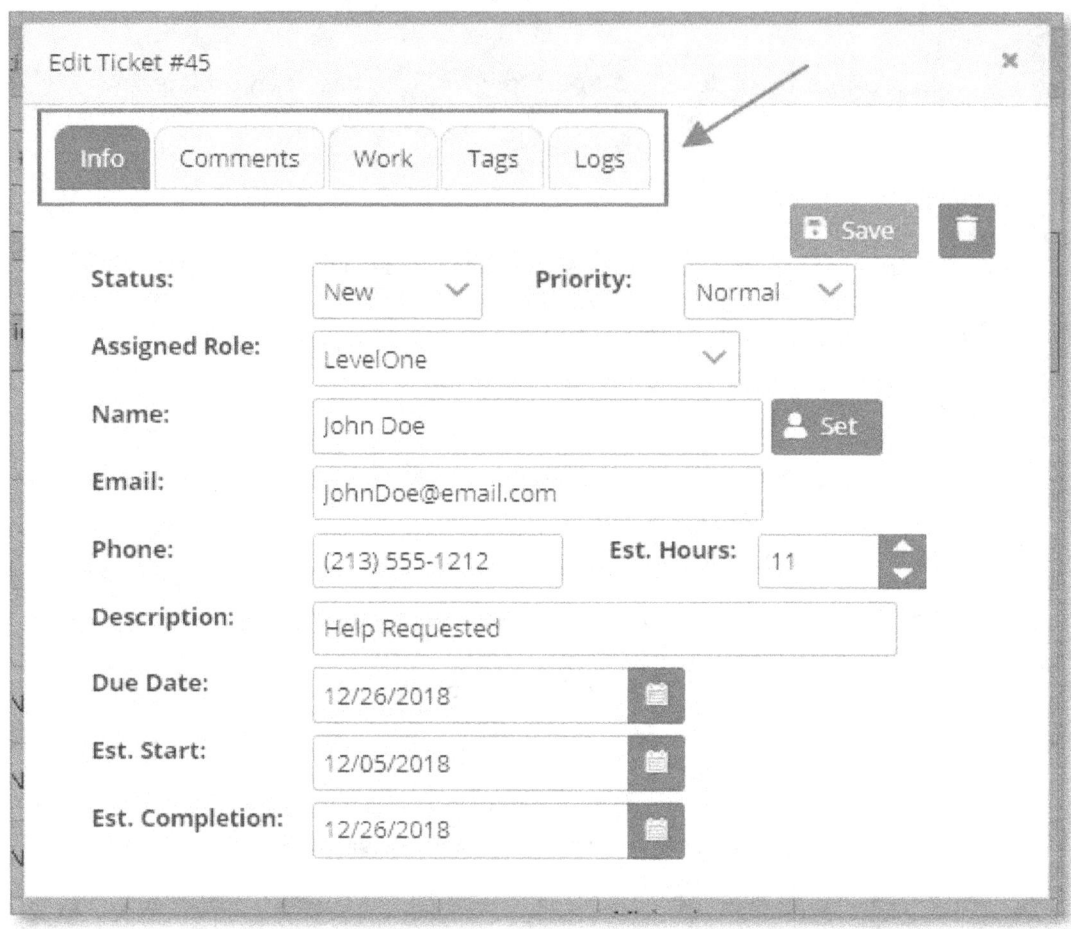

Users that are **Administrators** or members of a **Role** that a **Help Desk Ticket** is assigned to have the ability to alter any fields related to a **Ticket** and to view the **Logs** related to the **Ticket**.

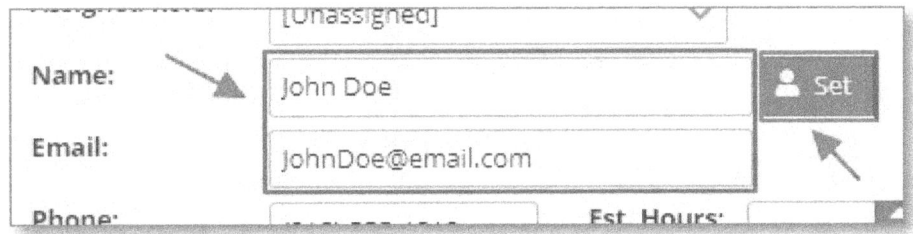

On the **Info** screen, the **Ticket Requester** can be set either by entering their name and **Email** address or by selecting a **User Account**.

To set the **Ticket Requester** to a **User Account**, click the **Set** button.

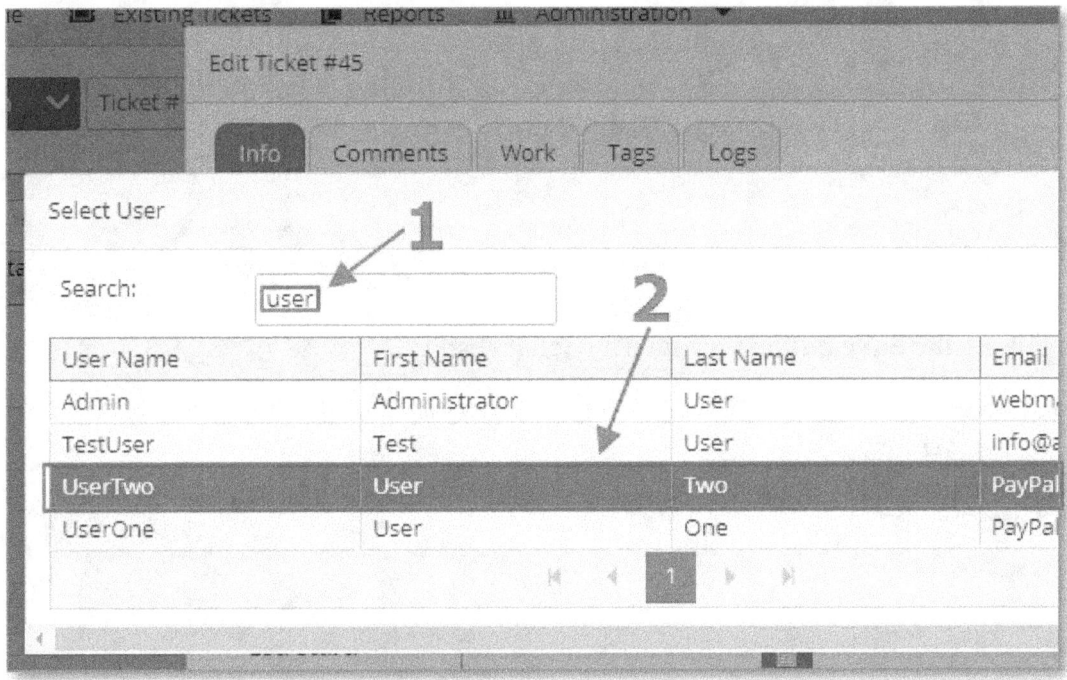

This will bring up the **Select User** screen. The **Search** box can be used to assist in searching for a **User Account**. Clicking on a **User Account** in the *results grid* will select that **User Account**.

ADefHelpDesk 4

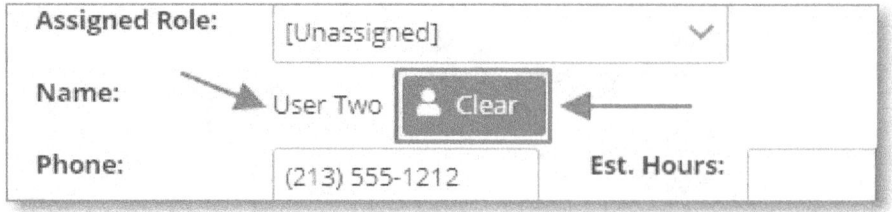

The **Ticket Requester** will now be set. The **Email** field will no longer display because the **Email** address attached to the **User Account** will be used for notification **Emails**.

Clicking the **Clear** button will clear the **Ticket Requester**.

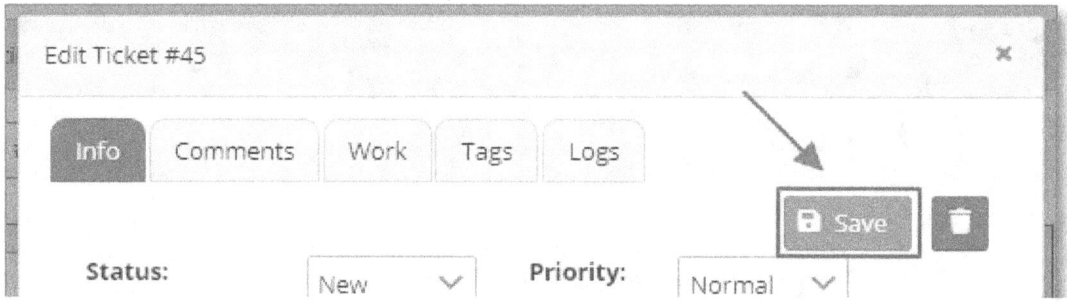

Clinking the **Save** button will save any changes.

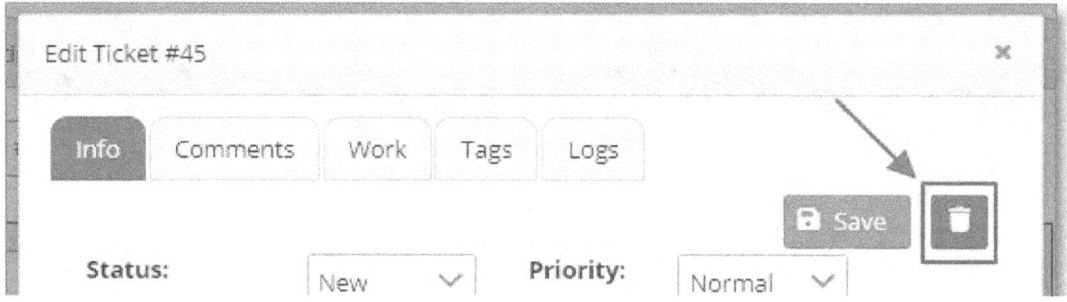

Clicking the **Red** *trash can* icon will delete the **Help Desk Ticket**.

Add and Edit Comments

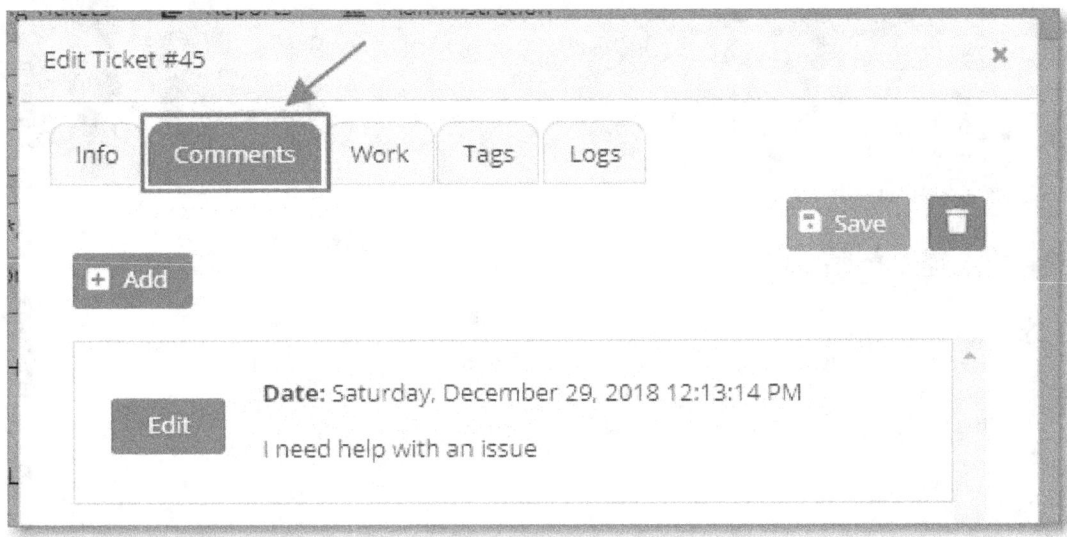

Comments are accessible by clicking the **Comments** tab.

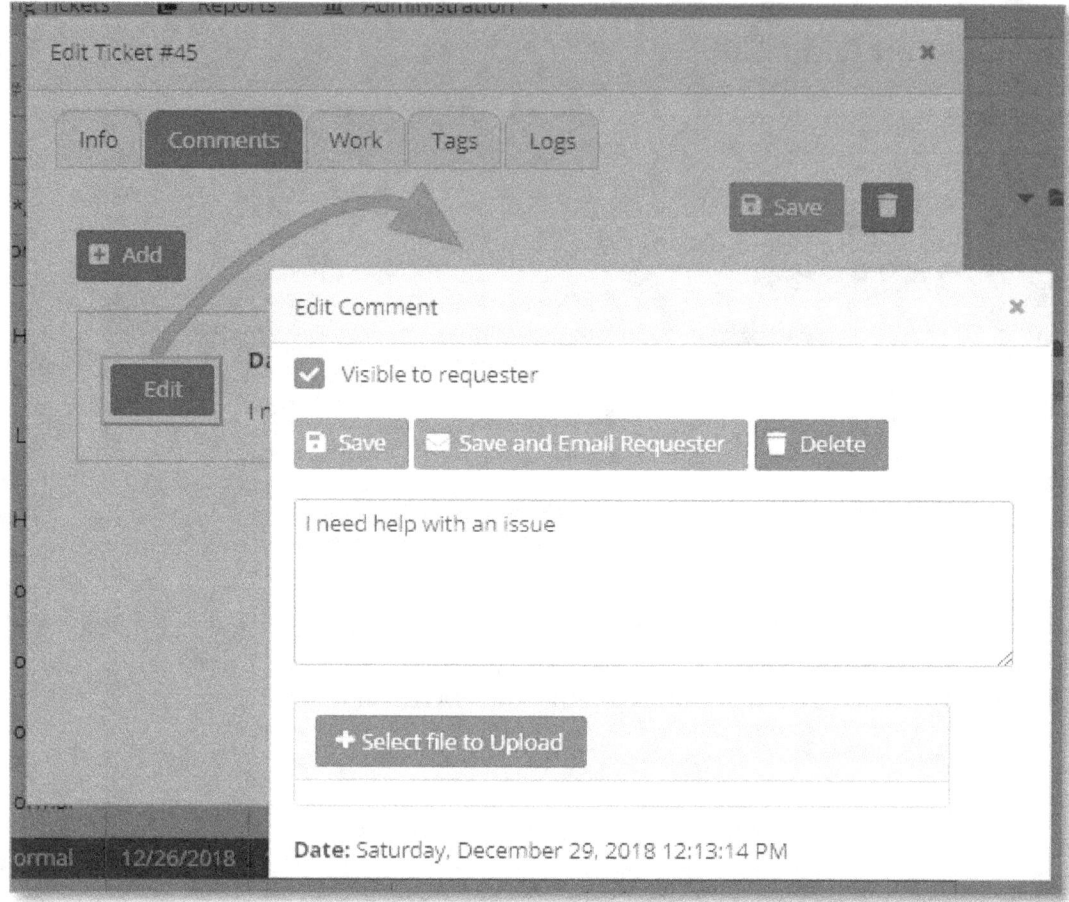

When the **Edit** button next to a **Comment** is clicked, the details of the **Comment** will show in the **Edit Comment** screen.

Users who are members of the **Role** assigned to a **Ticket** have the ability to enter or update **Comments** and upload files to attach to the **Comment**.

They can also check the **Visible to Requestor** box and click the **Save** or the **Save and Email Requestor** button to insert a **Comment** and send an **Email** containing the **Comment** to the **Ticket Requestor** and the other **Administrators** in the **Role** assigned to the **Ticket**.

The **Delete** button will allow them to delete the **Comment**.

Note: Users who are only **Ticket Requestors** are only able to see **Comments** that are marked **Visible to Requestor**.

Add and Edit Work Items

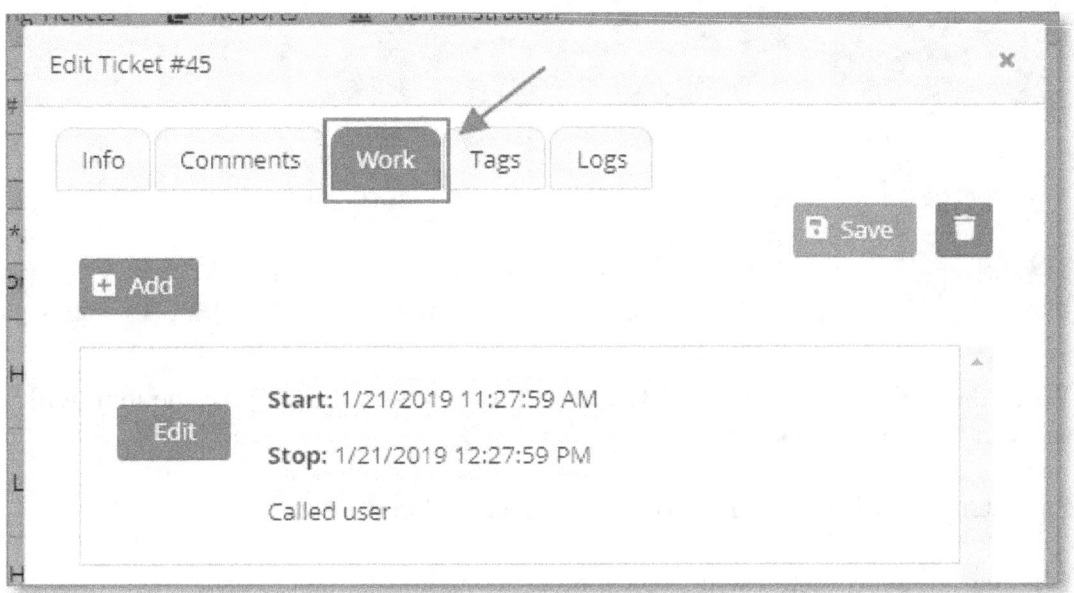

Work items are accessible by clicking the **Work** tab.

ADefHelpDesk 4

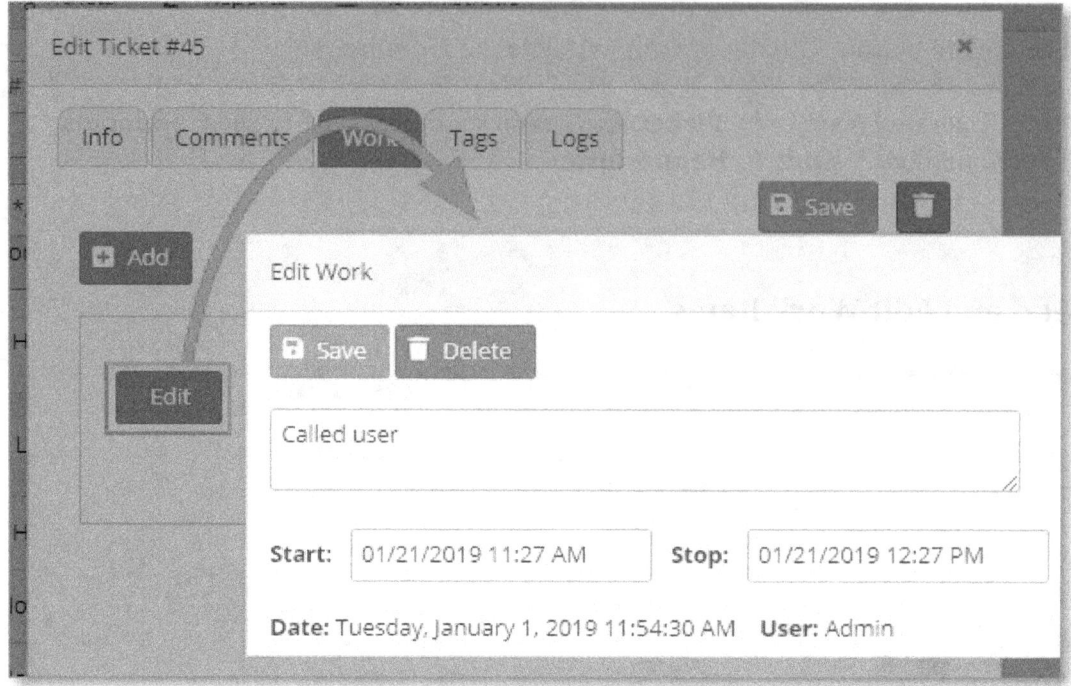

When the **Edit** button next to a **Work** item is clicked, the details of the item will show in the **Edit Work** screen.

Each item must include a **Description** and a **Start** and **Stop** time.

Clicking the **Add** button will allow a new **Work** item to be created.

The **Save** button will *save* any changes.

The **Delete** button will *delete* the item.

Edit Tags

Tags associated with a **Help Desk Ticket** are accessible by clicking the **Tags** tab.

Clicking the box next to each **Tag** will *enable* or *disable* that **Tag's** association with the **Help Desk Ticket**.

The **Save** button will *save* any changes.

Clicking the **Red** *trash can* icon will delete the **Help Desk Ticket**.

Note: Tags for the application can be administered by **Administrators** in **Administration/Tags**.

ADefHelpDesk 4

View Logs

Logs are accessible by clicking the **Logs** button.

The **Logs** screen will display all the log entries associated with the **Help Desk Ticket**, including who viewed the **Ticket** and what *roles* and **Users** in those *roles* have been assigned to administer it.

Chapter 4: Administration

Creating a Ticket for a User

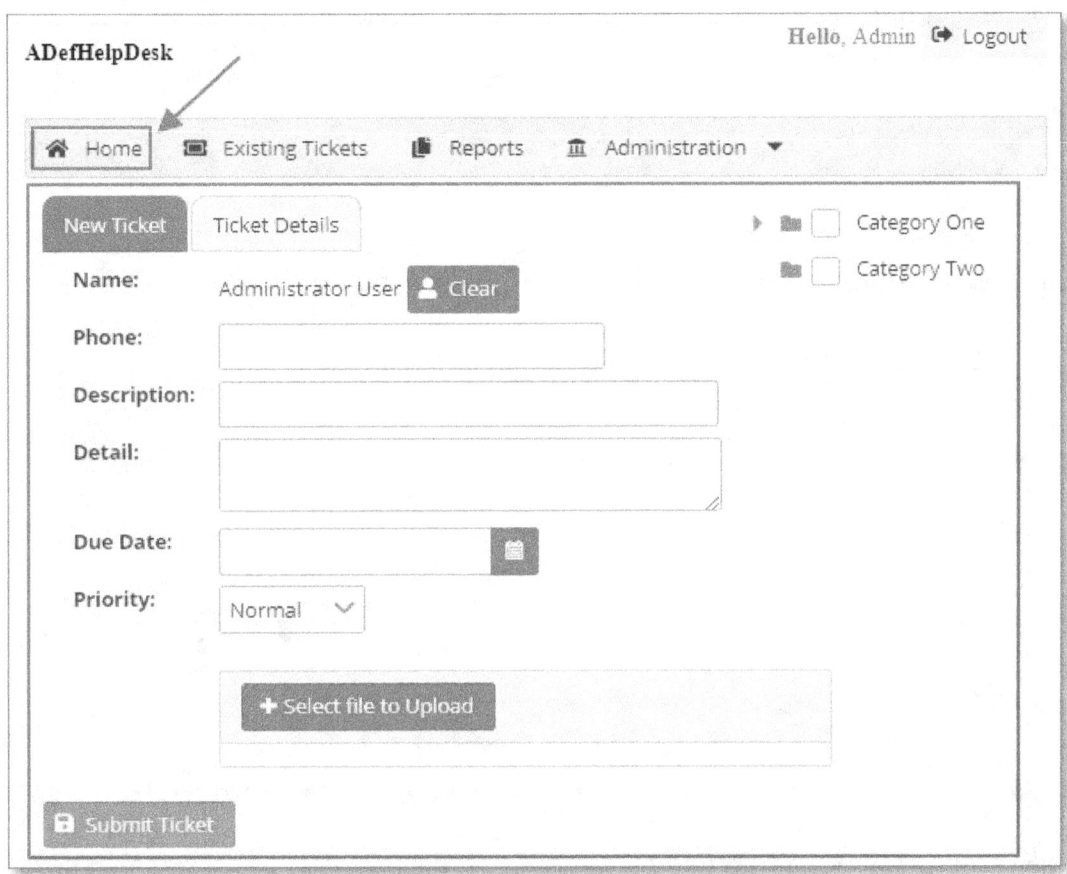

An **Administrator** (any **User** who has the **Is SuperUser** box checked in **Administration/User Manager**) or a user that is assigned to at least one **Role** (in **Administration/User Manager**) can create a **Ticket** for an **Anonymous user** or a **Ticket** for a **Registered user** by selecting the user using

ADefHelpDesk 4

the **Select User** section (which <u>only</u> appears on the **New Ticket** screen for **Administrators**).

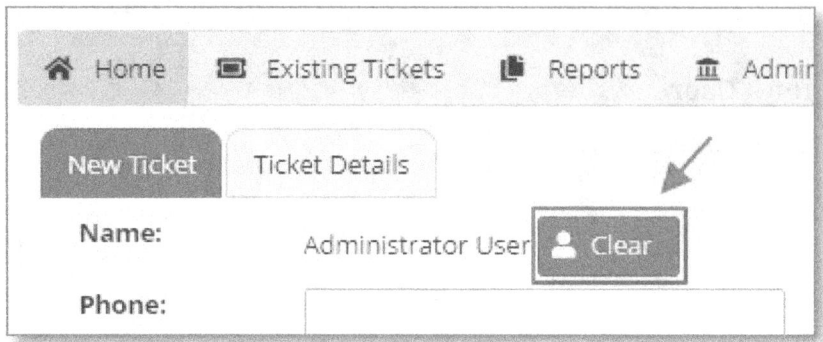

The **Select User** option will initially display a **Clear** button.

Clicking this button will allow a **User** to be selected.

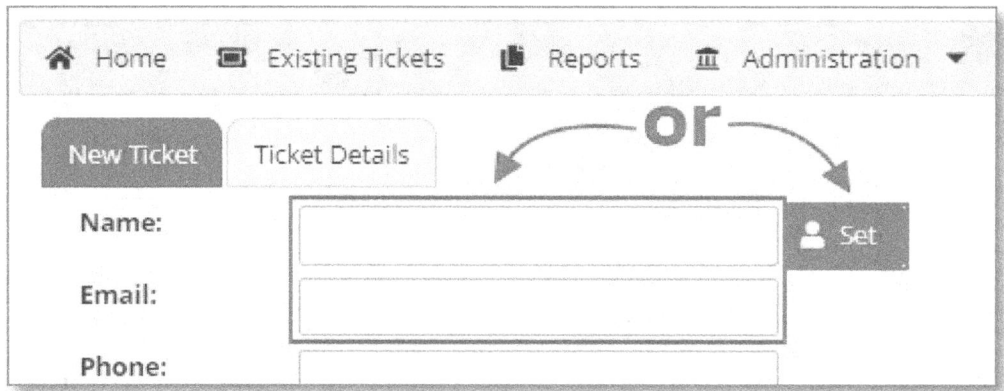

The current **User Selection** will be *cleared,* and the option will be presented to enter a **Name** and **Email** for an **Anonymous User**, <u>or</u> the **Set** button can be pressed to select an **Existing User**.

Note: An **Administrator** (any **User** who has the **Is SuperUser** box checked in **Administration/User Manager**) has the ability to create a *new* **User Account** in **Administration/User Manager**.

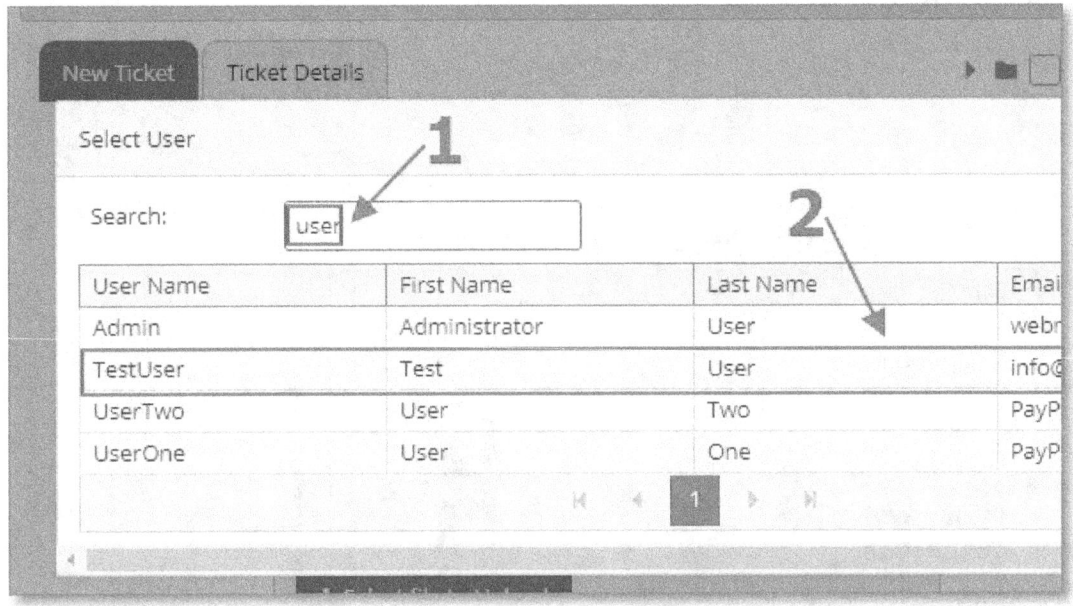

If the **Set** button is pressed, the **Select User** screen will display.

The **User** list can be *filtered* using the **Search** box. The desired **User** is selected by *clicking on the row* that they appear on.

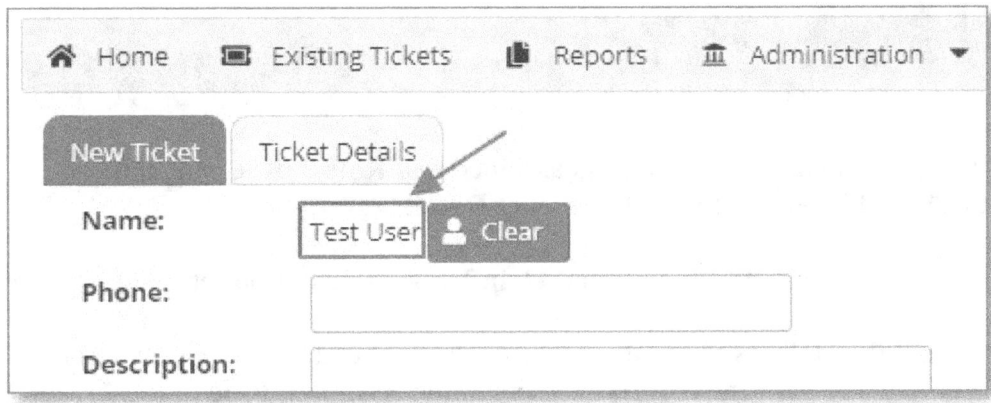

The **User** will now be set.

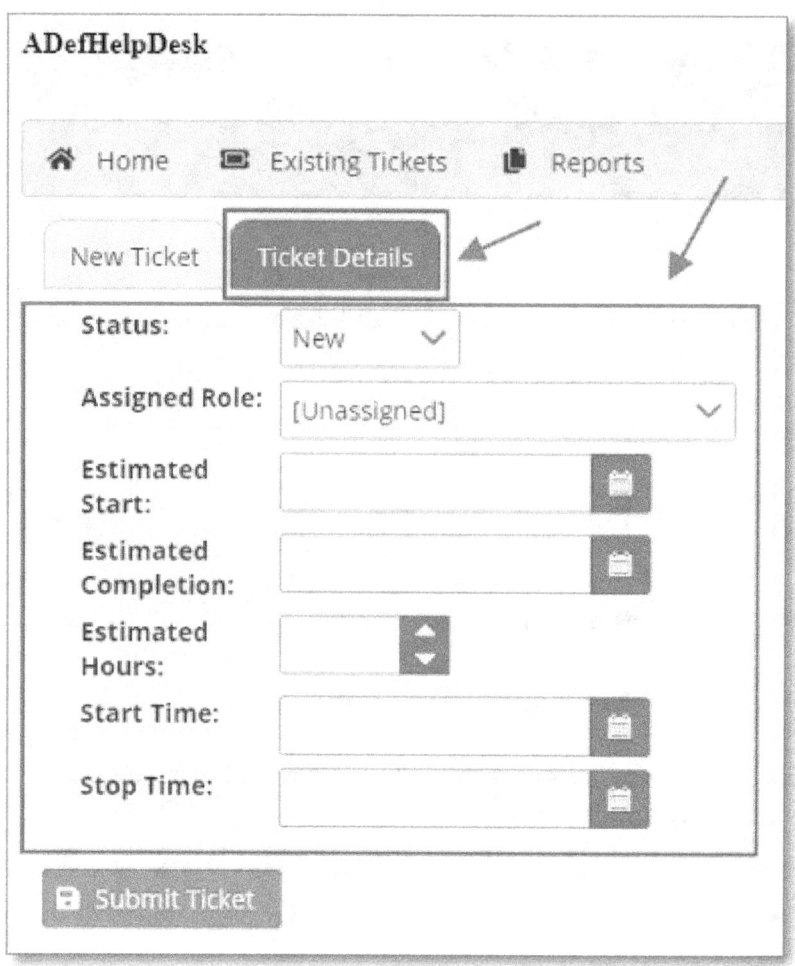

In addition, **Administrators**, and users assigned to a **Role** will see an *additional tab* on the **New Ticket** screen labeled **Ticket Details**.

This tab allows all the fields of an initial **Help Desk Ticket** to be set.

Clicking the **Submit Ticket** button will create the **Ticket** and *trigger* any **emails** to the **User** and any **Administrators** or users in the **Assigned Role** of the **Ticket** (if the **Assigned Role** dropdown is set).

Note:

- **Name**, **Email**, and **Description** are *required*. All other fields are *optional* and can be left blank.
- The **Tags**, displayed as a nested tree, with options that can be checked, will only display if the **Administrator** has created **Tags** in the **Administration/Tags** section
- **Emails** will be sent according to the rules described in the documentation covered in **Creating A Help Desk Ticket**.
- An **Administrator** (any **User** who has the **Is SuperUser** box checked in **Administration/User Manager**) *always* has the ability to **upload** a file to attach to a **Ticket**. Other users are only able to upload a file if the **Administrator** has enabled **file uploading** by setting the **File Upload Permission** to ALL in **Administration/Application Settings**.

Assigning Tickets to Groups

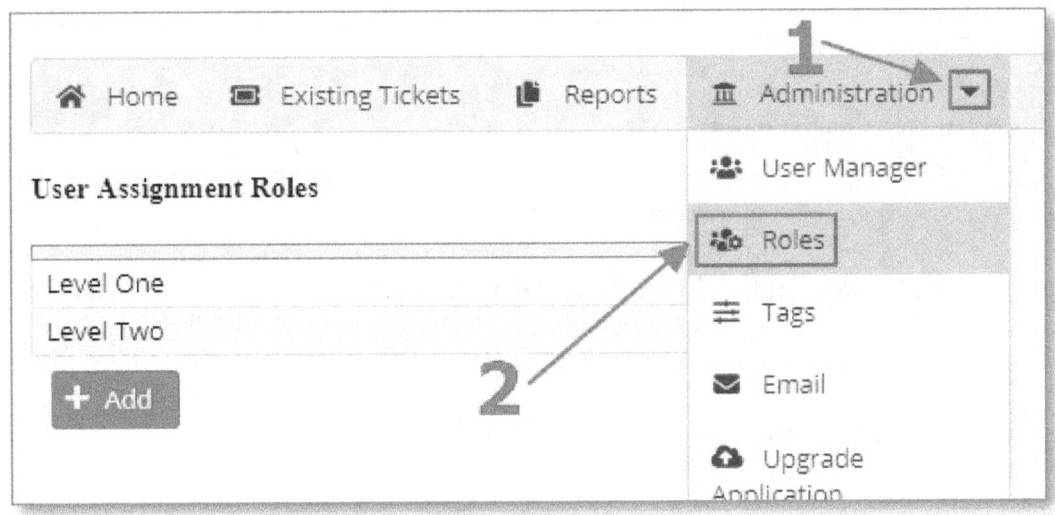

ADefHelpDesk 4

Roles allow **Help Desk Tickets** to be assigned to one or more users to be managed and eventually resolved. To implement this functionality, **Roles** must be *created*, *assigned* to **User Accounts**, and then **Help Desk Tickets** *assigned* to the **Roles**.

Note: Emails will be sent to **Users** in the **Role** assigned to a **Help Desk Ticket** according to the rules described in the documentation covered in **Creating A Help Desk Ticket**.

Creating Roles

An **Administrator** (any **User** who has the **Is SuperUser** box checked in **Administration/User Manager**) has the ability to create and manage **Roles** by selecting **Roles** from the **Administration** menu.

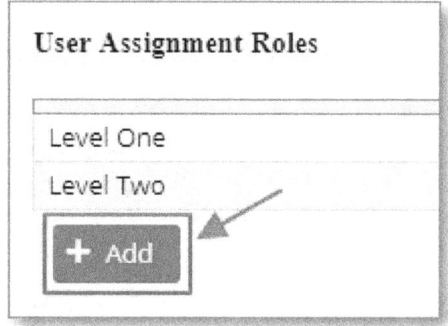

New **Roles** are created by clicking the **Add** button.

The **Role** name can be entered and *saved* by clicking the **Save** button.

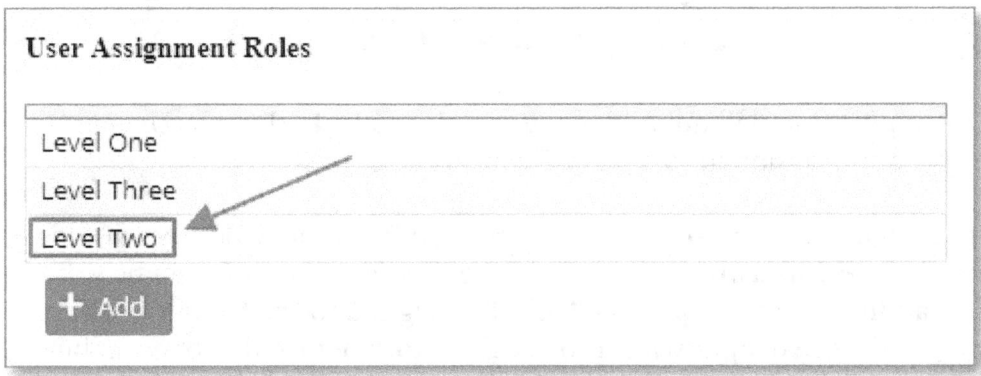

Existing Roles can be *edited* or *deleted* by first clicking on them in the **User Assignment Roles** list.

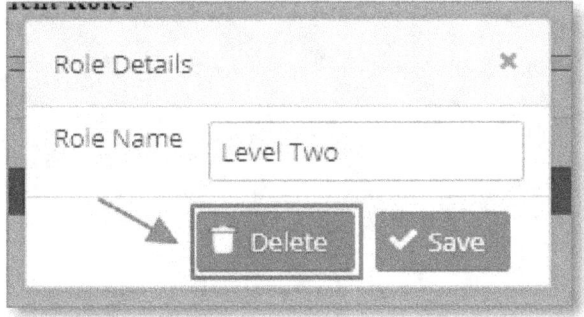

ADefHelpDesk 4

The **Role** can be *edited* and *saved* or *deleted*.

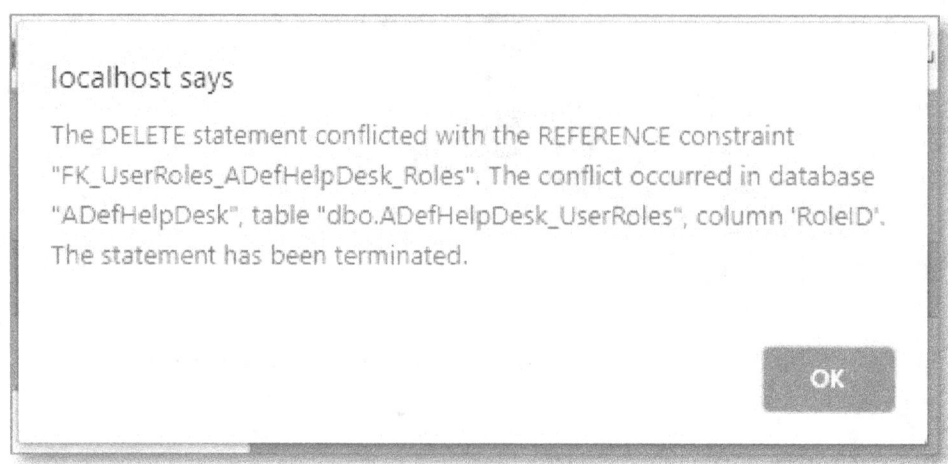

Note: The application will not allow you to delete a **Role** that has **Users** assigned to it or is assigned to a **Help Desk Ticket**.

All **Users** assigned to the **Role** must be removed from the **Role** (by editing each **User** in **Administration/User Manager**) before the **Role** can be *deleted*. In addition, any **Help Desk Tickets** assigned to the **Role** must have their **Assigned Role** dropdown set to another **Role** before this one can be *deleted*.

Assigning Users To Groups

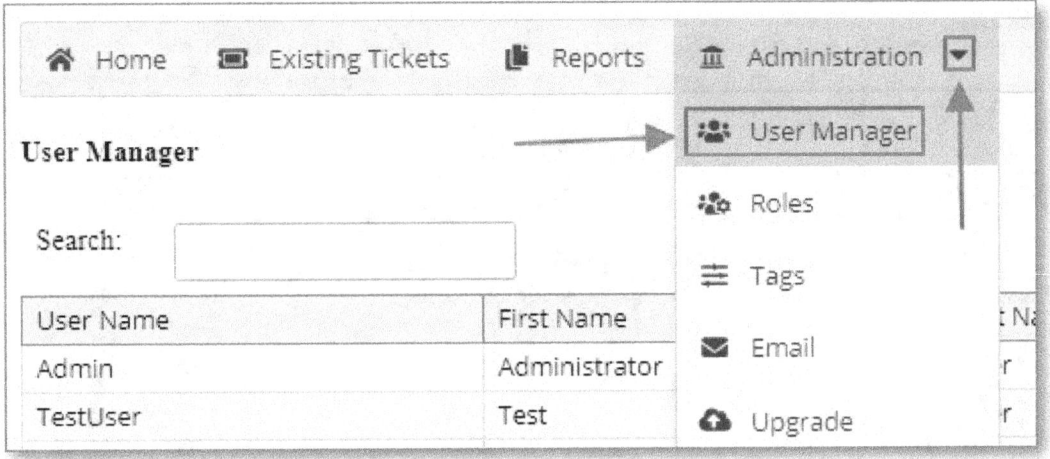

An **Administrator** (any **User** who has the **Is SuperUser** box checked in **Administration/User Manager**) has the ability to manage **Roles** for **Users** by selecting **User Manager** from the **Administration** menu.

ADefHelpDesk 4

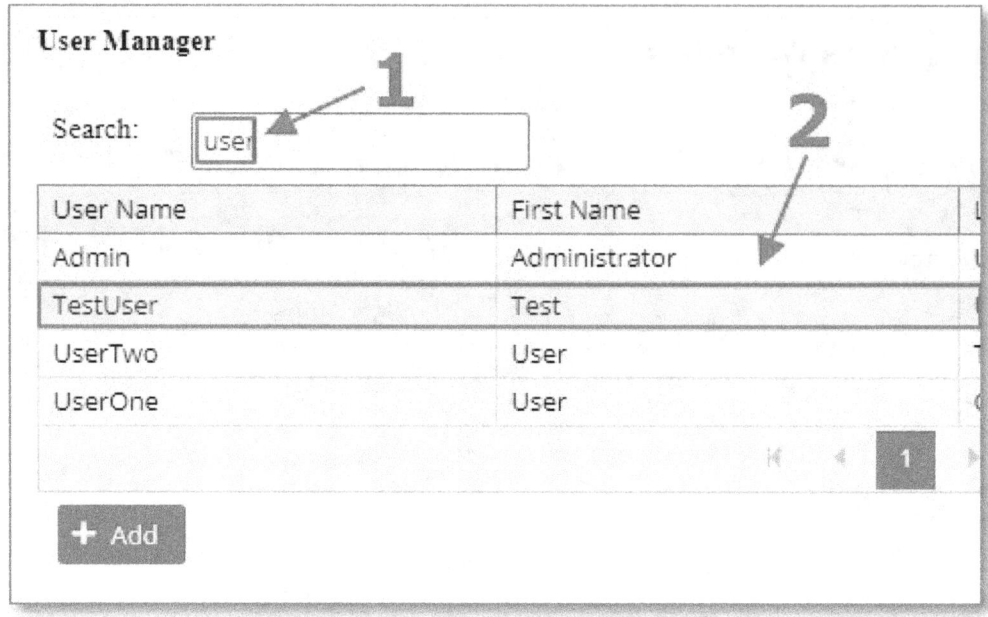

This will bring up the **Select User** screen. The **Search** box can be used to assist in searching for a **User Account**. Clicking on a **User Account** in the *results grid* will select that **User Account**.

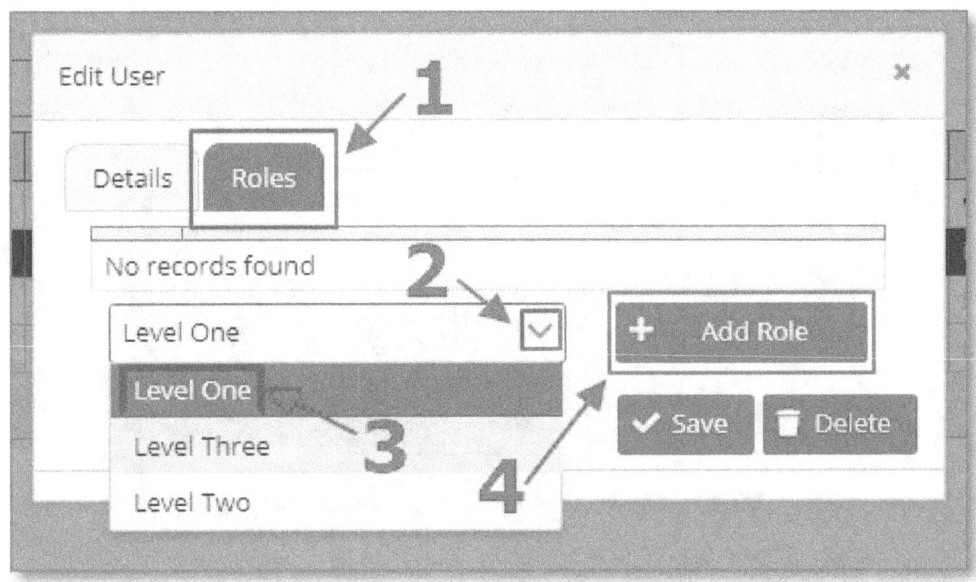

Clicking the **Roles** tab will navigate to **Role** selection. A previously created **Role** can be selected in the *drop down,* and the **Add Role** button can then be *clicked* to add it to the list.

The process can be repeated to add any additional **Roles**.

Clicking the *trashcan* icon to the left of a **Role** in the list will remove the **Role** from the **User**.

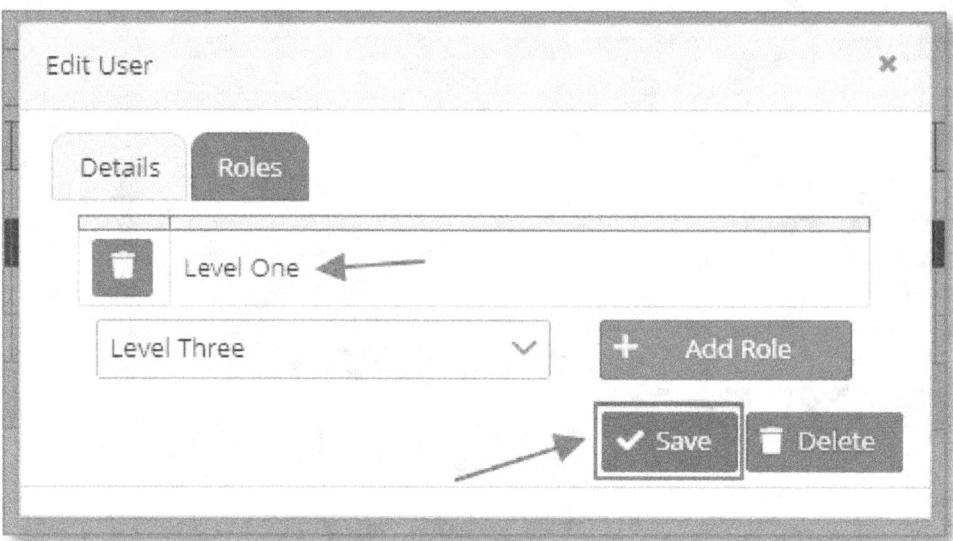

The **Save** button must be clicked to *save* any **Role** changes for the **User**.

Assigning Help Desk Tickets To Roles

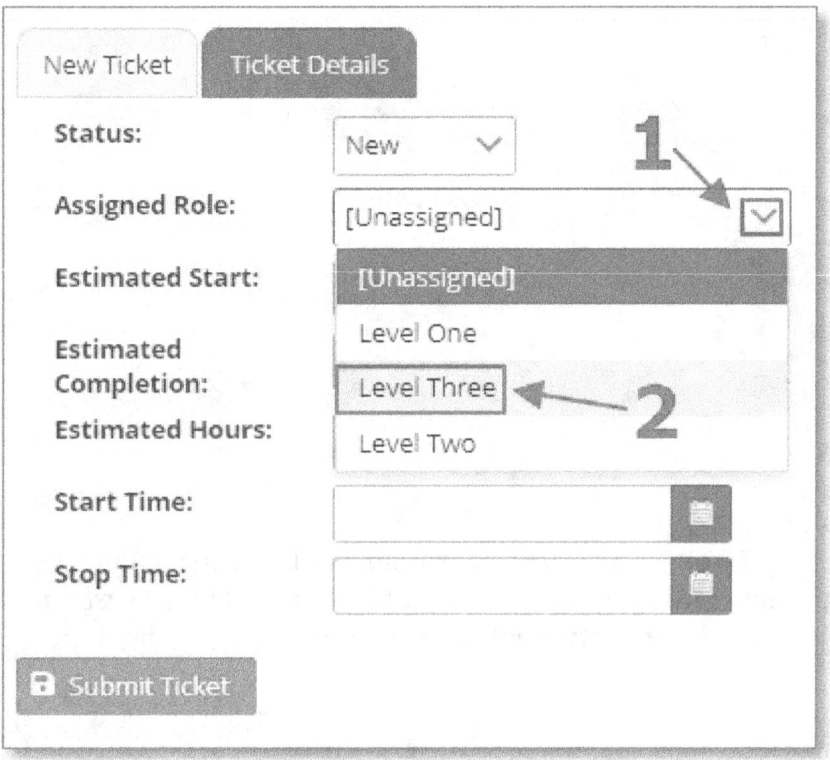

When *creating* or *editing* a **Help Desk Ticket**, a previously created **Role** can be assigned to a ticket by selecting it in the **Assigned Role** dropdown.

ADefHelpDesk 4

Reports

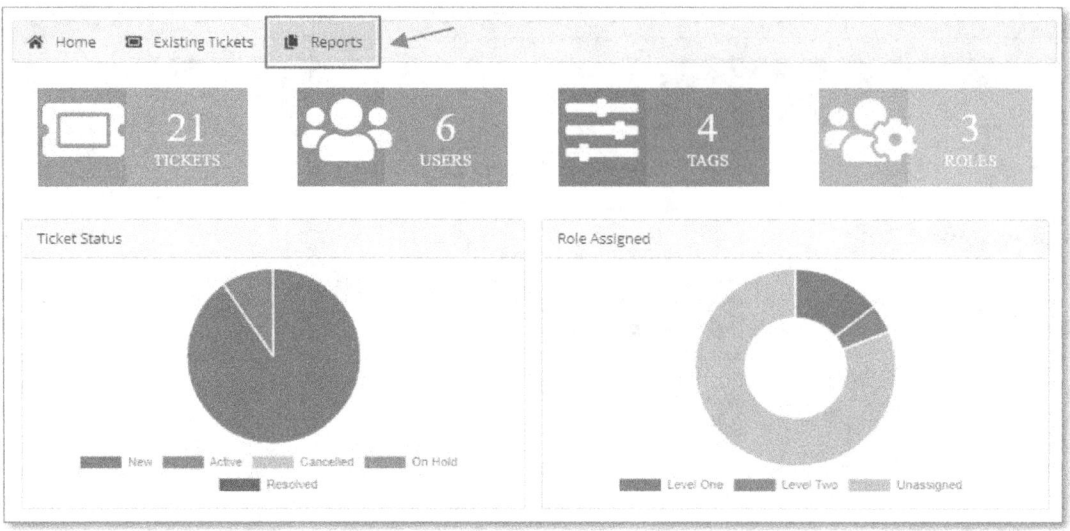

An **Administrator** (any **User** who has the **Is SuperUser** box checked in **Administration/User Manager**) or a user that is assigned to *at least one* **Role** (in **Administration/User Manager**) has the ability to access the **Reports** screen.

The **Reports** screen displays the counts of **Help Desk Tickets**, **Users**, **Tags**, and **Roles**.

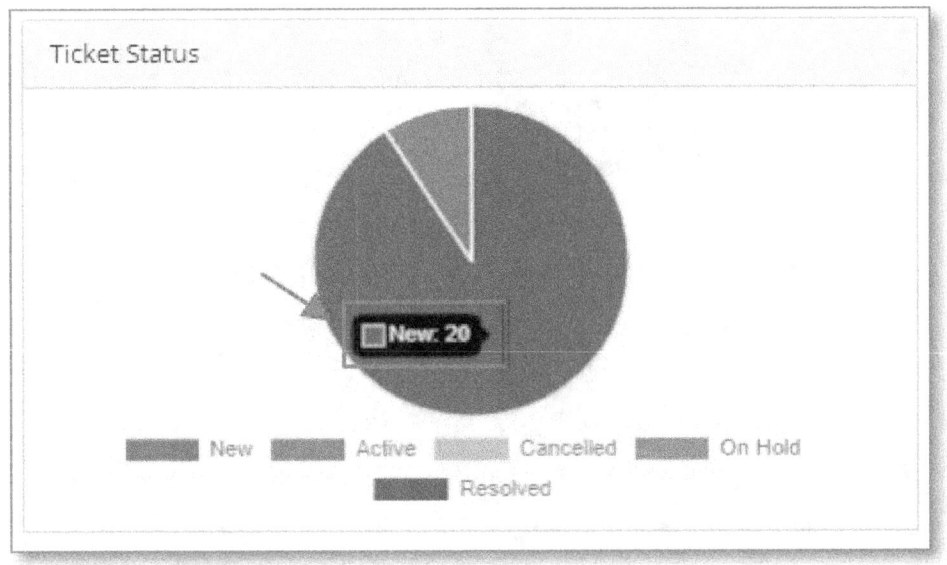

The percentage of **Help Desk Tickets** that are assigned to each **Status** are displayed in the **Ticket Status** section.

Hovering your *mouse pointer* over a section of the **pie chart** will display the actual count of **Help Desk Tickets**.

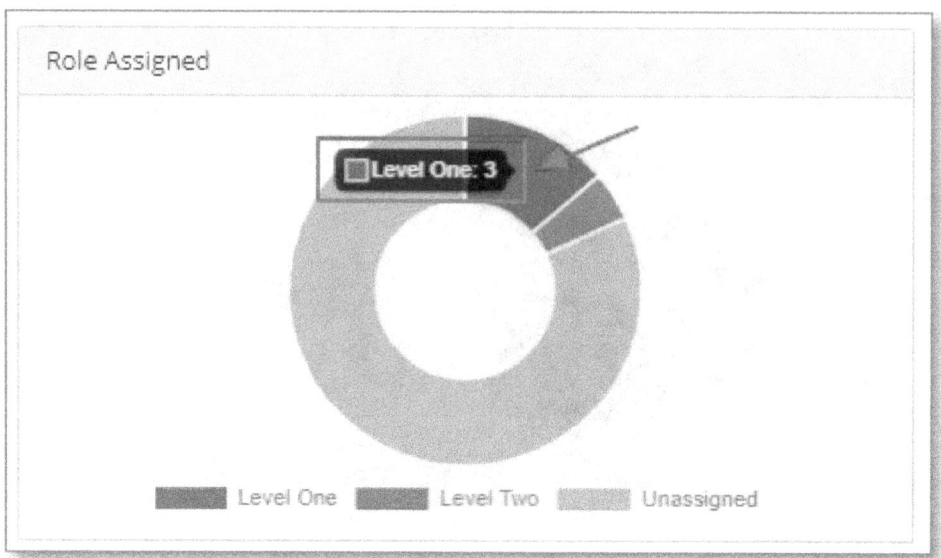

The percentage of **Help Desk Tickets** that are assigned to each **Role** are displayed in the **Role Assigned** section.

Hovering your *mouse pointer* over a section of the **donut chart** will display the actual count of **Help Desk Tickets**.

Chapter 5: Administration Settings

Application Settings

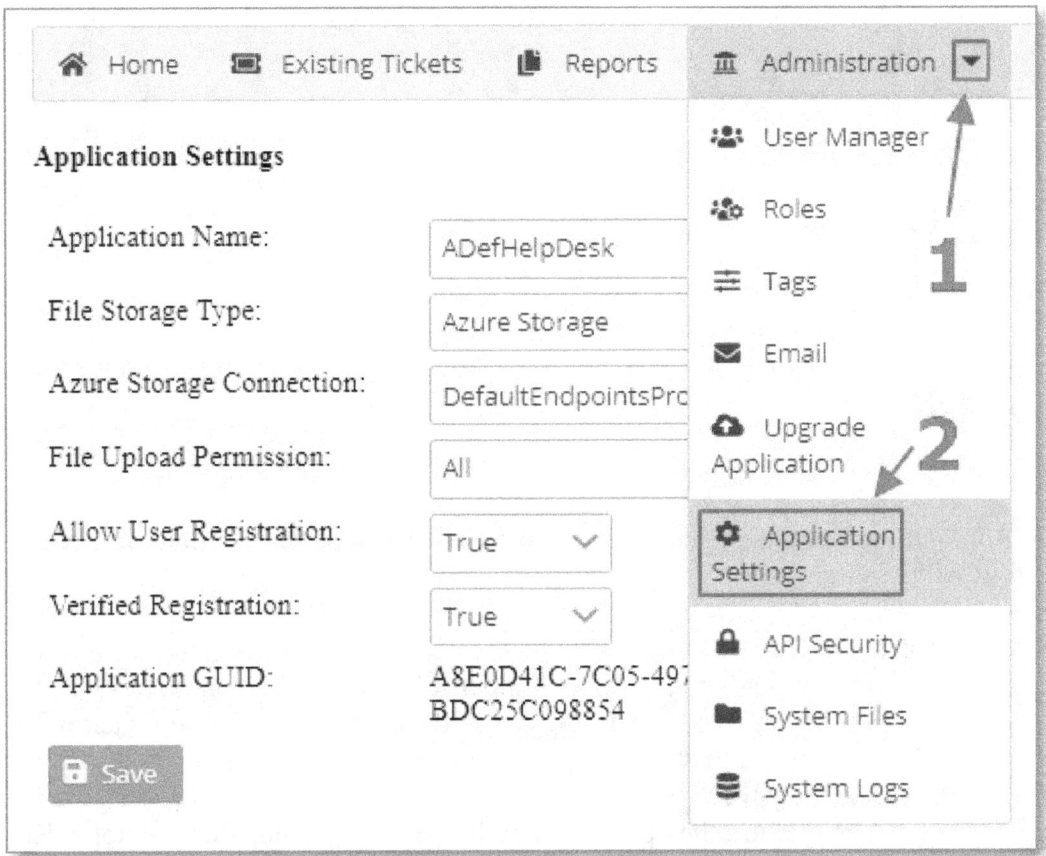

An **Administrator** (any **User** who has the **Is SuperUser** box checked in **Administration/User Manager**) has the ability to manage the settings for the application by selecting **Application Settings** from the **Administration** menu.

ADefHelpDesk 4

Application Settings

Application Name:	ADefHelpDesk
File Storage Type:	Azure Storage
Azure Storage Connection:	DefaultEndpointsProtocol=https;AccountNa
File Upload Permission:	All
Allow User Registration:	True
Verified Registration:	True
Application GUID:	A8E0D41C-7C05-4978-8CA5-BDC25C098854

Save

The Application Settings screen allows the **Administrator** to **view** and/or **update** the following values:

- **Application Name:**
    - The name displayed in the upper left corner of the application. Note, you will have to log out of the application and log back in to see this value change after updating it and saving it.
- **File Storage Type:**
    - The method the application will use to store files that are uploaded to be attached to **Help Desk Tickets**. Possible values are **File Storage** and **Azure Storage**.
- **File Upload Permission:**
    - Indicates what group of users will be allowed to upload files to attach to **Help Desk Tickets**. Possible values are **All** and **Administrator**.
- **Allow User Registration:**

- o If this is set to **True**, the **Register** option will be available, and an anonymous user will have the ability to create an account.
- **Application GUID:**
  - o This value is uniquely generated when the application is installed, and this value stored in the database. It is used to identify the application by external **Web API** clients when they connect to the application.

Note: The **Save** button must be pressed to save any changes to the screen.

File System Settings

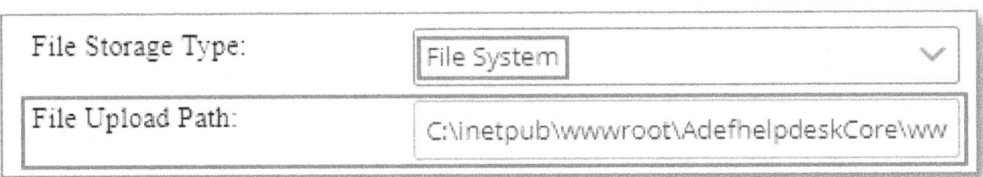

When **File System** is selected for **File Storage Type**, the **File Upload Path** setting will appear. The value entered for this setting must be a location for which the process under which the web application is running must have **read** and **write** permission.

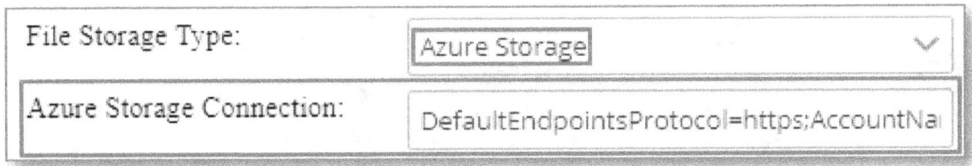

When **Azure Storage** is selected for **File Storage Type**, the **Azure Storage Connection** setting will appear. The value entered for this setting must be a valid **Microsoft Azure Storage** connection string.

User Registration Settings

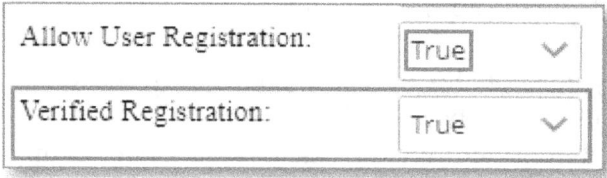

The **Verified Registration** setting option will only appear when the **Allow User Registration** value is set to **True**.

If the **Verified Registration** setting is set to **True**, when a user creates an account using the **Register** option, they will be sent an email with a code that they will have to use when they log on for the first time.

User Manager

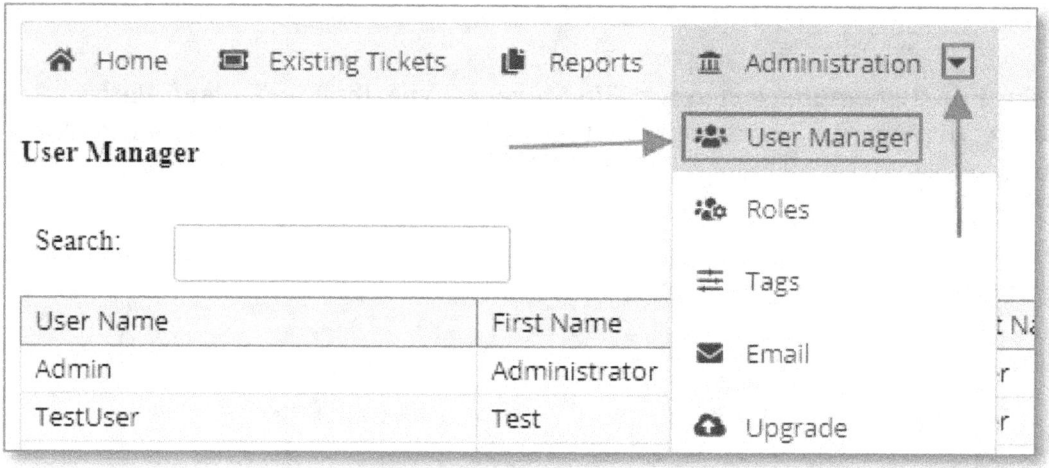

An **Administrator** (any **User** who has the **Is SuperUser** box checked in **Administration/User Manager**) has the ability to manage **Roles** for **Users** by selecting **User Manager** from the **Administration** menu.

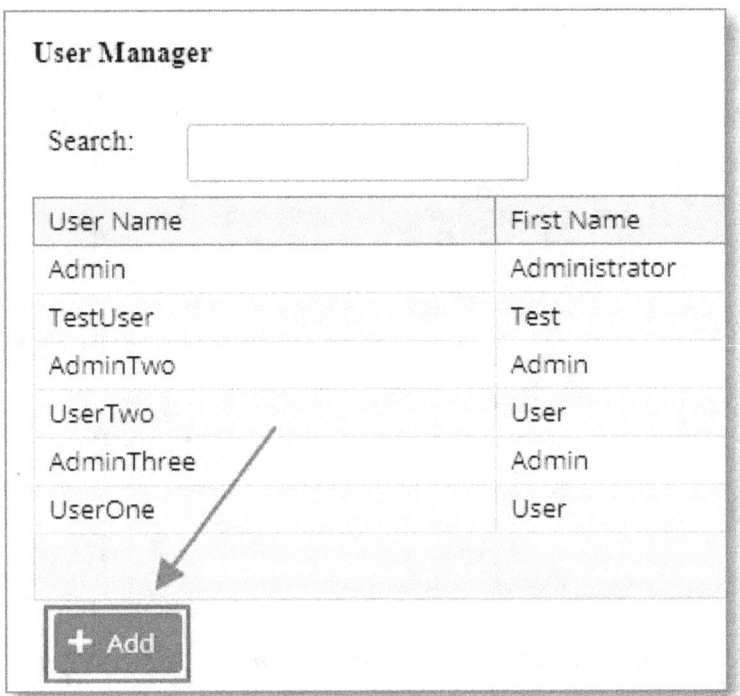

A *new* **User Account** can be created by clicking the **Add** button.

ADefHelpDesk 4

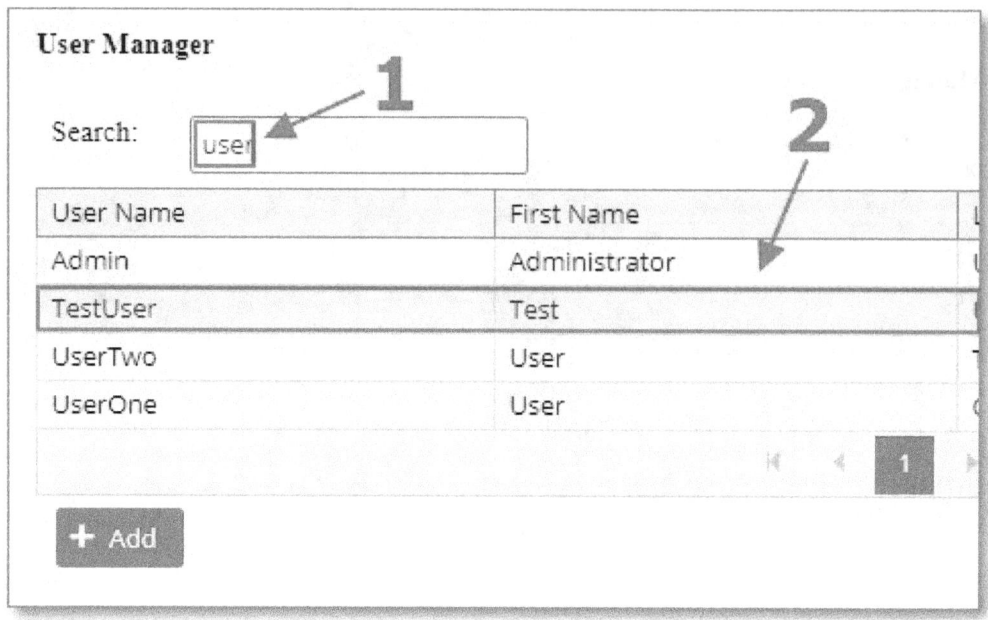

The **Search** box can be used to assist in searching for an *existing* **User Account**.

Clicking on a **User Account** in the *results grid* will select that **User Account**.

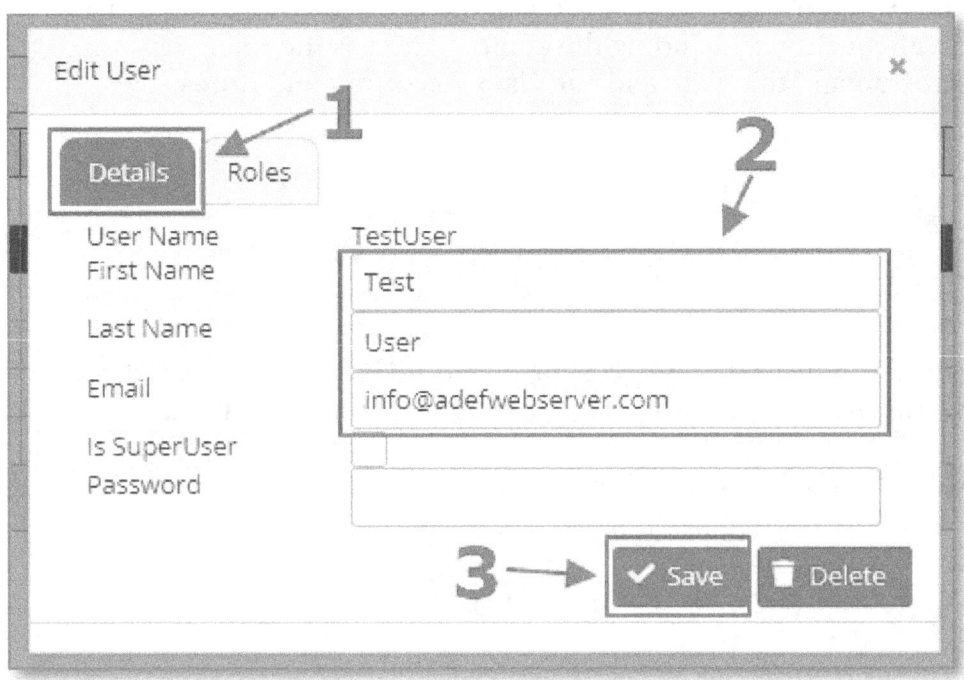

When a **User Account** is selected, clicking the **Details** tab will navigate to **Details** section.

Information can be altered in any of the *editable fields*. The **Save** button must be clicked to **Save** any changes.

Note: The **User Name** cannot be changed.

A user can be *deleted* at any time by clicking the **Delete** button.

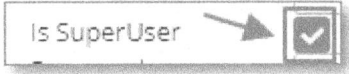

ADefHelpDesk 4

Clicking the **IS SuperUser** box will provide the **User Account** with the ability to perform all functions, including the ability to access the **User Administration** and to *create* and *edit* **User Accounts** and **Roles**.

The password is only updated if a value is entered into the **Password** box. Otherwise, the original password for the **User Account** is retained.

Note: A value for the **Password** box is required when creating a new **User Account**.

Role Management

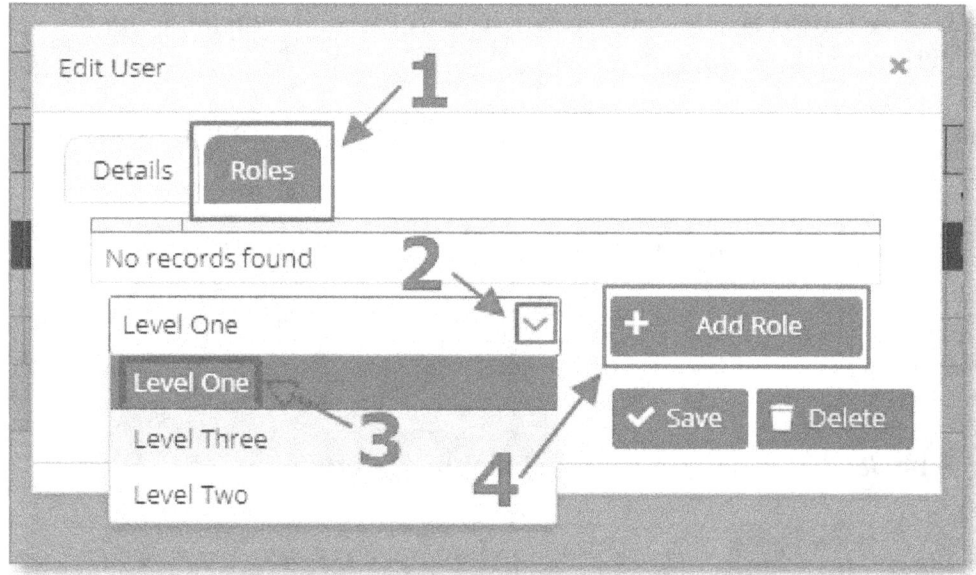

Clicking the **Roles** tab will navigate to **Role** selection. A previously created **Role** can be selected in the *drop down*, and the **Add Role** button can then be *clicked* to add it to the list.

The process can be repeated to add any additional **Roles**.

Clicking the *trashcan* icon to the left of a **Role** in the list will remove the **Role** from the **User Account**.

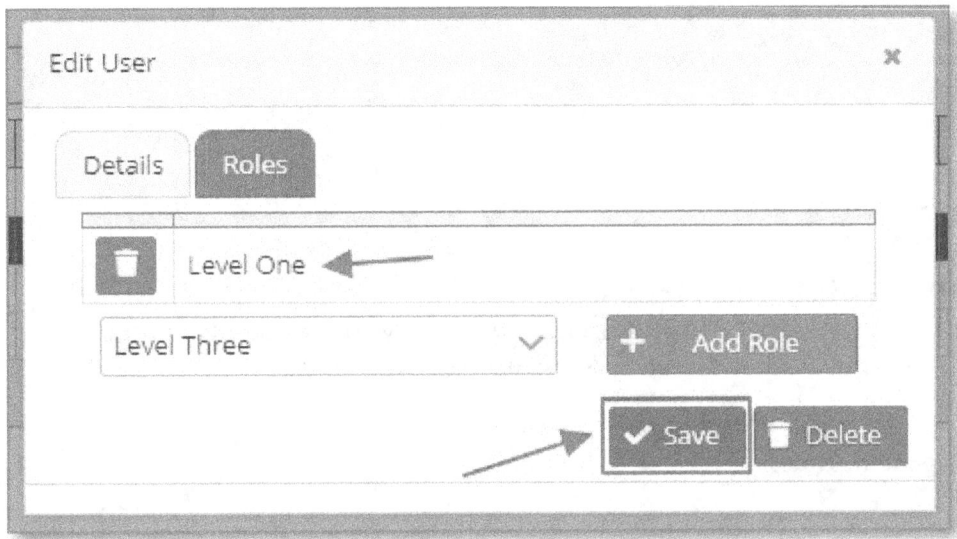

The **Save** button must be clicked to *save* any **Role** changes for the **User**.

ADefHelpDesk 4

Roles

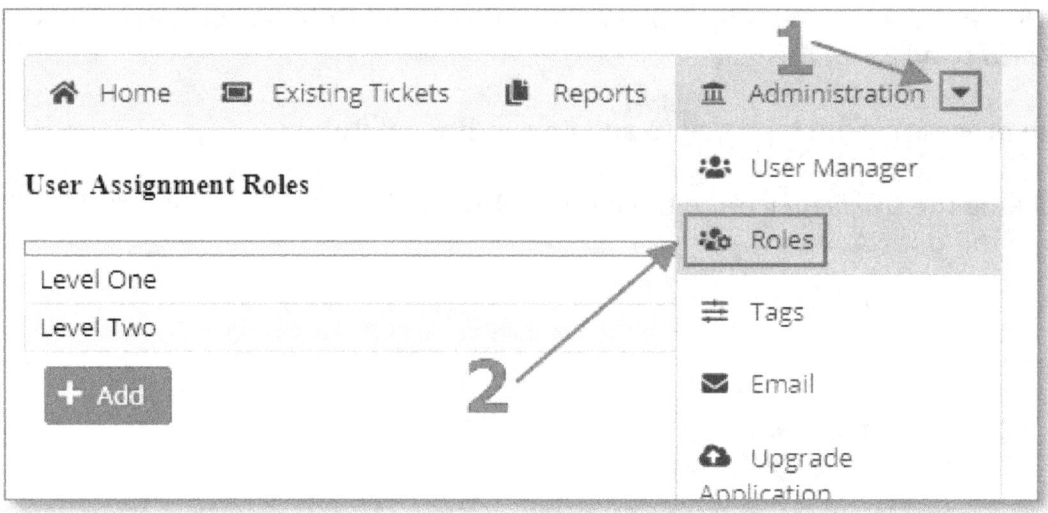

An **Administrator** (any **User** who has the **Is SuperUser** box checked in **Administration/User Manager**) has the ability to create and manage **Roles** by selecting **Roles** from the **Administration** menu.

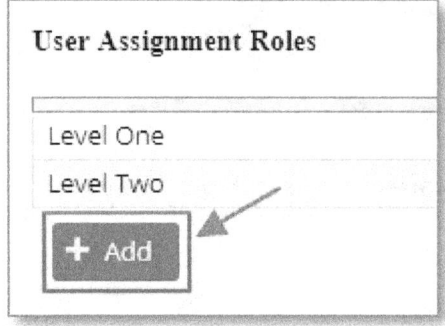

New **Roles** are created by clicking the **Add** button.

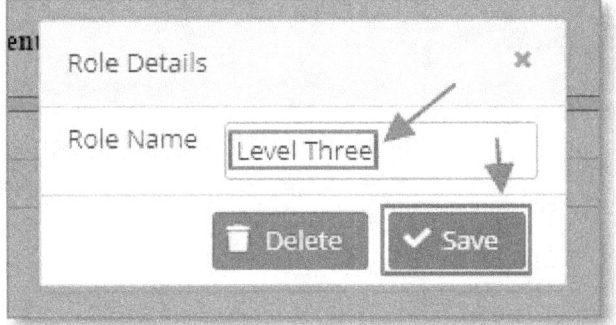

The **Role** name can be entered and saved by clicking the **Save** button.

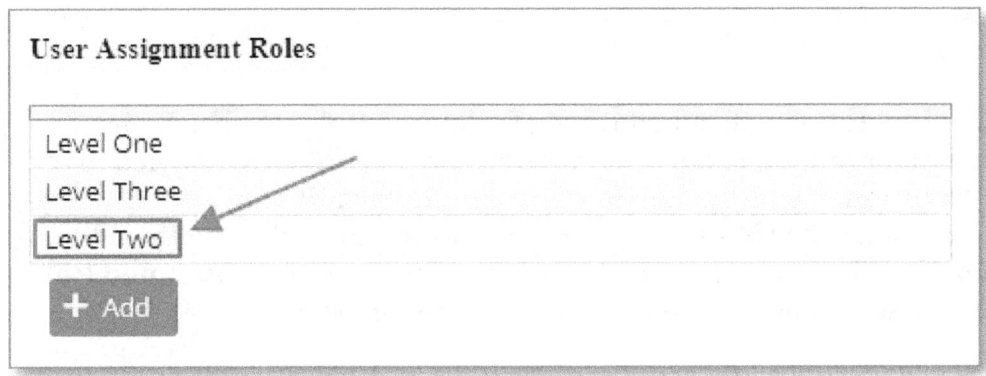

Existing Roles can be *edited* or *deleted* by first clicking on them in the **User Assignment Roles** list.

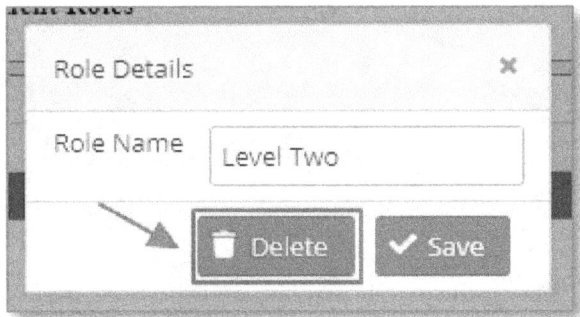

ADefHelpDesk 4

The **Role** can be *edited* and *saved* or *deleted*.

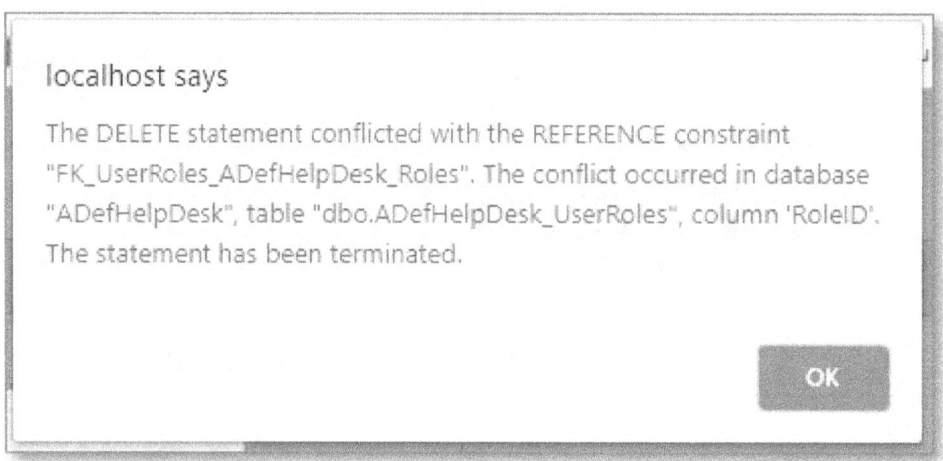

Note: The application will not allow you to delete a **Role** that has **Users** assigned to it or is assigned to a **Help Desk Ticket**. All **Users** assigned to the **Role** must be removed from the **Role** (by editing each **User** in **Administration/User Manager**) before the **Role** can be *deleted*. In addition, any **Help Desk Tickets** assigned to the **Role** must have their **Assigned Role** dropdown is set to another **Role** before this one can be *deleted*.

Tags

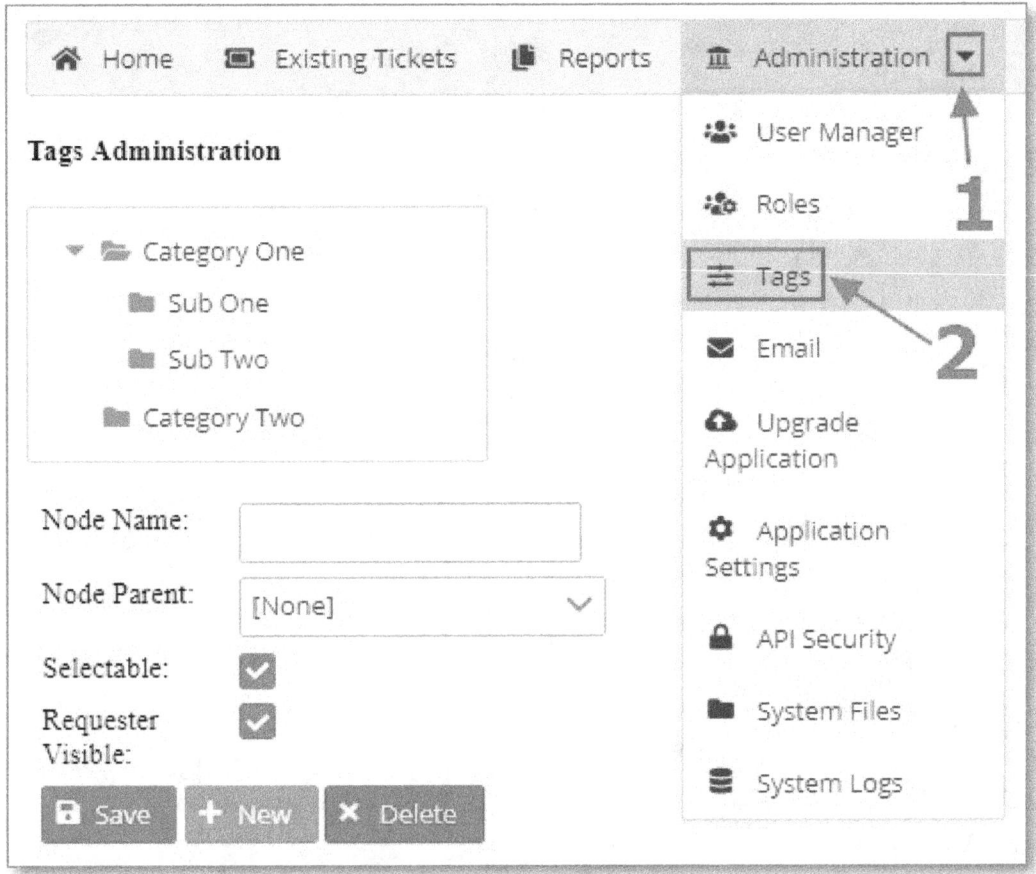

An **Administrator** (any **User** who has the **Is SuperUser** box checked in **Administration/User Manager**) has the ability to manage the **Tags** (also known as **Nodes**) for the application by selecting **Tags** from the **Administration** menu.

Tags are used to categorize **Tickets** to allow for *organization* and to facilitate *searching*. An unlimited number of **Tags** can be created and they can be nested to *unlimited levels*.

ADefHelpDesk 4

Tags can have their *visibility* to the **Requestor** set, so that certain tags can be used only for internal *routing* and *categorization* and will not be seen by non-**Administrators**.

Creating Tags

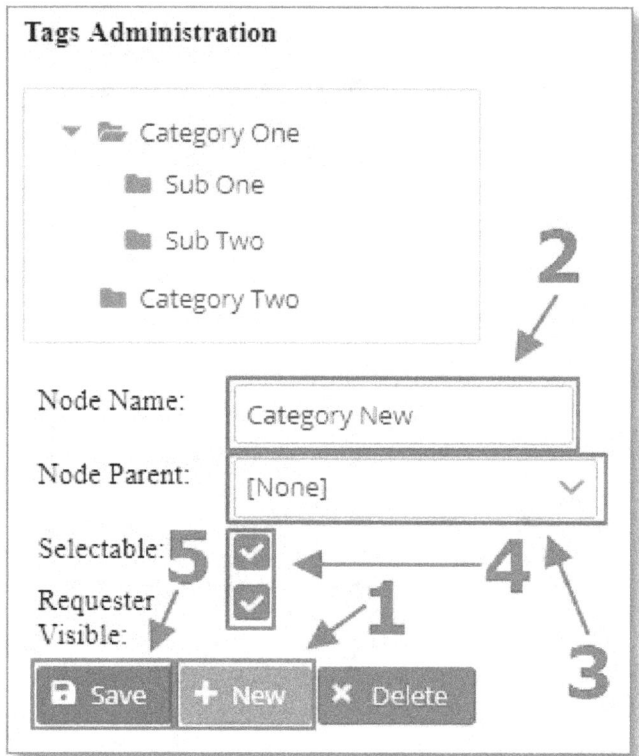

To create a **Tag**:

1. Click the **New** button.
2. Enter a name for the **Tag** in the **Node Name** box.
3. Select the *parent* for the **Tag** (select **[None]** if the **Tag** is to be a *root level* **Tag**).
4. Indicate if the **Tag** is **Selectable** (or just used to group children **Tags**) and if the **Tag** is **Requestor Visible** (non-Administrators can see it and select it when creating or editing **Help Desk Tickets**).

5. Click **Save** to *save* or *update* the **Tag.**

Editing Tags / Reordering Tags

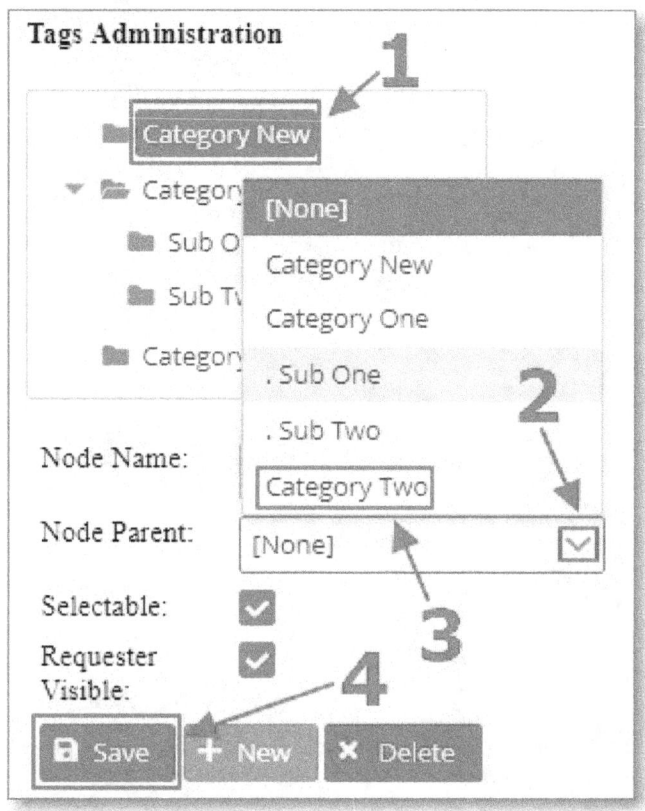

To edit or reorder or move a **Tag** to another position, click on the **Tag** in the **Tag** tree, and its properties will display in the **Tag** edit section.

Alter any of the *properties* and click the **Save** button to save the changes.

Note: If the position of a **Parent Tag** is changed, the **Tag** and all its child **Tags** will be reordered.

ADefHelpDesk 4

Note: Any **Help Desk Tickets** related to a **Tag** will retain that relationship even if the **Tag** is reordered in the **Tag** tree.

Deleting Tags

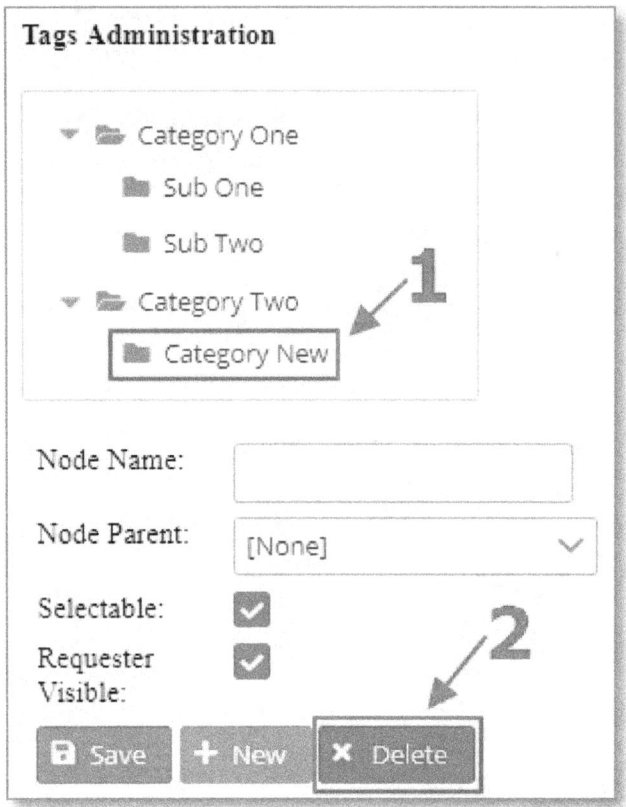

To delete a **Tag**, click on the **Tag** in the **Tag** tree, and its properties will display in the **Tag** edit section.

Click the **Delete** button, and the **Tag** will be deleted, and any child **Tags** will become children of the deleted **Tag's** parents (if any).

Email Settings

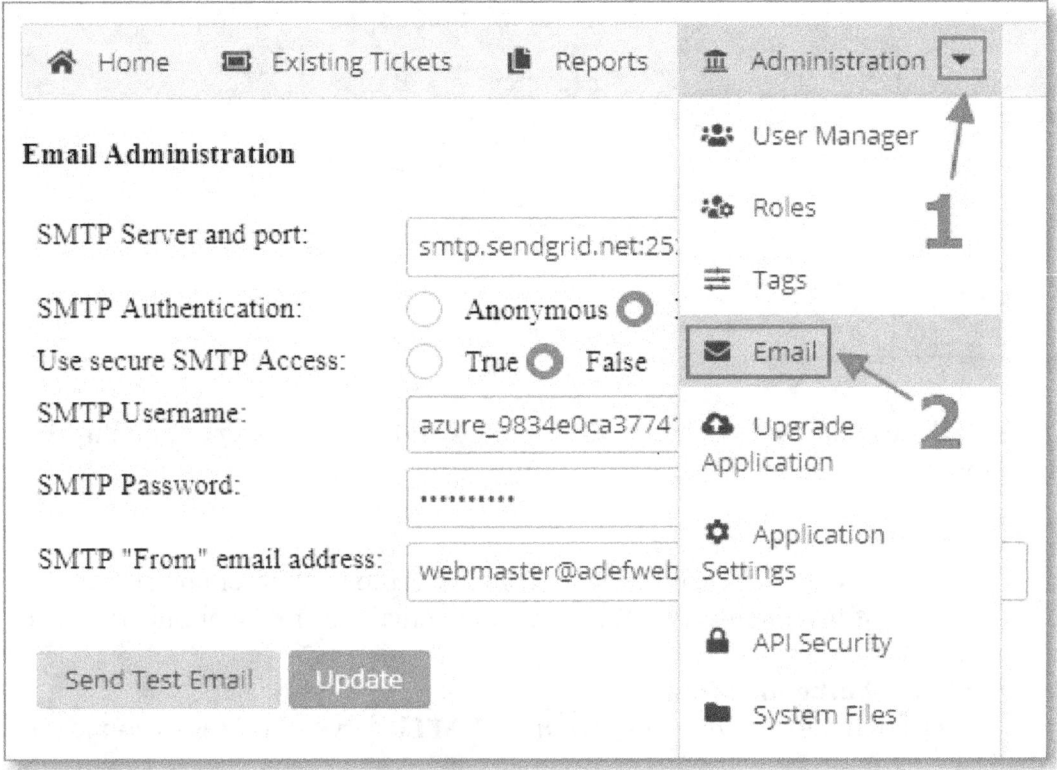

An **Administrator** (any **User** who has the **Is SuperUser** box checked in **Administration/User Manager**) has the ability to manage the email settings by selecting **Email** from the **Administration** menu.

ADefHelpDesk 4

Email Administration	
SMTP Server and port:	smtp.sendgrid.net:2525
SMTP Authentication:	● Anonymous ○ Basic ○ NTLM
Use secure SMTP Access:	○ True ● False
SMTP "From" email address:	webmaster@email.com

[Send Test Email] [Update]

The **Email Administration** screen allows the **Administrator** to **view** and **update** the following values:

- **SMTP Server and port:**
    - The **SMTP** (Simple Mail Transfer Protocol) server and server port of the email server through which emails from the application will be sent.
- **SMTP Authentication:**
    - The type of *authentication* the **SMTP** server requires to connect to it.
- **Use secure SMTP Access:**
    - Indicates if *secure* SMTP access is required or not.
- **SMTP "From" email address:**
    - The **email address** that all emails coming from the application will use.

Note: The **Update** button must be pressed to save any changes to the screen.

SMTP Authentication

SMTP Authentication:	○ Anonymous ◉ Basic ○ NTLM
Use secure SMTP Access:	○ True ◉ False
SMTP Username:	azure_9834jghjhjj7hg41c2e8jgjjhggjg8a
SMTP Password:	··········

When **SMTP Authentication** is set to **Basic** or **NTML**, the **SMTP Username** and **SMTP Password** options will appear.

These values will be used to authenticate with the **SMTP server**.

Send Test Email Button

The **Send Test Email** button can be pressed at any time to attempt to send a *test email* to the **email address** in the **SMTP "From" email address** setting using the current email settings.

You do not have to click the **Update** button before clicking the **Send Test Email** button; however, you will need to click the **Update** button to save any email settings.

ADefHelpDesk 4

Upgrade Application

See the **Upgrading** section in **Chapter 2: Installing and Upgrading**.

API Security(Swagger Rest API)

ADefHelpDesk features a full *REST based API* that exposes all the functionality to allow you to incorporate it with any external application.

In your **ADefHelpDesk** site there is a **Swagger page** (see: https://swagger.io/) that documents the *REST based API* endpoints in your **ADefHelpDesk** site at: ***http://{your default web address}/swagger/*** (for example: http://adefhelpdesk.azurewebsites.net/swagger/).

This allows a single installation of **ADefHelpDesk** to support unlimited external applications, yet your support personnel manages it all from one interface. This also allows processes such as auto responders to periodically check for new tickets and route them, and or update them, and trigger or send emails. Third parties can also create *services* and *custom integrations* such as artificial intelligent driven processes, custom data mining, and reporting.

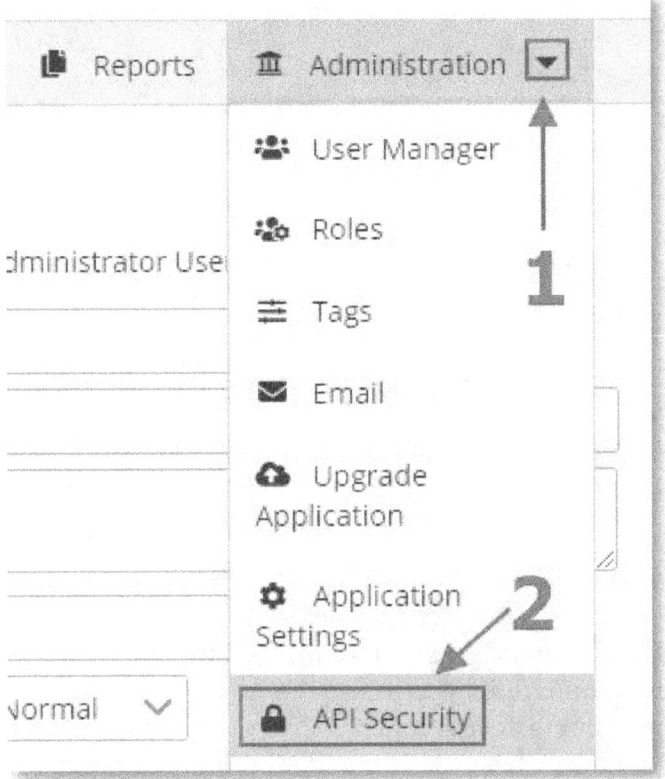

To enable and use the **API**, you create an account to call the **API** by accessing the **API Security** page.

Log in as a user who is marked in the **User Manager** as **Is SuperUser**.

From the menu bar, select **Administration** then **API Security**.

ADefHelpDesk 4

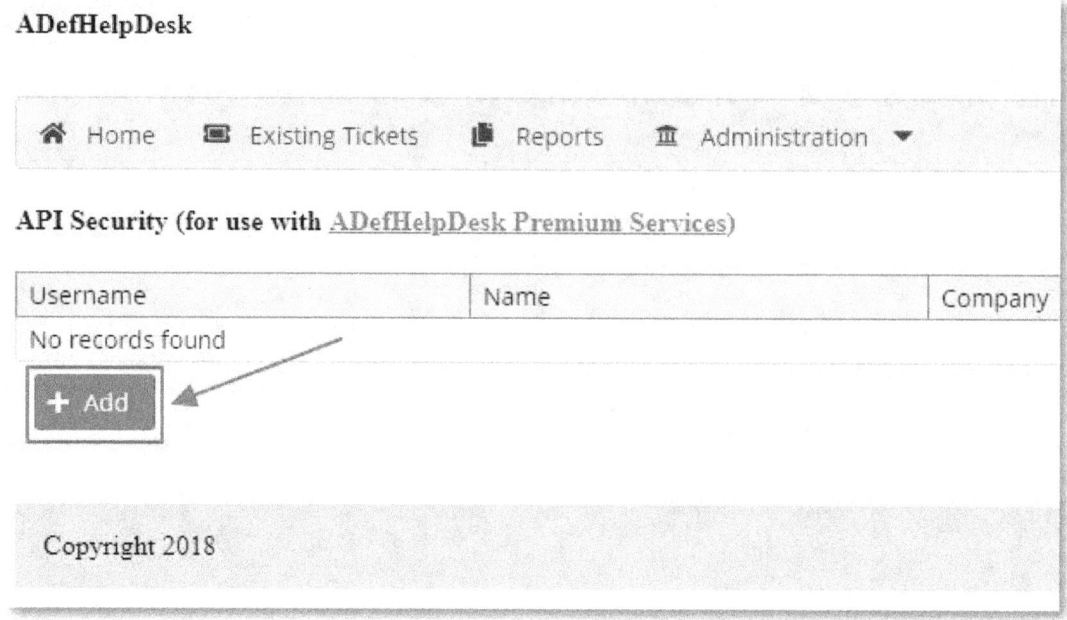

Note: ADefHelpDesk plans to provide *premium services* in the future that will use the API; however, they <u>are not</u> required for you to use the API. To use the API, you only need to create an account to access it.

To add a new account, click the **Add** button.

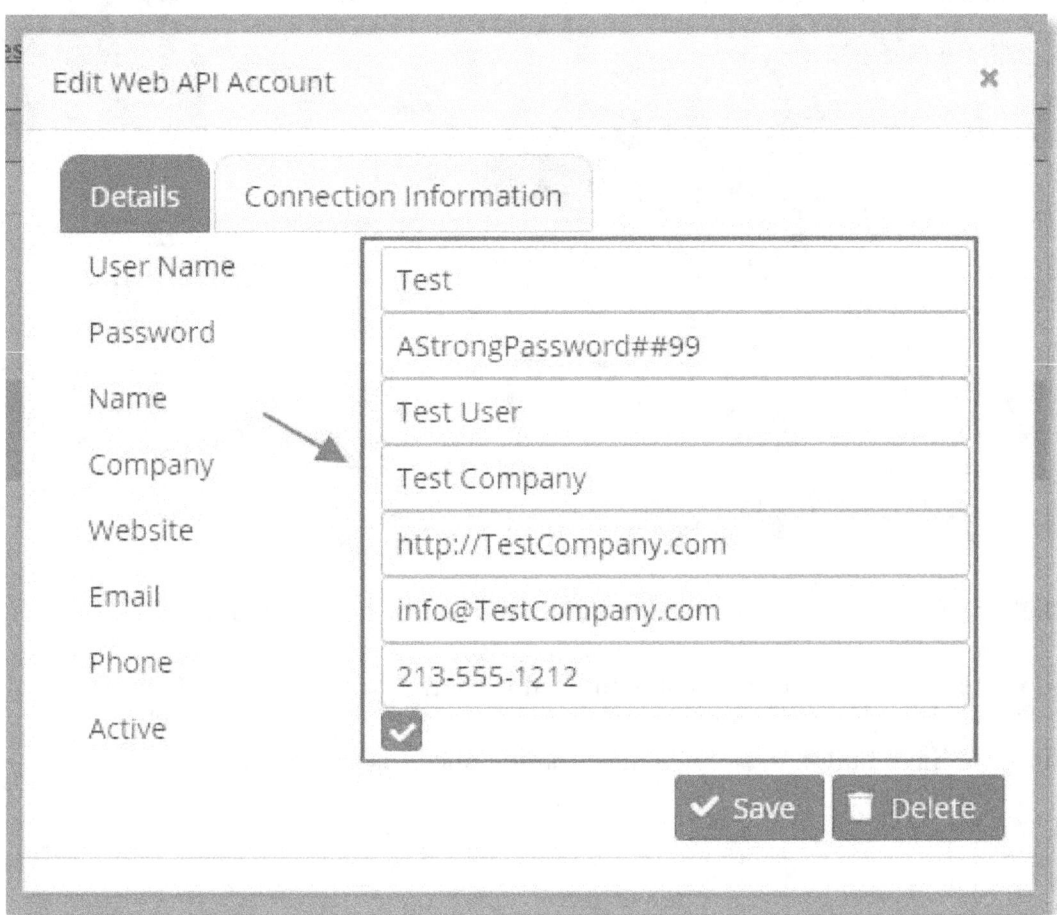

Enter the information for the account.

Ensure that the **Active** box is checked.

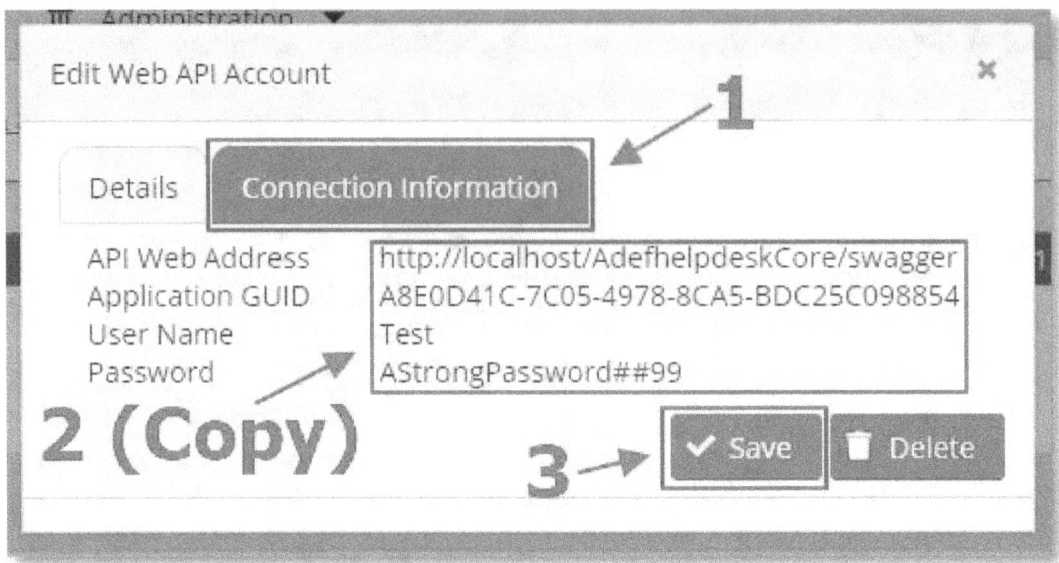

Click the **Connection Information** tab to display the connection information.

Copy the information down; you will need it later.

Click the **Save** button to save the information and close the box.

Using The Swagger End Point

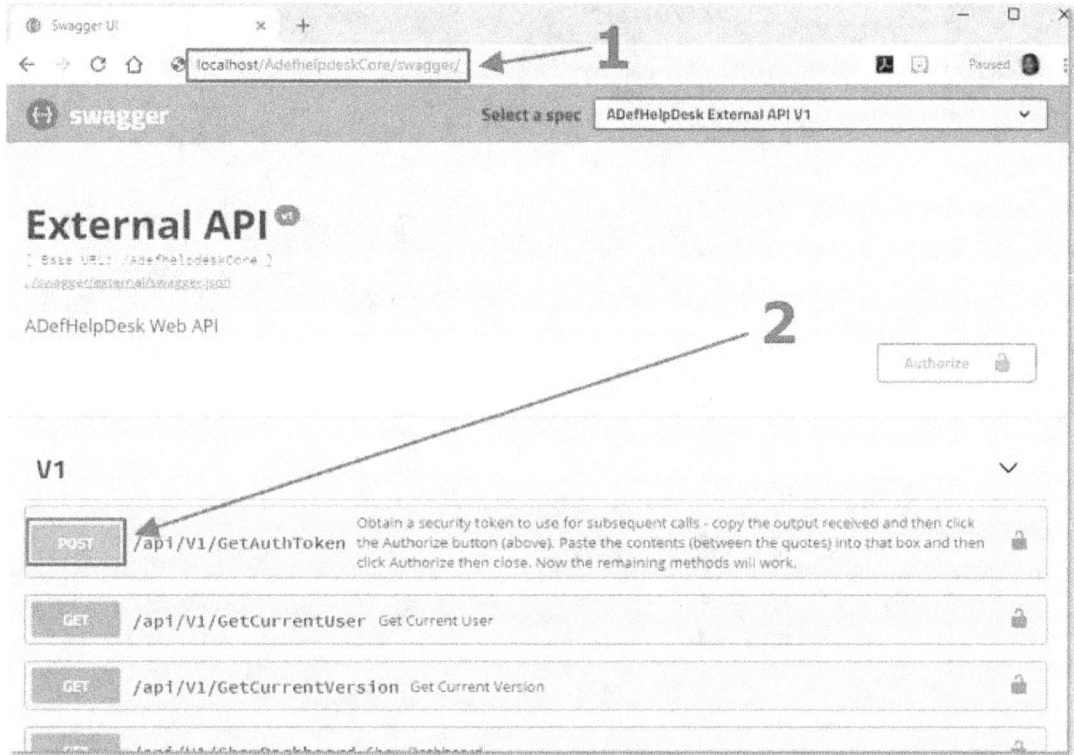

In your web browser, navigate to: ***http://{your default web address}/swagger/***

Click on the **Post** button on the **GetAuthToken** method.

ADefHelpDesk 4

Click the **Try it out** button.

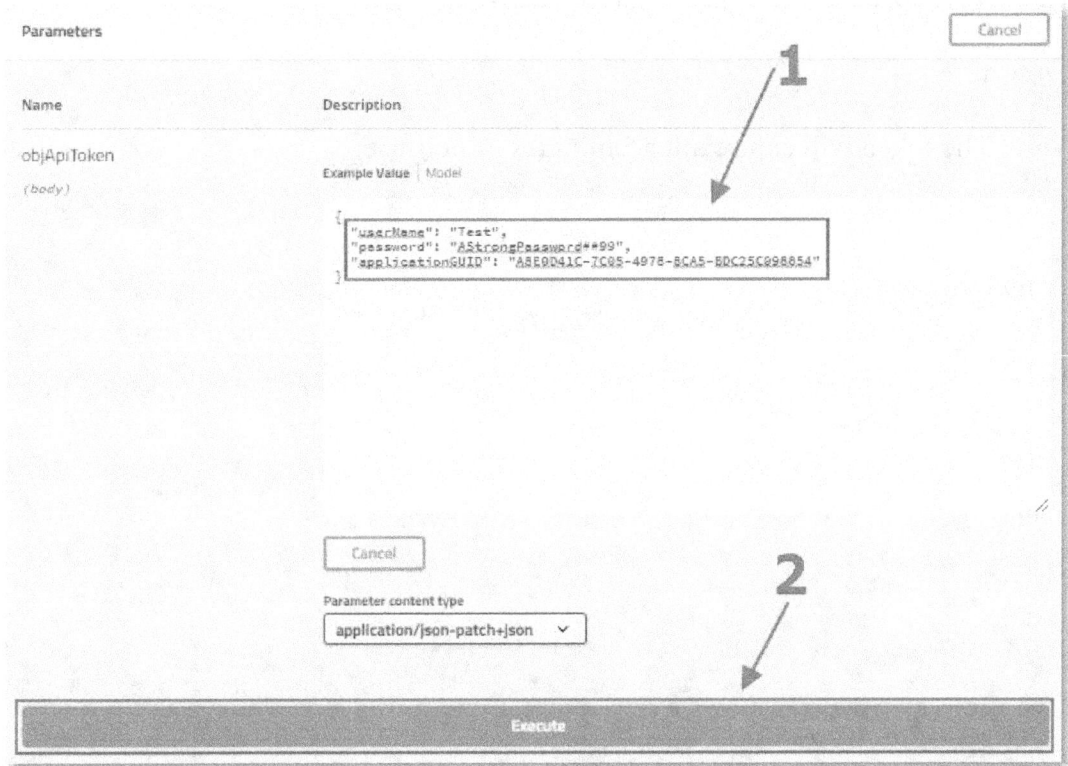

Enter the connection information obtained earlier and click the **Execute** button.

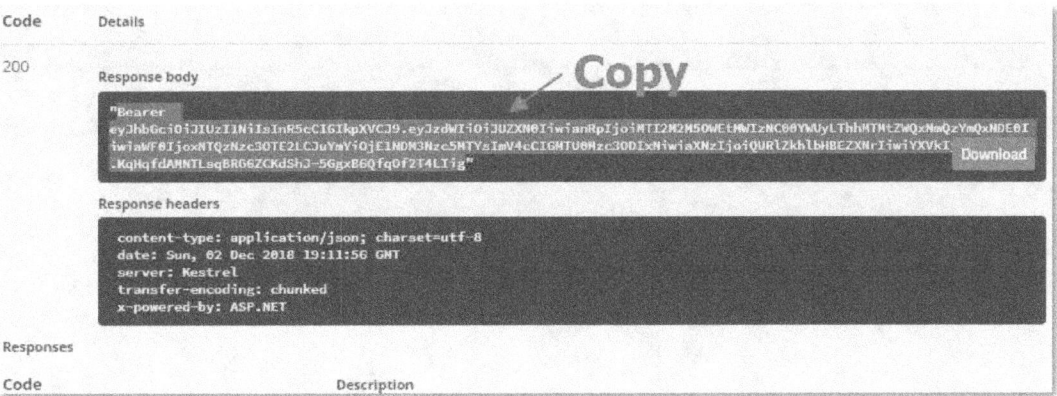

ADefHelpDesk 4

The *Bearer token* will display in the **Server response** section.

Copy it.

Note: The token will expire after 5 minutes of non-use.

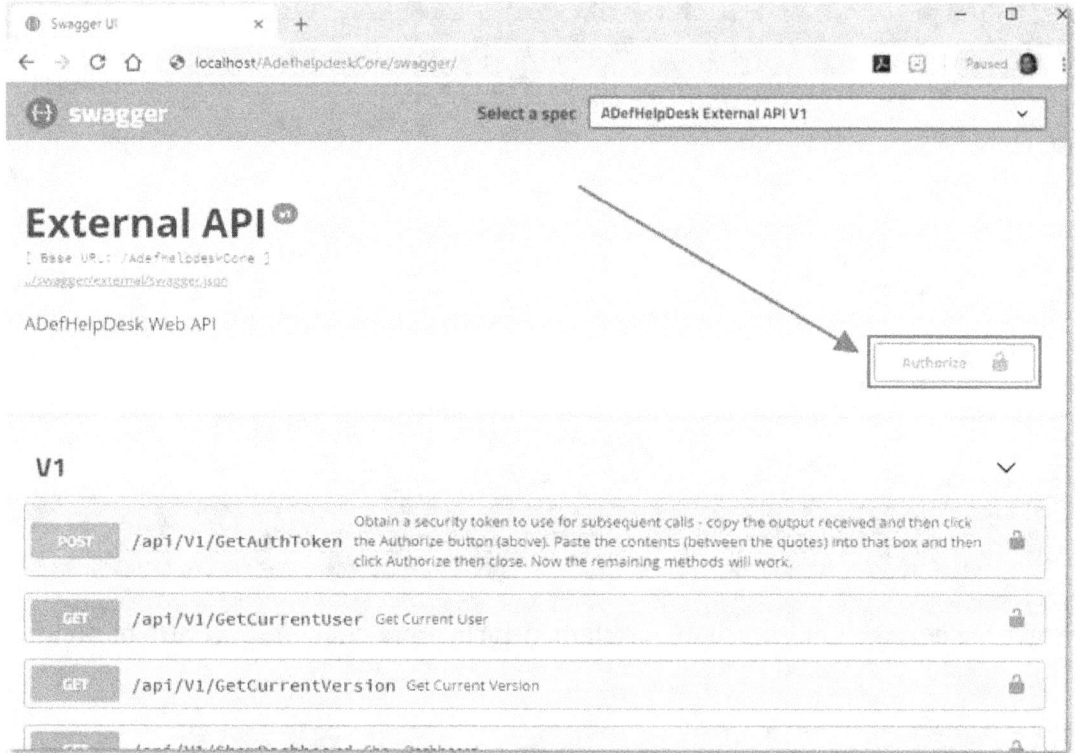

Click the **Authorize** button.

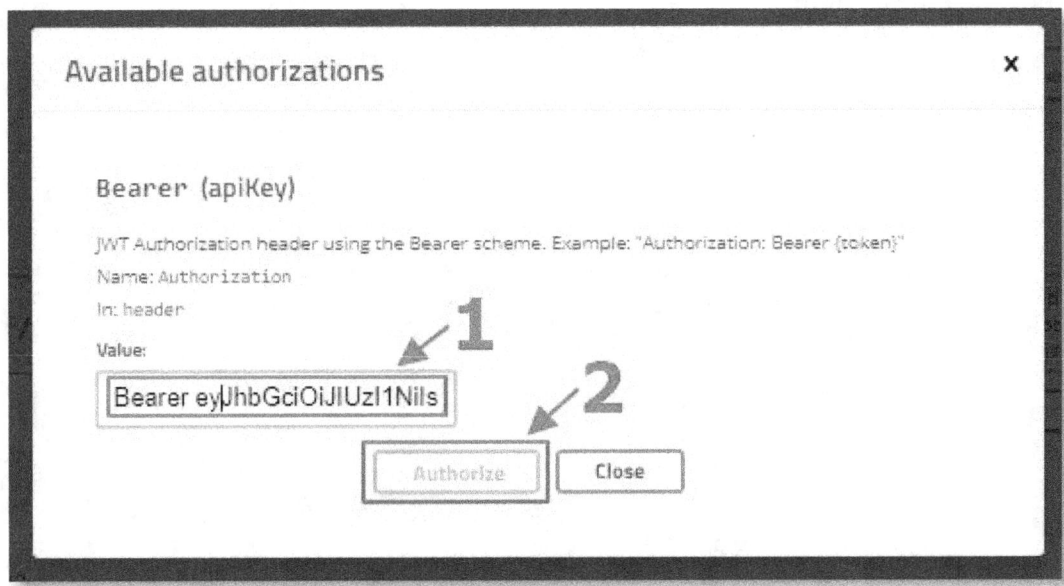

Enter the *Bearer token* and click the **Authorize** button.

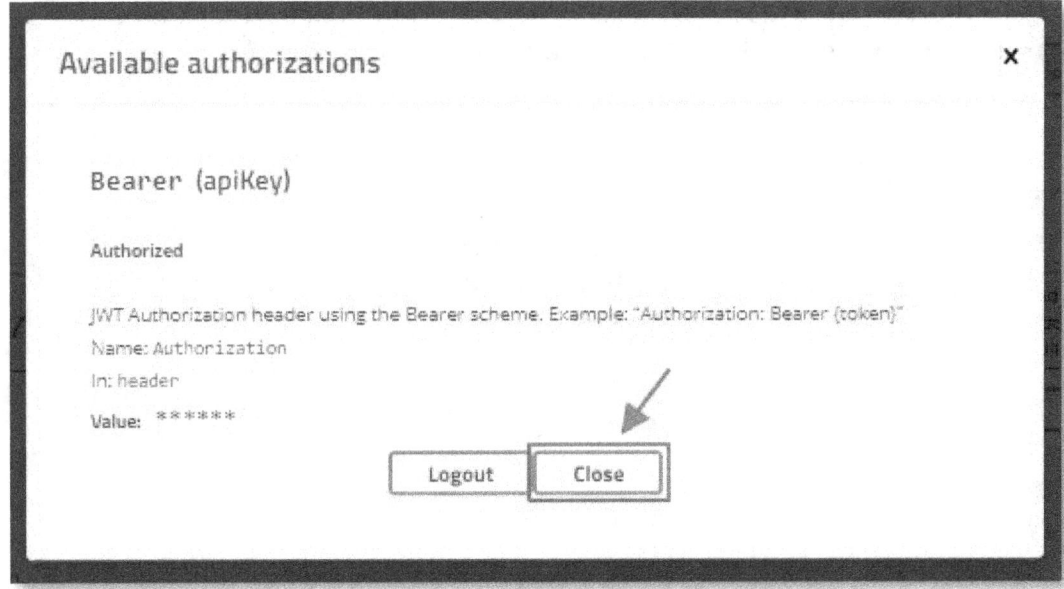

ADefHelpDesk 4

Click the **Close** button.

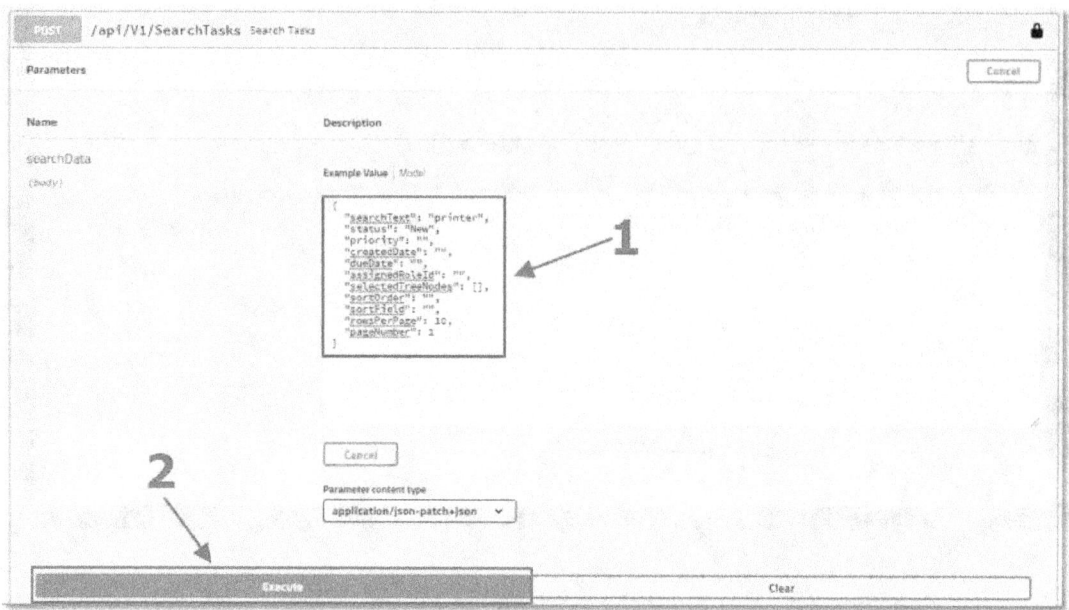

Expand the **SearchTasks** method, click the **Try it out** button, enter a query in the **searchData** box, and click the **Execute** button.

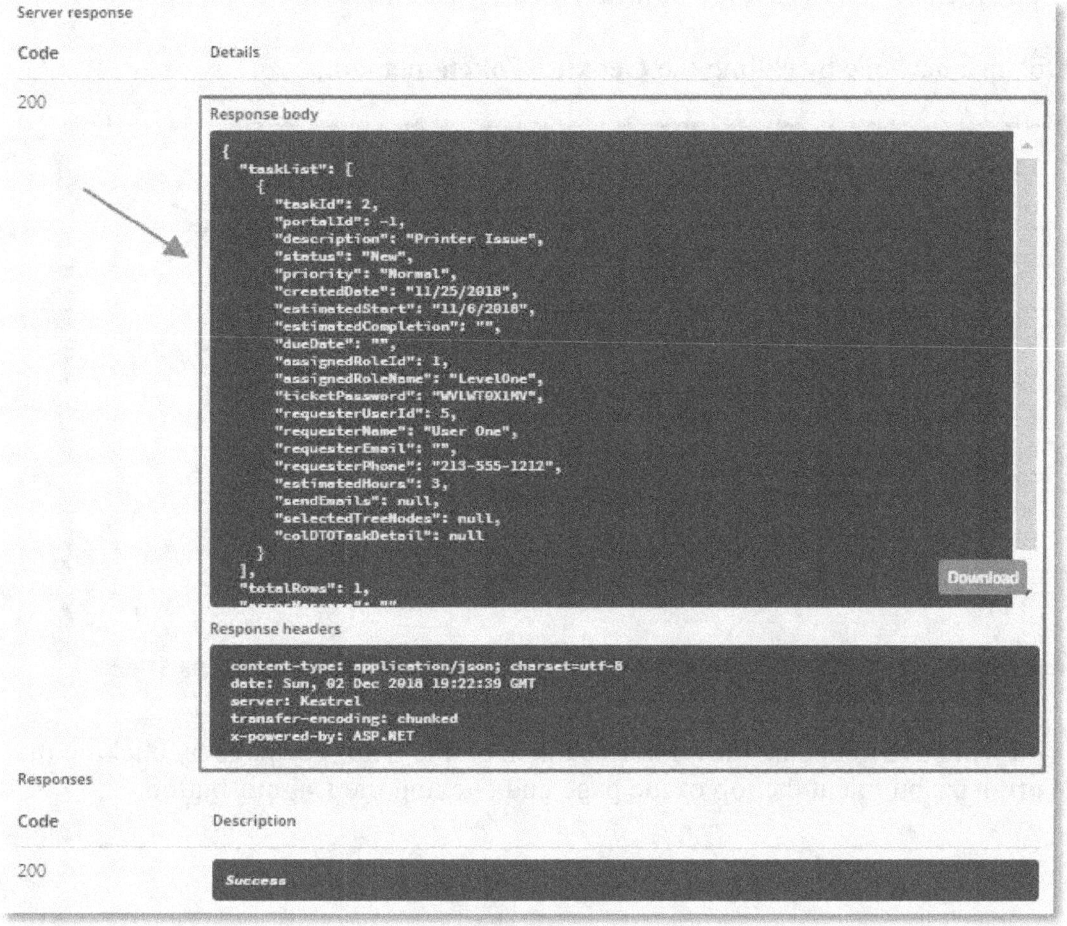

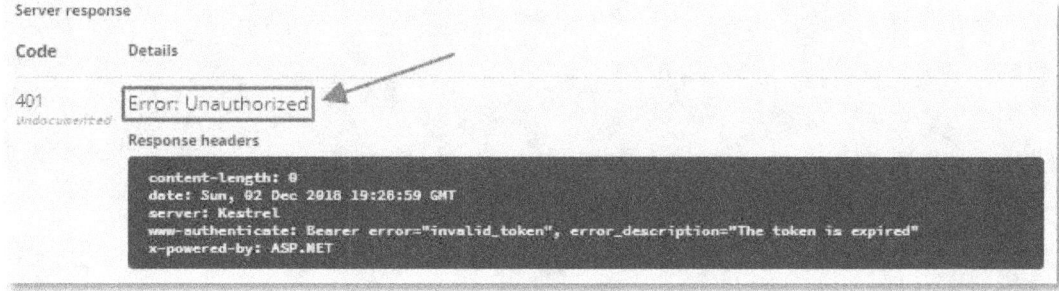

The results will display in the **Server response** section.

ADefHelpDesk 4

If any method returns a **401 Unauthorized** error, the token is expired.

Obtain a new one by calling the **GetAuthToken** method.

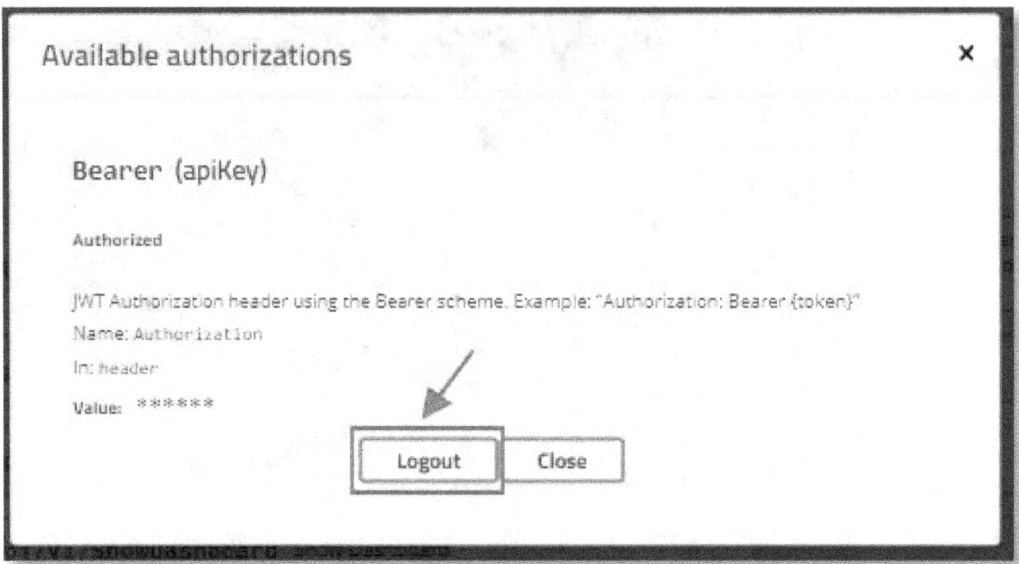

You will have to update the authorize token on the **Swagger** page by clicking the **Authorize** button at the top of the page and clicking the **Logout** button.

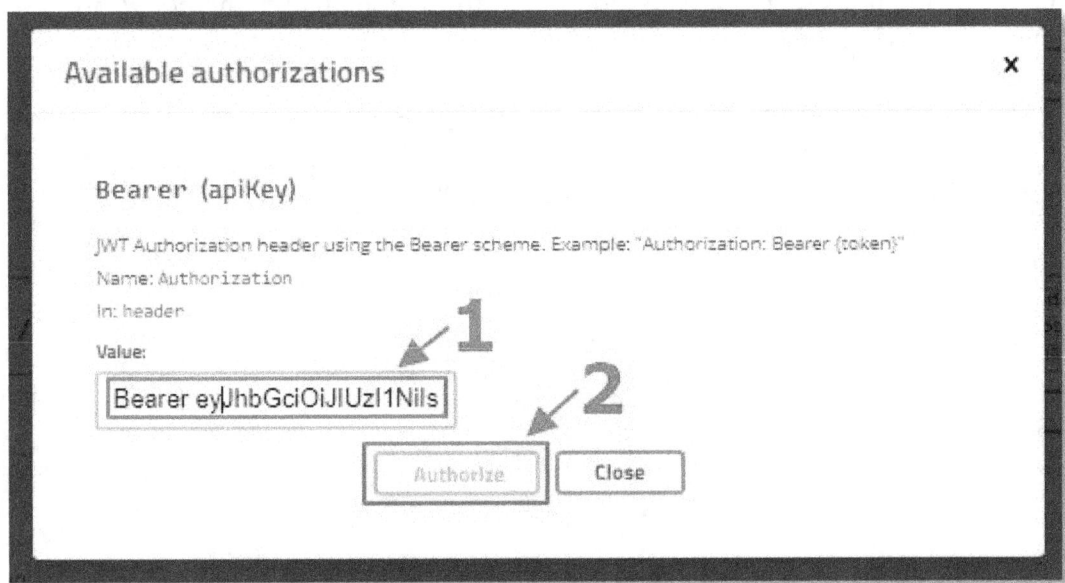

You can then enter the new token.

Consuming The Swagger API Definition For Custom Applications

To consume the *REST based API* endpoints from your custom applications, you can point them to the **Swagger** definition at:
http://{your default web address}/swagger/external/swagger.json

ADefHelpDesk 4

The following links will guide you to more information on creating *clients* to consume the API methods:

- **NSwag:** https://docs.microsoft.com/en-us/aspnet/core/tutorials/getting-started-with-nswag
- **AutoRest:** https://github.com/Azure/autorest

Systems Files

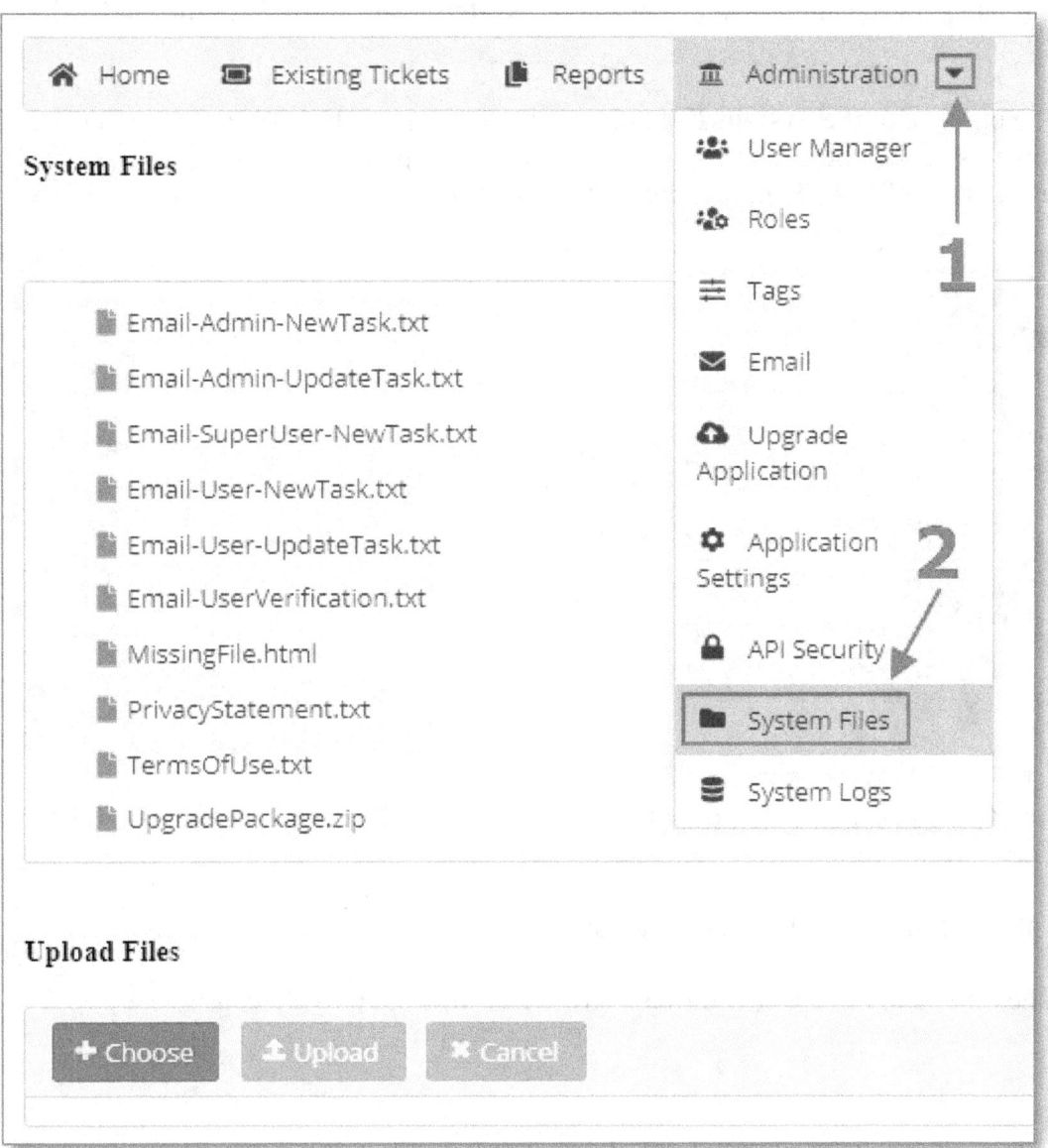

ADefHelpDesk 4

An **Administrator** (any **User** who has the **Is SuperUser** box checked in **Administration/User Manager**) has the ability to manage the system file templates for the application by selecting **System Files** from the **Administration** menu.

The purpose of the **System Files** page is to allow the **Administrator** to alter the contents of the **email templates**, the **Missing File** page, the **Privacy Statement**, and **Terms of Use**, by uploading updated templates.

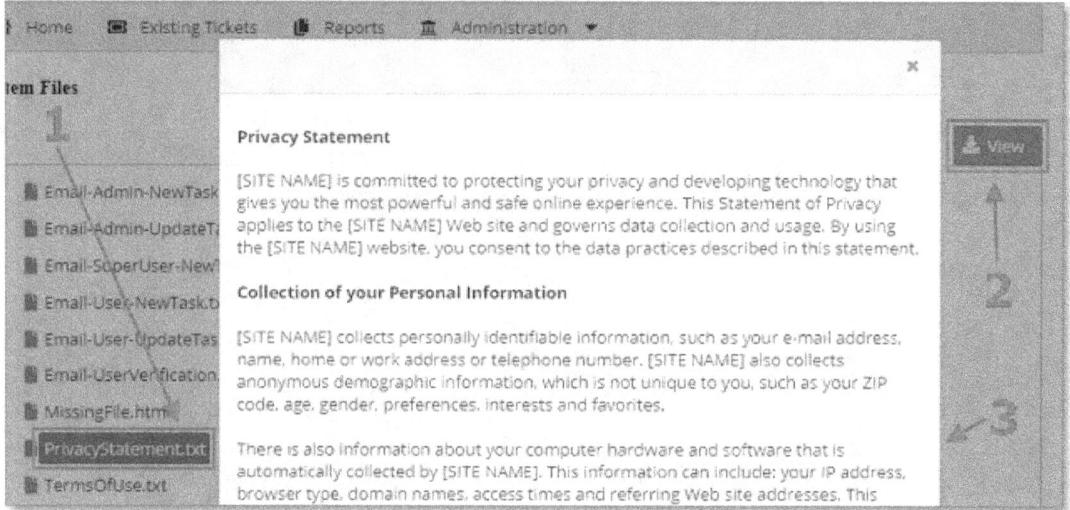

Any **text file** can be viewed by first selecting it in the file list, then *clicking* the **View** button.

The file contents will display in a popup.

Click the **X** in the upper right-hand corner of the popup to close it.

Updating Templates

A system file template can be *updated* by uploading a file with the exact same name.

This is done by first clicking the **Choose** button in the **Upload Files** section.

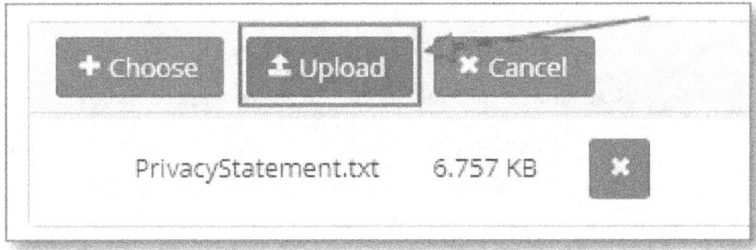

After the file is selected, click the **Upload** button to complete the process.

Note: You will want to first view the existing templates and use them as the starting point for any modifications you wish to make.

ADefHelpDesk 4

System Logs

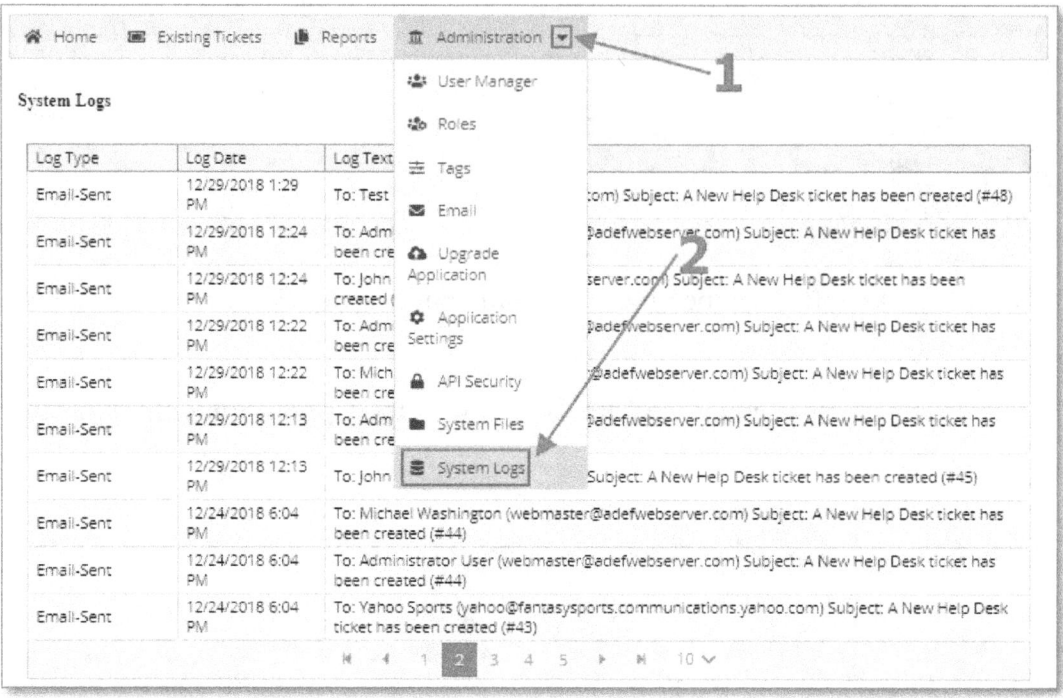

An **Administrator** (any **User** who has the **Is SuperUser** box checked in **Administration/User Manager**) has the ability to view the application-wide logs by selecting **System Logs** from the **Administration** menu.

Type of Logs

- Email-Error
- Email-Sent
- TaskDetail-Deletion
- File-Deletion
- File-Write-Error
- File-Read-Error

- File-Delete-Error
- Task-Creation-Error
- Task-Read-Error
- Task-Update-Error
- Task-Delete-Error
- WebAPI Account Created
- WebAPI Account Update
- WebAPI Account Deleted

Paging Options

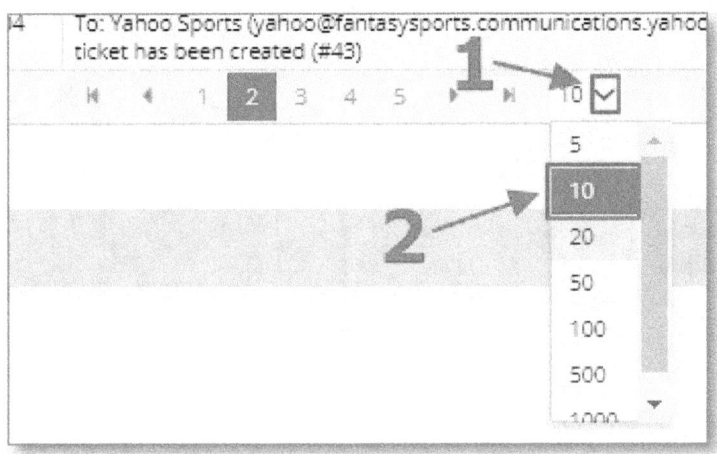

An **Administrator** can navigate through the logs using the **pager control** at the bottom of the **grid**. The number of records displayed on each page can be changed by clicking the downward arrow next to the *current records per page* setting and selecting a different number.

Chapter 6: Integrations

Creating a .Net Core Web Application to Create a Ticket

The sample code for this section can be obtained at the link "Calling a REST API from .Net Core Including Uploading Files" at http://lightswitchhelpwebsite.com/Downloads.aspx

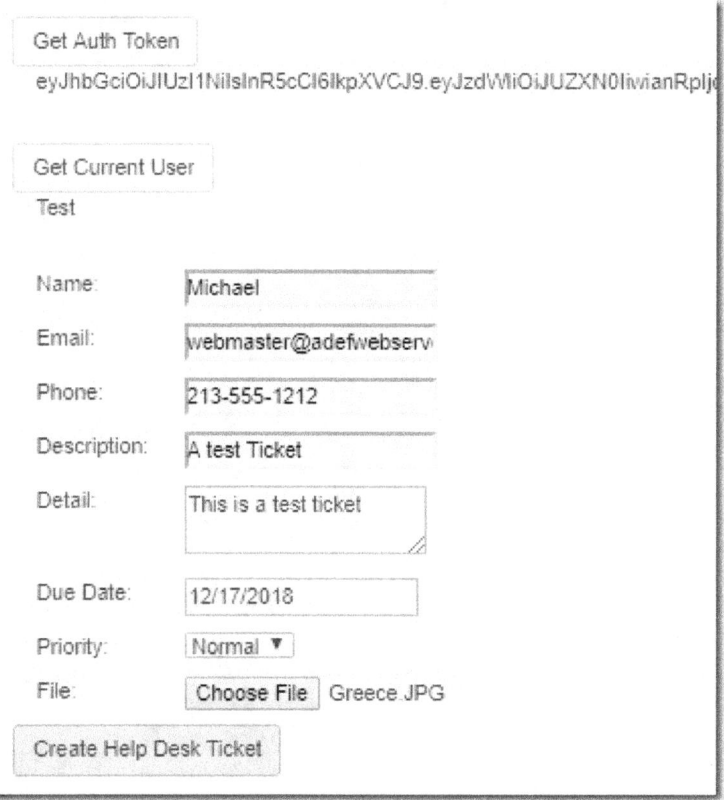

Calling a **REST based API** from **.Net Core** is usually more complicated than many of the samples you may have seen. The reason is that each **REST based API** can implement its own unique security measures. In addition, passing complex parameters, and uploading files though a **REST based API**, can prove challenging.

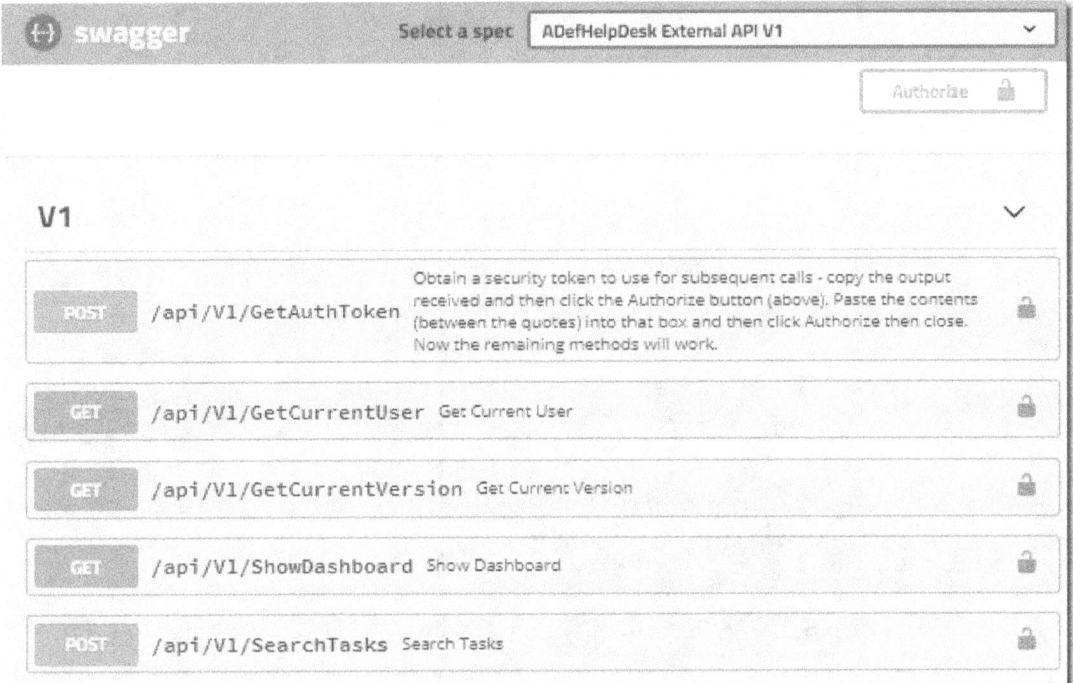

In this example, we will look at consuming the **REST Based API** in **ADefHelpDesk**. This API has the following features that we will explore:

- Requires callers to first obtain a **JSON Web Token (JWT)** (also called a *Bearer Token*) using a combination of a **UserName**, **Password**, and **Application GUID**. The token is then passed in the header of the subsequent requests to the other methods to authenticate the requests.
- Allows an external caller to create **Help Desk Tickets** (and perform all other functionality).
- As part of creating **Help Desk Tickets**, the API allows the external caller to upload files.

ADefHelpDesk 4

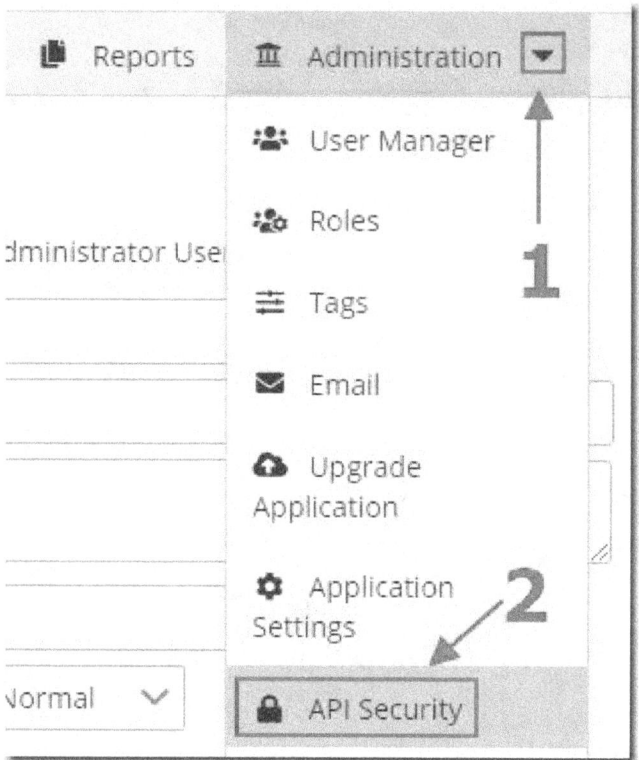

In **ADefHelpDesk**, follow the directions in the **API Security (Swagger Rest API)** section in **Chapter 5: Administration Settings**, to create an account that can call the **API**.

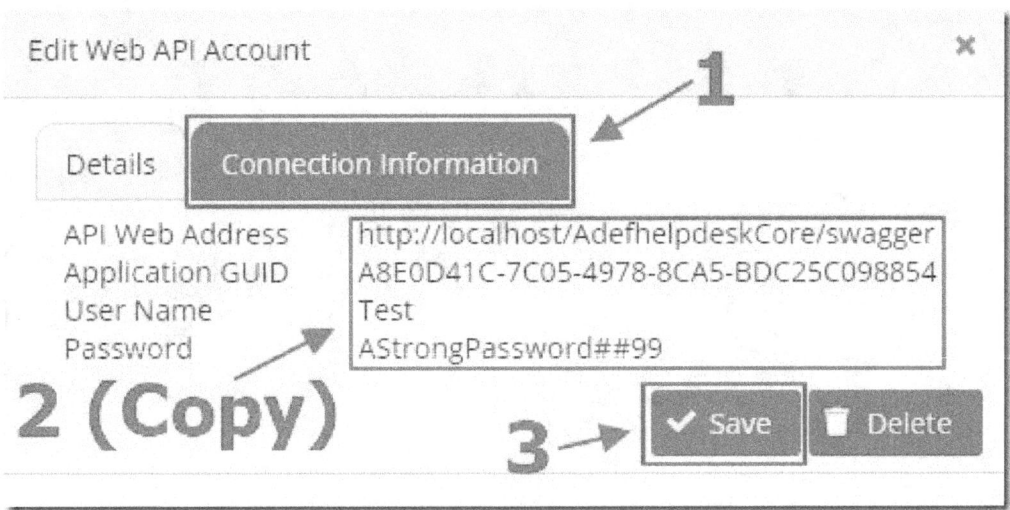

You will need to copy the information on the **Connection Information** tab to use later.

ADefHelpDesk 4

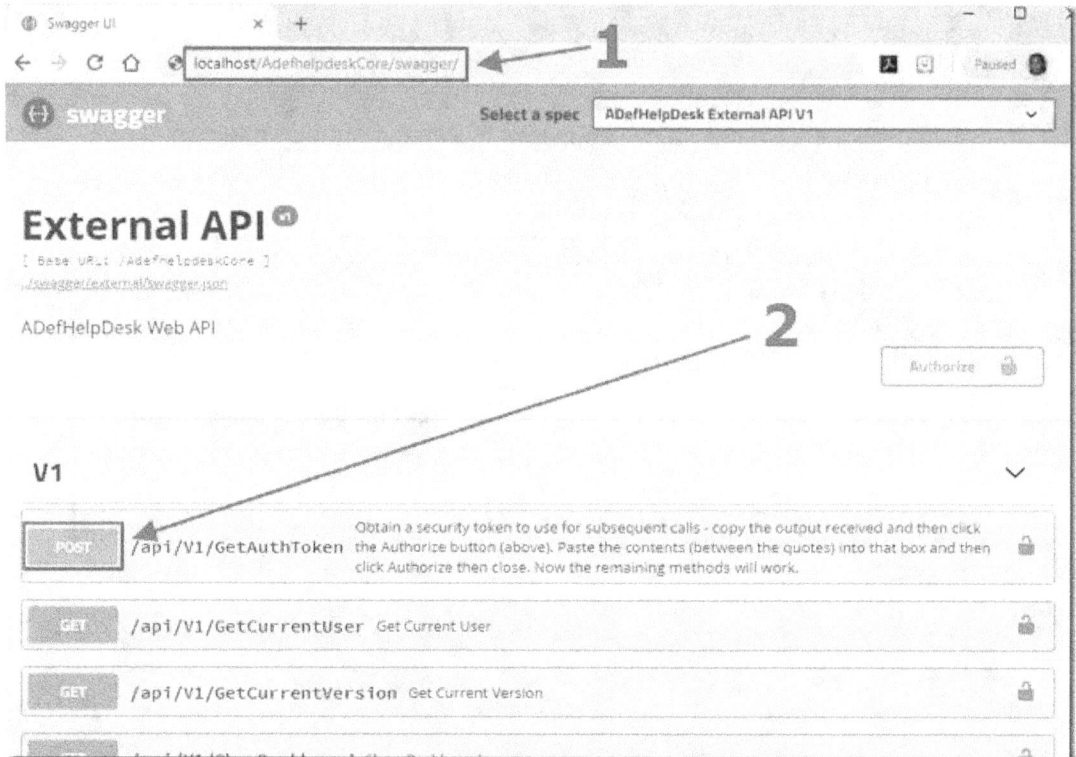

In the **ADefHelpDesk** site there is a **Swagger page** (see: https://swagger.io/) that documents the *REST based API* endpoints at: ***http://{your default web address}/swagger/*** (for example: http://adefhelpdesk.azurewebsites.net/swagger/).

We will refer to this page frequently.

Create The Application

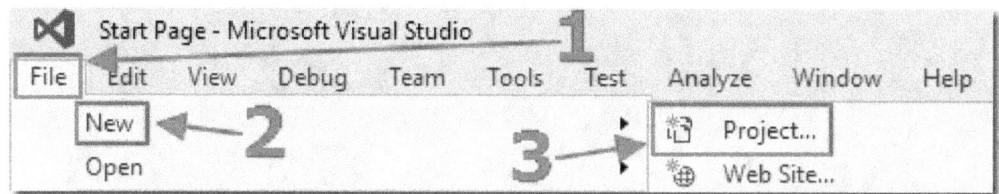

Open **Visual Studio** (Note: You can download the **Community Edition** free from https://www.visualstudio.com/vs/).

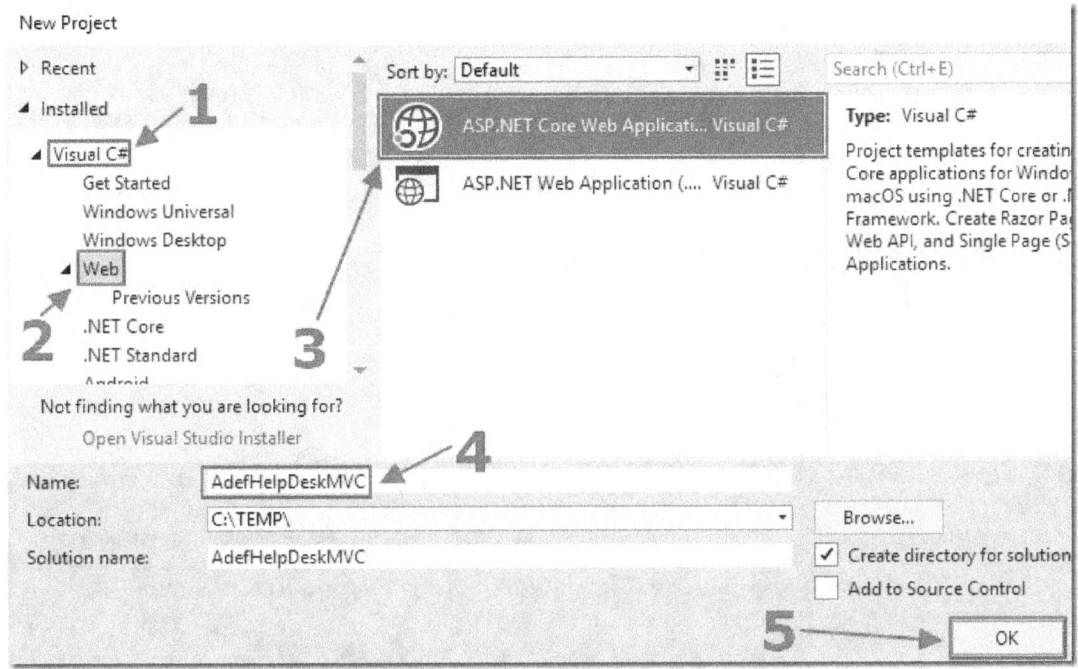

Select **Web**, then **ASP.NET Core Web Application**.

Enter **ADefHelpDesk MVC** for the **Name**.

Press **OK**.

ADefHelpDesk 4

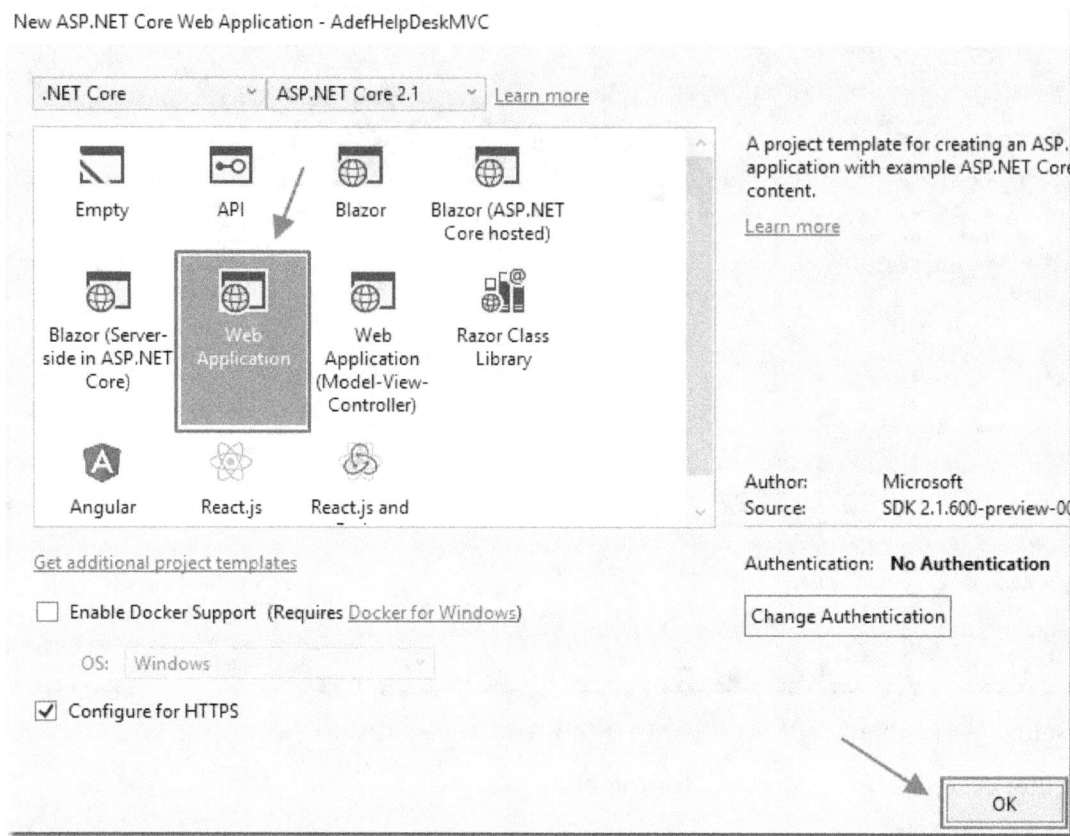

Select the **Web Application** template and press **OK**.

The project will be created.

Load Application Settings

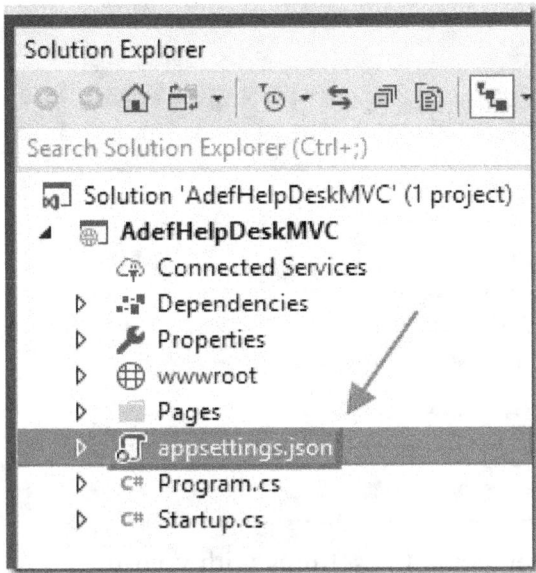

In the **Solution Explorer**, open the **appsettings.json** file.

ADefHelpDesk 4

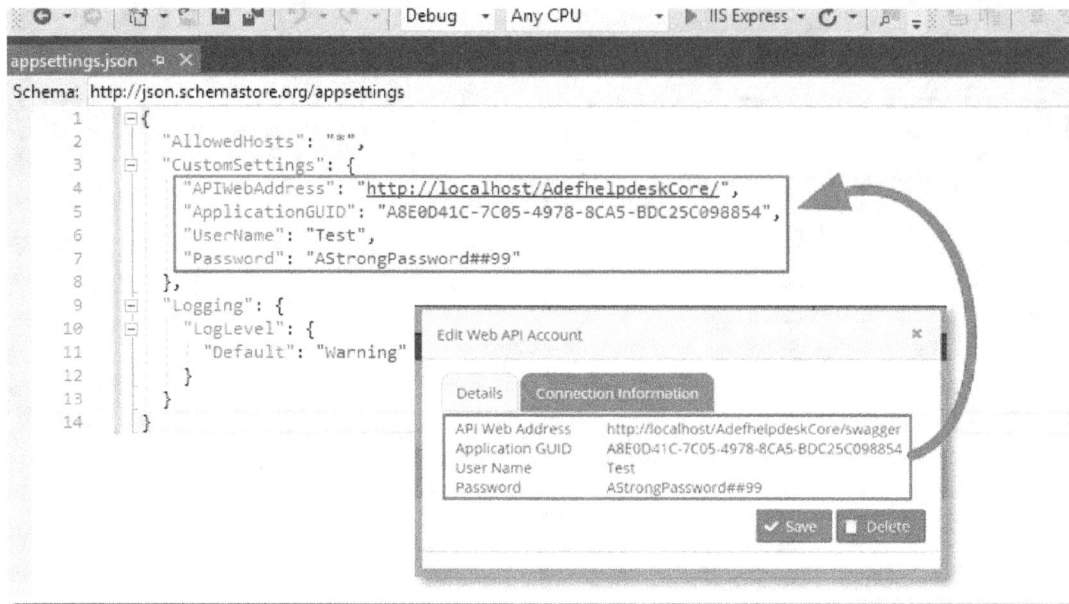

Replace the contents with the following (replacing the settings with your own values gathered earlier):

```
{
  "AllowedHosts": "*",
  "CustomSettings": {
    "APIWebAddress": "** Your Web Address **",
    "ApplicationGUID": "** Your ApplicationGUID **",
    "UserName": "** Your UserName **",
    "Password": "** Your Password **"
  },
  "Logging": {
    "LogLevel": {
      "Default": "Warning"
    }
  }
}
```

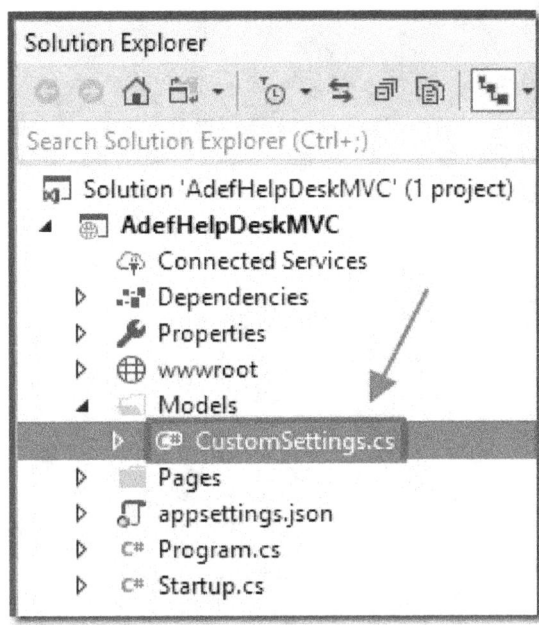

Add a folder called **Models** and a class file called **CustomSettings.cs** using the following code:

```
namespace AdefHelpDeskMVC.Models
{
    // This allows us to retrieve custom settings
    // from appsettings.json
    public class CustomSettings
    {
        public string APIWebAddress { get; set; }
        public string ApplicationGUID { get; set; }
        public string UserName { get; set; }
        public string Password { get; set; }
    }
}
```

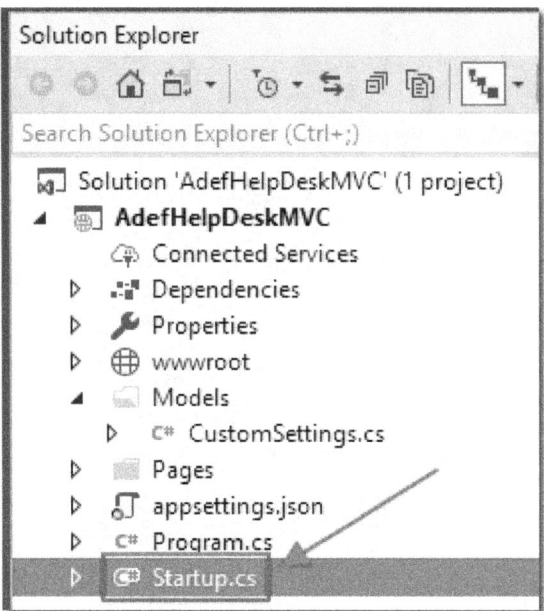

Next, open the **Startup.cs** file.

Change the **Startup** method to the following:

```
public Startup(IHostingEnvironment env)
{
    var builder = new ConfigurationBuilder()
        .SetBasePath(env.ContentRootPath)
        .AddJsonFile("appsettings.json", optional: true, reloadOnChange: true)
        .AddJsonFile($"appsettings.{env.EnvironmentName}.json", optional: true)
        .AddEnvironmentVariables();
    Configuration = builder.Build();
}
```

Change the **ConfigureServices** method to the following:

```csharp
public void ConfigureServices(IServiceCollection services)
{
    services.Configure<CookiePolicyOptions>(options =>
    {
        // This lambda determines whether user consent for non-essential cookies is
            needed for a given request.
        options.CheckConsentNeeded = context => true;
        options.MinimumSameSitePolicy = SameSiteMode.None;
    });
    services.AddMvc().SetCompatibilityVersion(CompatibilityVersion.Version_2_1);
    // Get the CustomSettings from appsettings.json
    // allow them to be passed to any class using dependency injection
    services.Configure<Models.CustomSettings>(
        Configuration.GetSection("CustomSettings"));
}
```

This will load the settings in the **appsettings.json** file and make them available through the **CustomSettings** class using *dependency injection*.

ADefHelpDesk 4

Get The JSON Web Token (JWT) (Authentication Token)

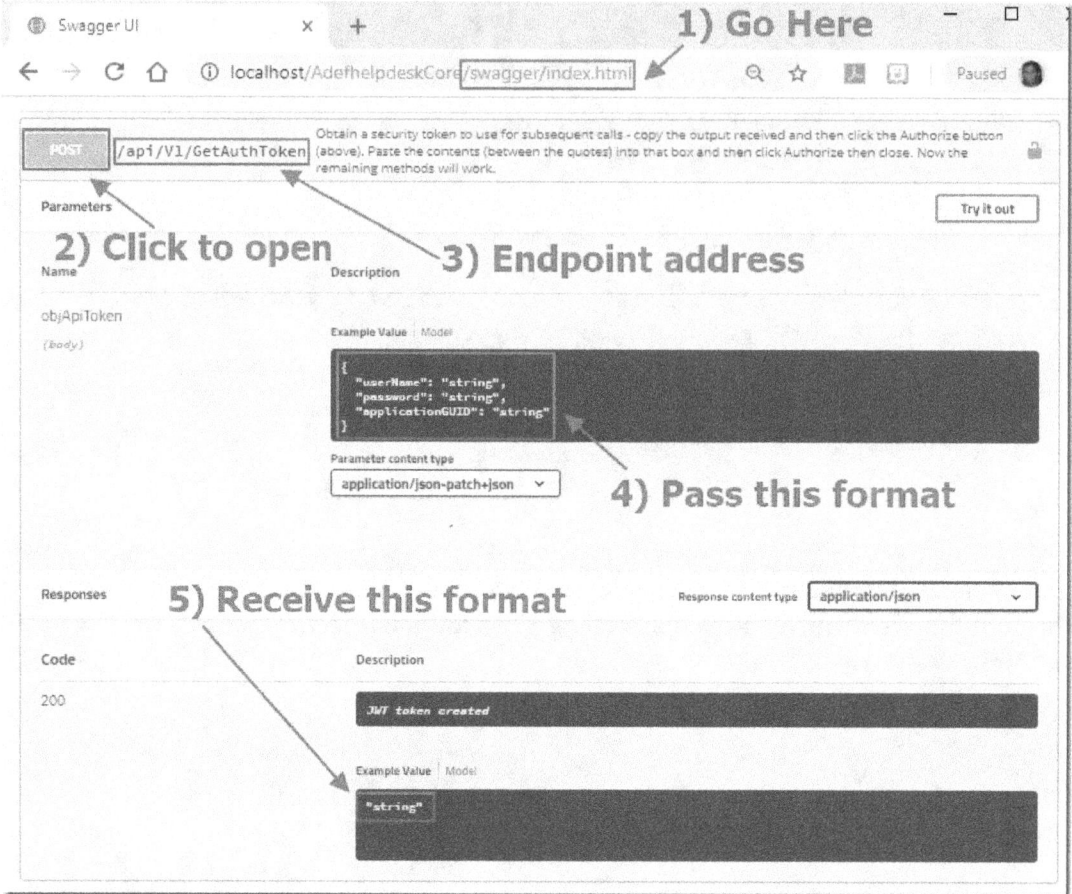

The **ADefHelpDesk API** requires that you use the **UserName** and **Password** to call the **/api/V1/GetAuthToken API** method to obtain a **JSON Web Token (JWT)** to use as authentication for subsequent calls to the other **API** methods.

Note that the method has the word **Post** in the green box. This indicates that it must be called by sending a *Post request*.

Note that the **JWT** will expire after a few minutes, and when it does, you will have to call the **/api/V1/GetAuthToken API** method again to obtain another **JWT**.

So, as the first step, we will create code to allow a **JWT** to be retrieved.

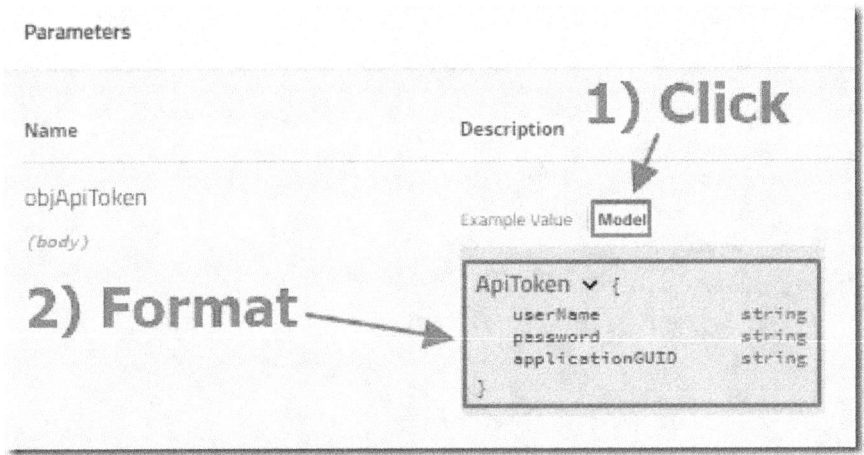

The **Swagger** page will provide the format (the class definition) of the parameter the endpoint requires.

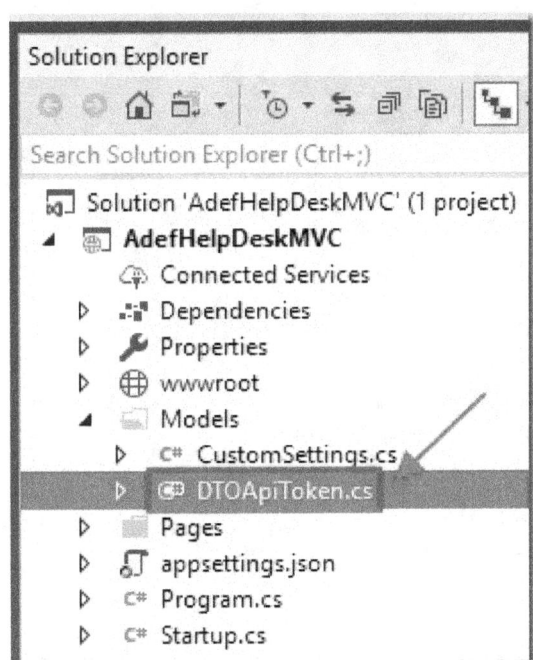

Create a class file called **DTOApiToken.cs** using the following code:

167

```csharp
namespace AdefHelpDeskMVC.Models
{
    public class DTOApiToken
    {
        public string userName { get; set; }
        public string password { get; set; }
        public string applicationGUID { get; set; }
    }
}
```

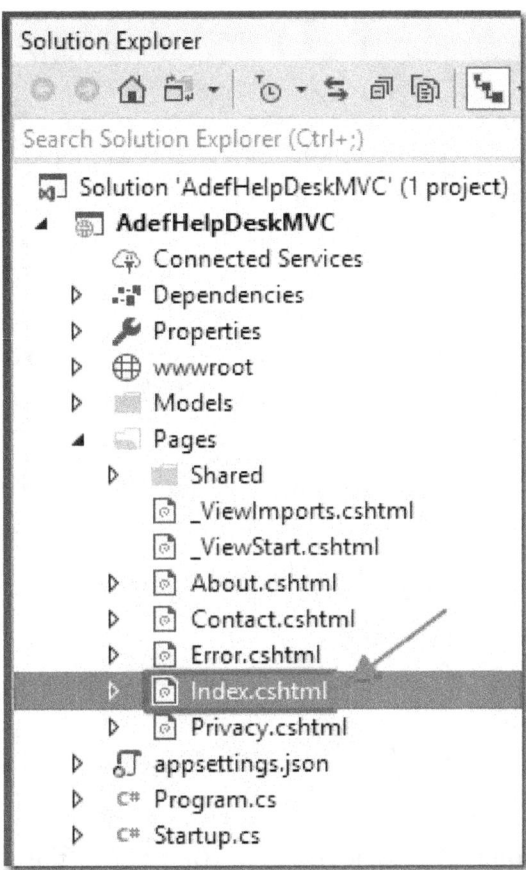

Next, open the page at **Pages/Index.cshtml** and change all the code to the following:

ADefHelpDesk 4

```
@page
@model IndexModel
@addTagHelper *, Microsoft.AspNetCore.Mvc.TagHelpers
@{
    ViewData["Title"] = "ADefHelpDesk API Client";
}
<div class="row">
    <div class="col-md-12">
        <h4>ADefHelpDesk API Client</h4>
        <p class="clearfix"><b>@Model.Message</b></p>
    </div>
</div>
<div class="row">
    <form asp-page-handler="AuthToken" method="post">
        <button class="btn btn-default">Get Auth Token</button>
    </form>
</div>
<div class="row">
    <p class="col-md-12">@Model.BearerToken</p>
</div>
<br />
```

This creates the page layout with a button that will retrieve the **Auth Token** (the **JWT**) and a label to display it.

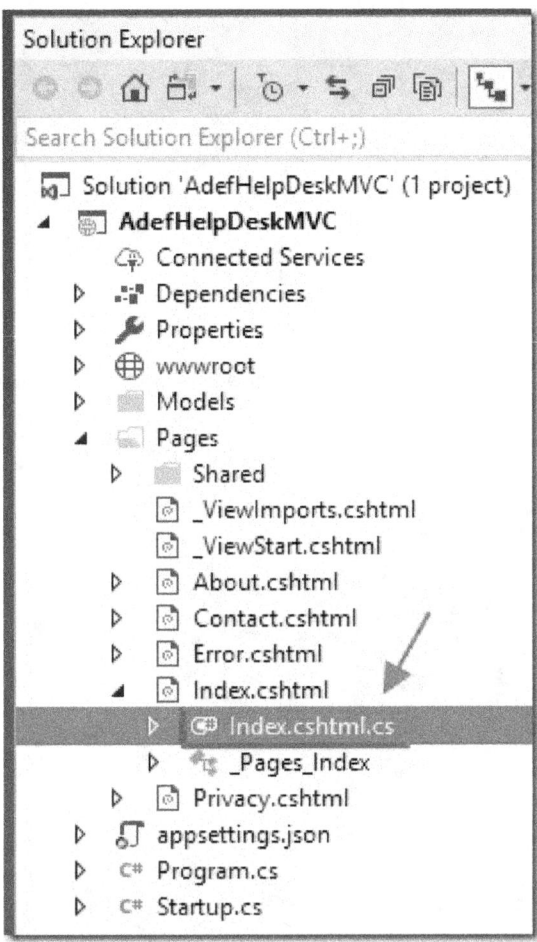

Finally, open the **Index.cshtml.cs** file and change all the code to the following:

ADefHelpDesk 4

```csharp
using System;
using System.Collections.Generic;
using System.Globalization;
using System.Linq;
using System.Net.Http;
using System.Net.Http.Headers;
using System.Text;
using System.Threading.Tasks;
using AdefHelpDeskMVC.Models;
using Microsoft.AspNetCore.Http;
using Microsoft.AspNetCore.Mvc;
using Microsoft.AspNetCore.Mvc.RazorPages;
using Microsoft.AspNetCore.Mvc.Rendering;
using Microsoft.AspNetCore.WebUtilities;
using Microsoft.Extensions.Options;
using Newtonsoft.Json;
using Newtonsoft.Json.Linq;
namespace AdefHelpDeskMVC.Pages
{
    [BindProperties]
    public class IndexModel : PageModel
    {
        // Used to make REST calls
        public static HttpClient client;
        // To store the settings from the appsettings.json file
        private CustomSettings _CustomSettings;
        // To hold any error messages
        public string Message { get; set; }
        // To store the JWT (Authentication token)
        public string BearerToken { get; set; }
        // This method is called when this class is initialized
        public IndexModel(IOptions<CustomSettings> CustomSettings)
        {
            // Get the custom settings using dependency injection
            _CustomSettings = CustomSettings.Value;
        }
    }
}
```

This provides the code to load the **CustomSettings**, using *dependency injection*, which were registered in the **Startup.cs** file.

Add the following methods:

```csharp
private void InitializeForm()
{
    // Initialization code to be added later...
}
// This method called when the page is loaded
public void OnGet()
{
    InitializeForm();
}
```

Now, to implement the code to handle the button click (to retrieve the **JWT**), add the following method:

```csharp
public async void OnPostAuthTokenAsync()
{
    // Instantiate the DTOApiToken class and set the parameters
    // using the values from CustomSettings
    DTOApiToken paramApiToken = new DTOApiToken();
    paramApiToken.userName = _CustomSettings.UserName;
    paramApiToken.password = _CustomSettings.Password;
    paramApiToken.applicationGUID = _CustomSettings.ApplicationGUID;
    // Call the GetAuthToken method and retrieve the BearerToken (JWT - Auth Token)
    // The BearerToken will then display on the page because it has
    // the following code: @Model.BearerToken
    BearerToken = await GetAuthToken(_CustomSettings.APIWebAddress, paramApiToken);
    InitializeForm();
}
```

Finally, add the following code to implement the **GetAuthToken** method:

```csharp
private static async Task<string> GetAuthToken(string APIWebAddress, DTOApiToken
                                    paramApiToken)
{
    // Store the final result
    string strResult = "";
    // Use the HttpClient
    using (client)
    {
        // Initialize the HttpClient
        client = new HttpClient();
        // Create a new REST request
        using (var request = new HttpRequestMessage())
        {
            // The Swagger page indicates this must be a "Post"
            request.Method = HttpMethod.Post;
            // Set the destination to the method indicated on the Swagger page
            // to: api/V1/GetAuthToken
            request.RequestUri = new Uri($"{APIWebAddress}api/V1/GetAuthToken");
            // Convert the parameters to JavaScript Object Notation (JSON) format
            var json = JsonConvert.SerializeObject(paramApiToken);
            request.Content = new StringContent(json, Encoding.UTF8,
            "application/json");
            // Make the request to the API endpoint on the ADefHelpDesk site
            var response = client.SendAsync(request).Result;
            // Receive the response
            var JsonDataResponse =
                await response.Content.ReadAsStringAsync();
            // Convert the response (the JWT (Auth Token)) to a String value
            strResult =
                JsonConvert.DeserializeObject<string>(JsonDataResponse);
            // Strip the word Bearer from the token
            strResult = strResult.Replace("Bearer ", " ");
        }
    }
    // Return the JWT
    return strResult;
}
```

ADefHelpDesk 4

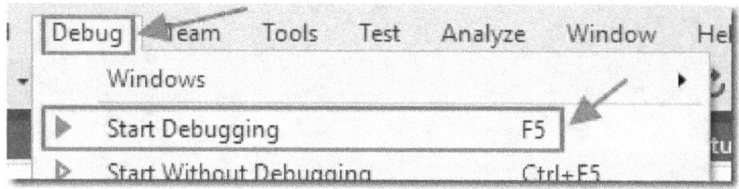

Hit **F5** to run the project.

You can now click the **Get Auth Token** button, and the code will call the **API** method on the **ADefHelpDesk** site, passing the **UserName**, **Password**, and **ApplicationGUID**, and retrieving the **JWT** that will then be displayed on the page.

Retrieve The Current User

To demonstrate how the **JWT** is used to authenticate a request, we will call the **GetCurrentUser API** method.

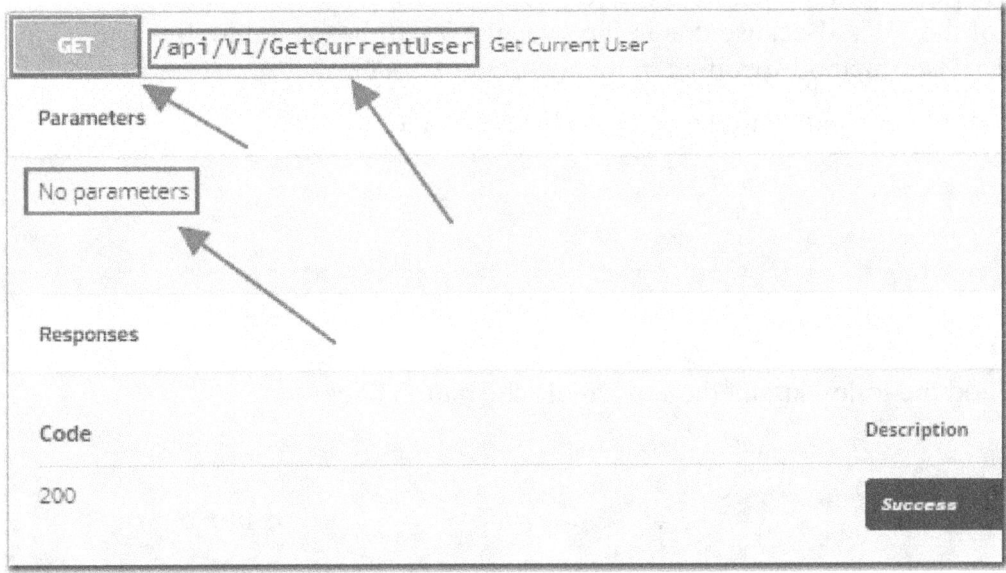

When we look at the **Swagger** page, we can get the **API** endpoint address see that we call it as a **Get**, and that we pass no parameters.

However, we will need to pass a valid and unexpired **JWT** in the *header* of the request, otherwise we will get an *unauthorized* response.

Add the following code to the **Index.cshtml** page:

```
<div class="row">
    <form asp-page-handler="CurrentUser" method="post">
        <input type="hidden" name="paramBearerToken" value="@Model.BearerToken" />
        <button class="btn btn-default">Get Current User</button>
    </form>
</div>
<div class="row">
    <p class="col-md-12">@Model.CurrentAPIUser</p>
</div>
```

This will create a button to click to retrieve the name of the **API User** and a *div* to display it.

ADefHelpDesk 4

Note that there is a hidden field called **paramBearerToken** that contains the value of the **JWT**. Because it is in the *form* tag it will be passed to the **CurrentUser** method specified in the *asp-page-handler* tag.

Add the following code to the **Index.cshtml.cs** page:

```csharp
// Store the name of the current API User
public string CurrentAPIUser { get; set; }
```

Next, add the following method to handle the button click:

```
public async void OnPostCurrentUserAsync(string paramBearerToken)
{
    // paramBearerToken is passed to this method (when the button is clicked)
    // by the hidden field
    if (paramBearerToken == null)
    {
        // Set error message
        Message = "The Auth Token is required";
    }
    else
    {
        // Call the API
        var response =
            await GetCurrentUser(_CustomSettings.APIWebAddress, paramBearerToken);
        if (response == "Unauthorized")
        {
            // Set error message
            Message = "The Auth Token is expired or invalid";
        }
        else
        {
            // Return the Current User
            CurrentAPIUser = response;
            // Save the Bearer Token
            BearerToken = paramBearerToken;
        }
    }
    InitializeForm();
}
```

Finally, add the following code to implement the **GetCurrentUser** method that is being called by the code above:

ADefHelpDesk 4

```csharp
private static async Task<string> GetCurrentUser(string APIWebAddress, string
                                                 paramBearerToken)
{
    // Store the final result
    string strResult = "";
    // Use the HttpClient
    using (client)
    {
        // Initialize the HttpClient
        client = new HttpClient();
        // Create a new REST request
        using (var request = new HttpRequestMessage())
        {
            // The Swagger page indicates this must be a "Post"
            request.Method = HttpMethod.Get;
            // Set the destination to the method indicated on the Swagger page
            // to: api/V1/GetCurrentUser
            request.RequestUri = new Uri($"{APIWebAddress}api/V1/GetCurrentUser");
            // Pass the JWT in the 'header' of the request with the word "Bearer" in
            // front
            client.DefaultRequestHeaders.Authorization =
                new AuthenticationHeaderValue("Bearer", paramBearerToken);
            // Make the request to the API endpoint on the ADefHelpDesk site
            var response = client.SendAsync(request).Result;
            // Handle if the JWT is expired
            if (response.StatusCode == System.Net.HttpStatusCode.Unauthorized)
            {
                return "Unauthorized";
            }
            // Receive the response
            var JsonDataResponse =
                await response.Content.ReadAsStringAsync();
            // Convert the response to a String value
            strResult =
                JsonConvert.DeserializeObject<string>(JsonDataResponse);
        }
    }
    // Return the response
    return strResult;
}
```

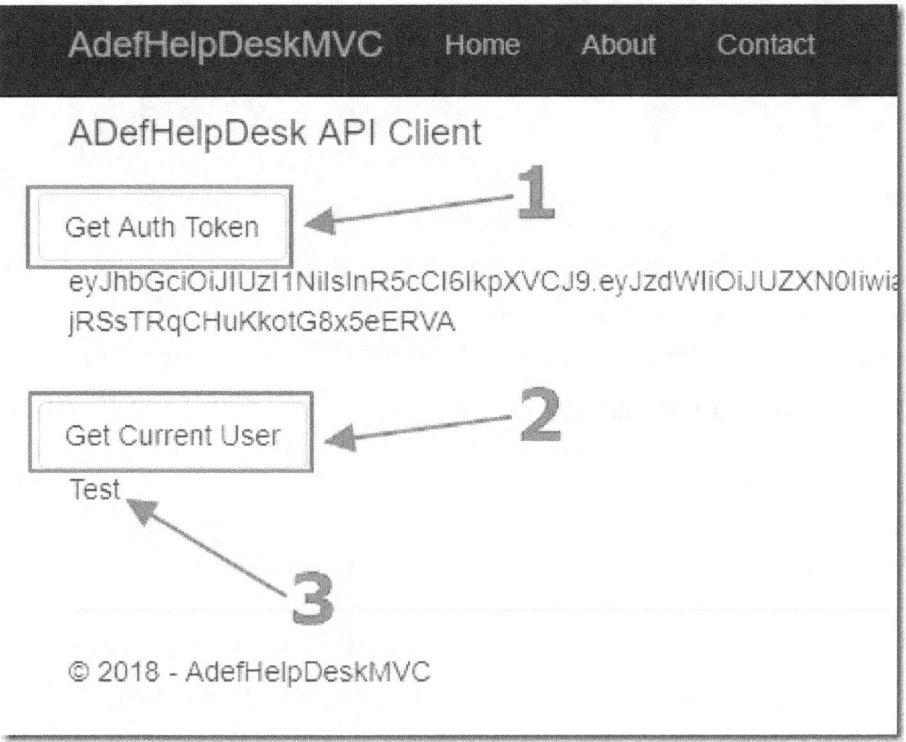

When we run the application, we first click the **Get Auth Token** button to get a **JWT**, then we click the **Get Current User** button to pass the **JWT** to the method that will retrieve the name of the current **API** user.

Create A Help Desk Ticket

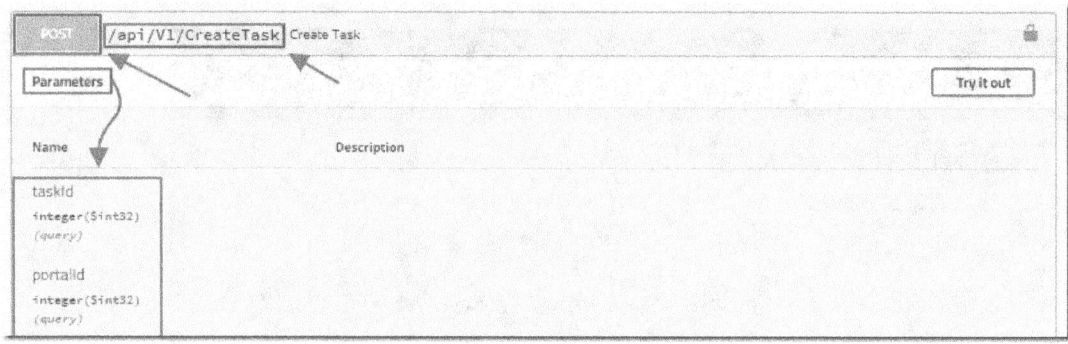

We will now create a **Help Desk Ticket** by calling the **CreateTask** method.

We see that this one has a lot of parameters.

```
DTOTask ∨ {
    taskId                  integer($int32)
    portalId                integer($int32)
    description             string
    status                  string
    priority                string
    createdDate             string
    estimatedStart          string
    estimatedCompletion     string
    dueDate                 string
    assignedRoleId          integer($int32)
    assignedRoleName        string
    ticketPassword          string
    requesterUserId         integer($int32)
    requesterName           string
    requesterEmail          string
    requesterPhone          string
    estimatedHours          integer($int32)
    sendEmails              boolean
    selectedTreeNodes
                            > [...]
    colDTOTaskDetail
                            > [...]
}

DTOTaskDetail ∨ {
    detailId                integer($int32)
    detailType              string
    contentType             string
    insertDate              string
    userId                  integer($int32)
    userName                string
    description             string
    emailDescription        string
    startTime               string
    stopTime                string
    sendEmails              boolean
    colDTOAttachment
                            > [...]
}
```

The parameters are a combination of the **DTOTask** class and the **DTOTaskDetail** class.

Their full definition for the classes is available by scrolling down toward the bottom of the **Swagger** page.

ADefHelpDesk 4

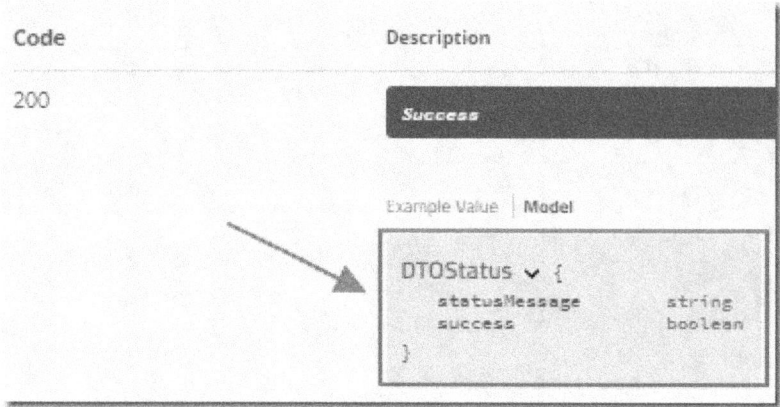

We can also see the class that the method will return.

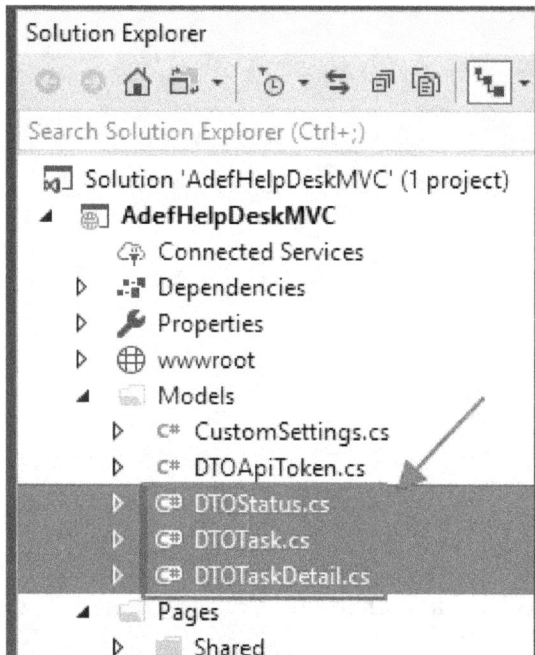

To represent these classes, add three class files to the **Models** folder using the following code:

DTOStatus.cs

```csharp
namespace AdefHelpDeskMVC.Models
{
    public class DTOStatus
    {
        public string StatusMessage { get; set; }
        public bool Success { get; set; }
    }
}
```

DTOTask.cs

ADefHelpDesk 4

```csharp
using System.Collections.Generic;
namespace AdefHelpDeskMVC.Models
{
    public class DTOTask
    {
        public int? taskId { get; set; }
        public int? portalId { get; set; }
        public string description { get; set; }
        public string status { get; set; }
        public string priority { get; set; }
        public string createdDate { get; set; }
        public string estimatedStart { get; set; }
        public string estimatedCompletion { get; set; }
        public string dueDate { get; set; }
        public int? assignedRoleId { get; set; }
        public string assignedRoleName { get; set; }
        public string ticketPassword { get; set; }
        public int? requesterUserId { get; set; }
        public string requesterName { get; set; }
        public string requesterEmail { get; set; }
        public string requesterPhone { get; set; }
        public int? estimatedHours { get; set; }
        public bool? sendEmails { get; set; }
        public List<int> selectedTreeNodes { get; set; }
        public List<DTOTaskDetail> colDTOTaskDetail { get; set; }
    }
}
```

DTOTaskDetail.cs

```
using System.Collections.Generic;
namespace AdefHelpDeskMVC.Models
{
    public class DTOTaskDetail
    {
        // Note: this field is renamed from description to
        // taskDetailDescription to prevent collision when passed
        // as a parameter with the field description in the Task object
        public string taskDetailDescription { get; set; }
        public int detailId { get; set; }
        public string detailType { get; set; }
        public string contentType { get; set; }
        public string insertDate { get; set; }
        public int userId { get; set; }
        public string userName { get; set; }
        public string emailDescription { get; set; }
        public string startTime { get; set; }
        public string stopTime { get; set; }
        public bool? sendEmails { get; set; }
    }
}
```

To create a form that will allow the **Ticket** to be input, add the following code to the **Index.cshtml** page:

ADefHelpDesk 4

```html
<div>
    <form asp-page-handler="CreateTicket" method="post" enctype="multipart/form-data">
        <input type="hidden" name="paramBearerToken" value="@Model.BearerToken" />
        <div class="row">
            <p class="col-md-1">Name:</p>
            <p class="col-md-11">
            <input asp-for="@Model.TicketForm.Name" /></p>
        </div>
        <div class="row">
            <p class="col-md-1">Email:</p>
            <p class="col-md-11">
            <input type="email" asp-for="@Model.TicketForm.Email" /></p>
        </div>
        <div class="row">
            <p class="col-md-1">Phone:</p>
            <p class="col-md-11">
            <input type="tel" asp-for="@Model.TicketForm.Phone" /></p>
        </div>
        <div class="row">
            <p class="col-md-1">Description:</p>
            <p class="col-md-11">
            <input asp-for="@Model.TicketForm.Description" /></p>
        </div>
        <div class="row">
            <p class="col-md-1">Due Date:</p>
            <p class="col-md-11">
            <input type="date" asp-for="@Model.TicketForm.DueDate" /></p>
        </div>
        <div class="row">
            <p class="col-md-1">Priority:</p>
            <p class="col-md-11">
            <select asp-for="@Model.TicketForm.Priority" asp-items="Model.Options"></select></p>
        </div>
        <div class="row">
            <button class="btn btn-default">Create Help Desk Ticket</button>
        </div>
    </form>
</div>
```

Add the following class (*outside* of the **IndexModel** class but inside the **AdefHelpDeskMVC** *namespace*) to the **Index.cshtml.cs** file:

```
public class Ticket
{
    public string Name { get; set; }
    public string Email { get; set; }
    public string Phone { get; set; }
    public string Description { get; set; }
    public string Detail { get; set; }
    public DateTime? DueDate { get; set; }
    public string Priority { get; set; }
}
```

Add this *extension method* class that will be used later to serialize parameters to append to the URL:

ADefHelpDesk 4

```csharp
public static class ObjectExtensions
{
    // From: https://bit.ly/2A5R70I
    public static IDictionary<string, string> ToKeyValue(this object metaToken)
    {
        if (metaToken == null)
        {
            return null;
        }
        JToken token = metaToken as JToken;
        if (token == null)
        {
            return ToKeyValue(JObject.FromObject(metaToken));
        }
        if (token.HasValues)
        {
            var contentData = new Dictionary<string, string>();
            foreach (var child in token.Children().ToList())
            {
                var childContent = child.ToKeyValue();
                if (childContent != null)
                {
                    contentData = contentData.Concat(childContent)
                        .ToDictionary(k => k.Key, v => v.Value);
                }
            }
            return contentData;
        }
        var jValue = token as JValue;
        if (jValue?.Value == null)
        {
            return null;
        }
        var value = jValue?.Type == JTokenType.Date ?
            jValue?.ToString("o", CultureInfo.InvariantCulture) :
            jValue?.ToString(CultureInfo.InvariantCulture);
        return new Dictionary<string, string> { { token.Path, value } };
    }
}
```

Add the following properties inside the **IndexModel** class:

```csharp
// To hold values for the Ticket form
public Ticket TicketForm { get; set; }
// To hold values for the dropdown on the Ticket form
public List<SelectListItem> Options { get; set; }
```

Change the **InitializeForm** method to the following:

```csharp
private void InitializeForm()
{
    // Instatiate the values for the form
    TicketForm = new Ticket();
    // Create options for the dropdown on the form
    Options = new List<SelectListItem>();
    Options.Add(new SelectListItem { Value = "Normal", Text = "Normal" });
    Options.Add(new SelectListItem { Value = "High", Text = "High" });
    Options.Add(new SelectListItem { Value = "Low", Text = "Low" });
    // Set the default Priority value
    TicketForm.Priority = "Normal";
}
```

Next, add the method that will handle the button click when the form is submitted:

ADefHelpDesk 4

```
public async void OnPostCreateTicketAsync(string paramBearerToken)
{
    if (paramBearerToken == null)
    {
        // Set error message
        Message = "The Auth Token is required";
    }
    else
    {
        // Format the fields
        DTOTask objDTOTask = new DTOTask();
        DTOTaskDetail objDTOTaskDetail = null;
        IFormFile objIFormFile = null;
        objDTOTask.createdDate = DateTime.Now.ToShortDateString();
        objDTOTask.requesterUserId = -1;
        objDTOTask.status = "New";
        objDTOTask.sendEmails = true;
        // Set values from form
        objDTOTask.description = TicketForm.Description;
        objDTOTask.dueDate = TicketForm.DueDate?.ToShortDateString();
        objDTOTask.priority = TicketForm.Priority;
        objDTOTask.requesterEmail = TicketForm.Email;
        objDTOTask.requesterName = TicketForm.Name;
        objDTOTask.requesterPhone = TicketForm.Phone;
        // Call the API
        var response = await CreateTicket(
            objDTOTask,
            objDTOTaskDetail,
            objIFormFile,
            _CustomSettings.APIWebAddress,
            paramBearerToken);
        if (response.StatusMessage == "Unauthorized")
        {
            // Set error message
            Message = "The Auth Token is expired or invalid";
        }
        else
        {
            // Save the Bearer Token
            BearerToken = paramBearerToken;
            if (response.Success)
            {
                Message = "Ticket Created!";
            }
            else
            {
                Message = response.StatusMessage;
            }
        }
    }
    InitializeForm();
}
```

Finally, add the code to implement the **CreateTicket** method that the code above calls:

ADefHelpDesk 4

```csharp
private static async Task<DTOStatus> CreateTicket(
    DTOTask paramDTOTask,
    DTOTaskDetail paramDTOTaskDetail,
    IFormFile paramIFormFile,
    string APIWebAddress,
    string paramBearerToken)
{
    HttpResponseMessage response;
    DTOStatus Result = new DTOStatus();
    using (client)
    {
        client = new HttpClient();
        using (var request = new HttpRequestMessage())
        {
            client.DefaultRequestHeaders.Authorization =
                new AuthenticationHeaderValue("Bearer", paramBearerToken);
            // Add Task parameters
            var TaskParameters = paramDTOTask.ToKeyValue();
            // If there are Task Details add them
            if (paramDTOTaskDetail != null)
            {
                var TaskDetailParameters = paramDTOTaskDetail.ToKeyValue();
                foreach (var item in TaskDetailParameters)
                {
                    TaskParameters.Add(item);
                }
            }
            request.RequestUri =
                new Uri(QueryHelpers.AddQueryString(
                    $"{APIWebAddress}api/V1/CreateTask"
                    , TaskParameters));
            request.Method = HttpMethod.Post;
            // Send request
            response = client.SendAsync(request).Result;
            if (response.StatusCode == System.Net.HttpStatusCode.Unauthorized)
            {
                Result.Success = false;
                Result.StatusMessage = "Unauthorized";
                return Result;
            }
            var JsonDataResponse =
                await response.Content.ReadAsStringAsync();
            Result =
                JsonConvert.DeserializeObject<DTOStatus>(JsonDataResponse);
        }
    }
    return Result;
}
```

Note, the **IFormFile** *paramIFormFile* parameter is being passed but is not being implemented yet. We will use it to upload a file in the final section of this tutorial.

When we run the project, we can obtain an **Auth Token**, fill out the form, and submit a new **Help Desk Ticket**.

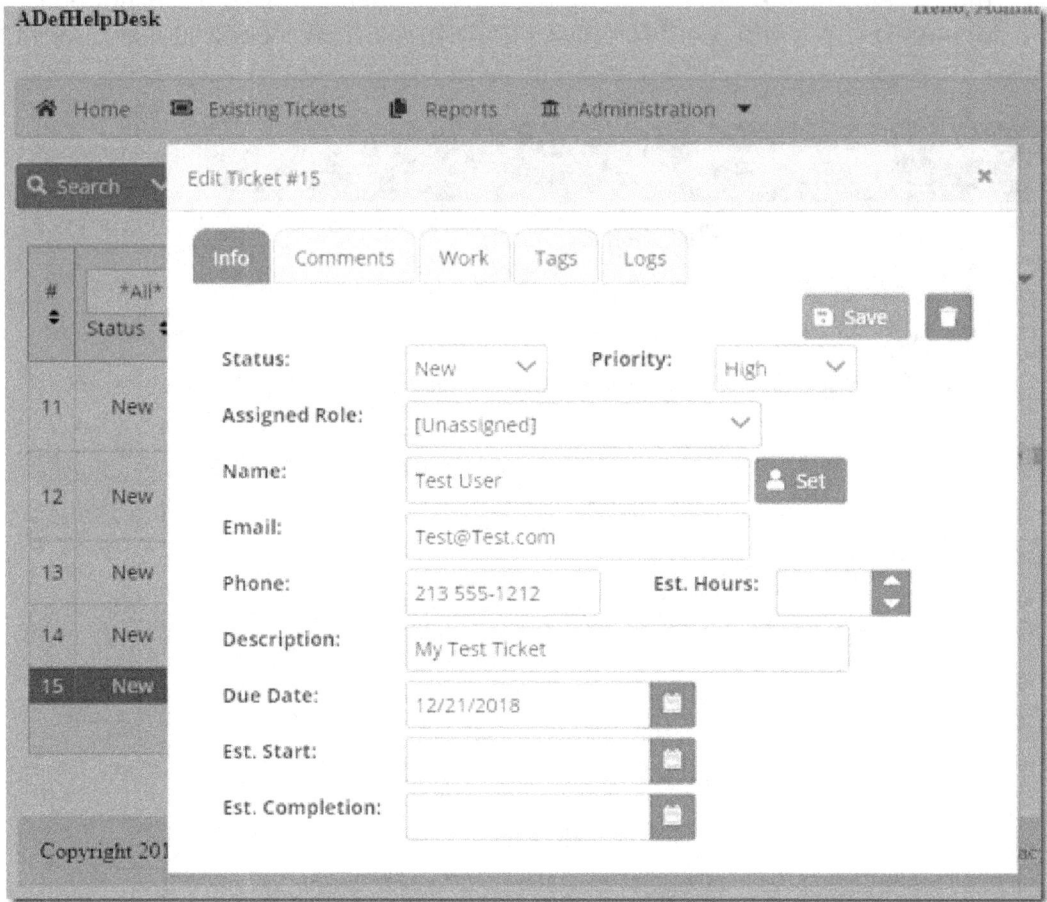

If we log into the **ADefHelpDesk** application, we can see the new **Ticket**.

Note: In this instance, the user specified in the **Email** parameter would be emailed a special link to the **Ticket** that allowed them to view and add comments to it. You can set a property to suppress emails on a per **Ticket** basis if needed. You also have the option to call the **API** method to create an account for a user and connect the **Ticket** to that account.

Upload A File

The **ADefHelpDesk API** allows a file to be uploaded when creating (or updating) a **Help Desk Ticket**.

It requires the file to be attached to a **Task Detail** object.

To hold the optional **Detail** text for the **Task Detail** object, add the following code to the form on the **Index.cshtml** page:

```
<div class="row">
    <p class="col-md-1">Detail:</p>
    <p class="col-md-11">
    <textarea asp-for="@Model.TicketForm.Detail"></textarea></p>
</div>
```

Also, add the following code to the form to allow a file to be uploaded:

```
<div class="row">
    <p class="col-md-1">File:</p>
    <p class="col-md-11">
    <input type="file" asp-for="@Model.TicketForm.FormFile" /></p>
</div>
```

In the **Index.cshtml.cs** file, add the following property to the **Ticket** class to hold the value of the file:

```
public IFormFile FormFile { get; set; }
```

Add the following code to the **OnPostCreateTicketAsync** method:

ADefHelpDesk 4

```
// If there is a file we need a Task Detail
if (TicketForm.FormFile != null)
{
    objDTOTaskDetail = new DTOTaskDetail();
    // Note: this field is renamed from description to
    // taskDetailDescription to prevent collision when passed
    // as a parameter with the field description in the Task object
    objDTOTaskDetail.taskDetailDescription = TicketForm.FormFile.FileName;
    // Set File
    objIFormFile = TicketForm.FormFile;
}
```

Finally, in the **CreateTicket** method, remove the line:

```
response = client.SendAsync(request).Result;
```

Replace it with:

```csharp
if (paramIFormFile != null)
{
    using (var readStream = paramIFormFile.OpenReadStream())
    {
        MultipartFormDataContent _multiPartContent =
            new MultipartFormDataContent();
        // Serialize Request
        StreamContent _fileData =
            new StreamContent(readStream);
        _fileData.Headers.ContentType =
            new MediaTypeHeaderValue("application/octet-stream");
        ContentDispositionHeaderValue _contentDispositionHeaderValue =
            new ContentDispositionHeaderValue("form-data");
        _contentDispositionHeaderValue.Name = "objFile";
        _contentDispositionHeaderValue.FileName = paramIFormFile.FileName;
        _fileData.Headers.ContentDisposition =
                                        _contentDispositionHeaderValue;
        _multiPartContent.Add(_fileData, "objFile");
        // Set content
        request.Content = _multiPartContent;
        // Send request
        response = client.SendAsync(request).Result;
    }
}
else
{
    // Send request
    response = client.SendAsync(request).Result;
}
```

ADefHelpDesk 4

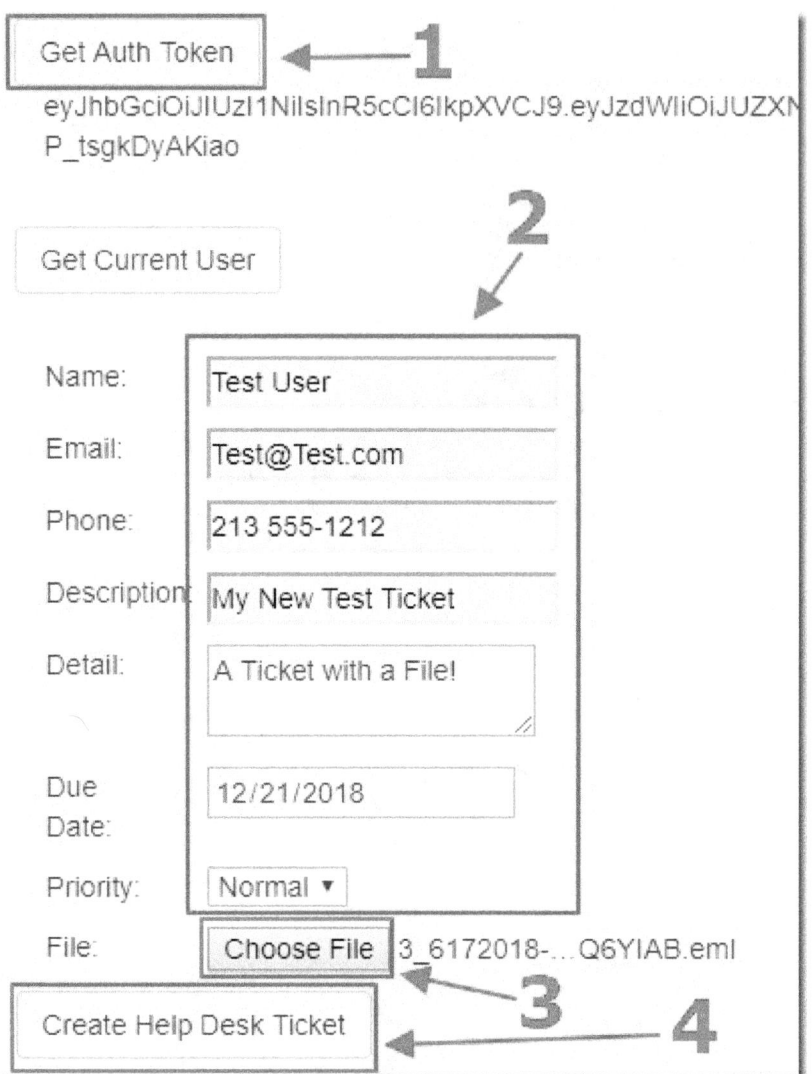

Now we can upload a file when creating a new **Help Desk Ticket**.

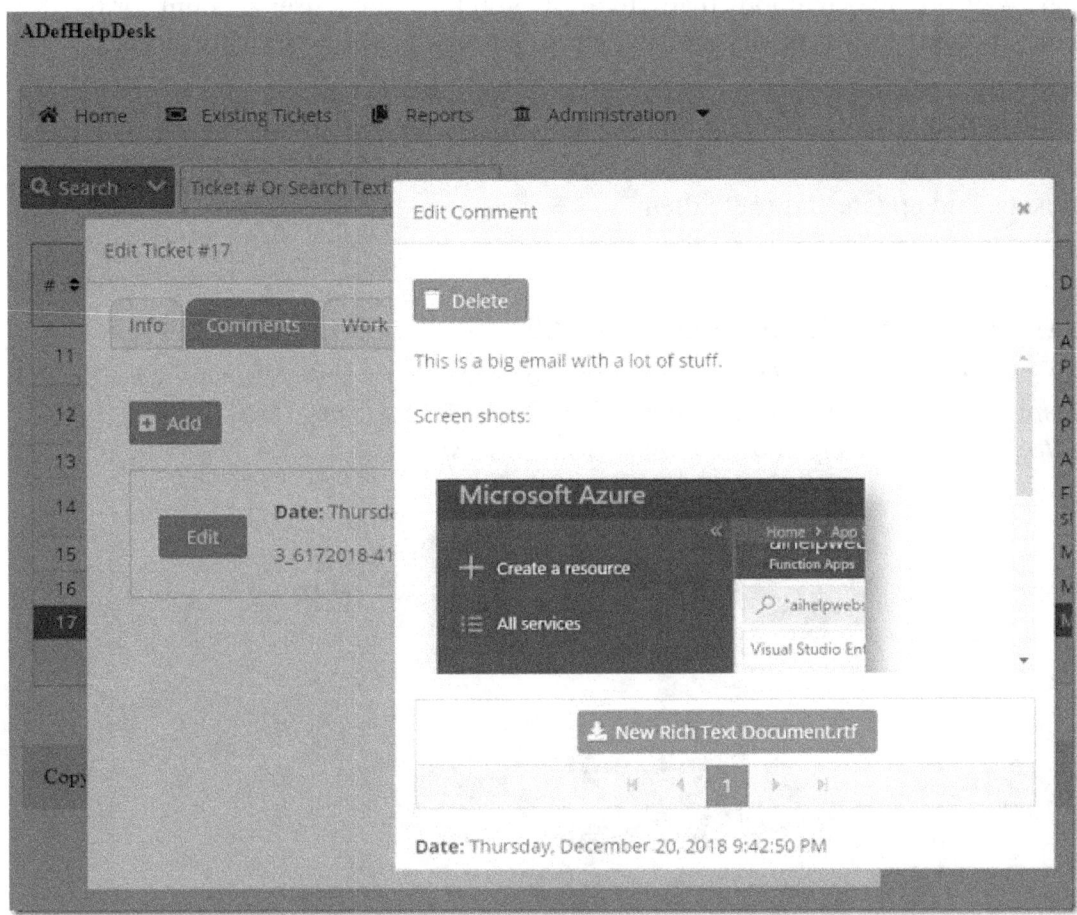

If we upload a **.EML file**, we can see its contents displayed in **ADefHelpDesk**, and any attachments in the **.EML** file will have download links.

If we upload a file that is not a **.EML** file, that file will display a download link.

Advantages Of A REST API

The **ADefHelpDesk API** demonstrates the power of using **REST APIs**. Rather than having multiple **Help Desk** applications to support your various applications that require your users to exit the application to create a **Ticket**, you can use the **API** to allow your users to create tickets from *inside* those applications.

ADefHelpDesk 4

The **API** provides methods that will allow you to create a user account for the user, if needed, so their tickets can be tracked, and email notifications sent.

This allows a single installation of **ADefHelpDesk** to support unlimited applications; yet, your support personnel manage it all from one interface. This also allows processes such as auto responders to periodically check for new tickets, and update and route them.

Creating an Azure Function to Retrieve Emails and Create Tickets

The sample code for this section can be obtained at the link "Retrieve Emails Using Azure Functions and Create Help Desk Tickets Using API" at http://lightswitchhelpwebsite.com/Downloads.aspx

You can create an **Azure** function that will retrieve emails every 5 minutes from a **Pop3** email account and create **Help Desk Tickets**.

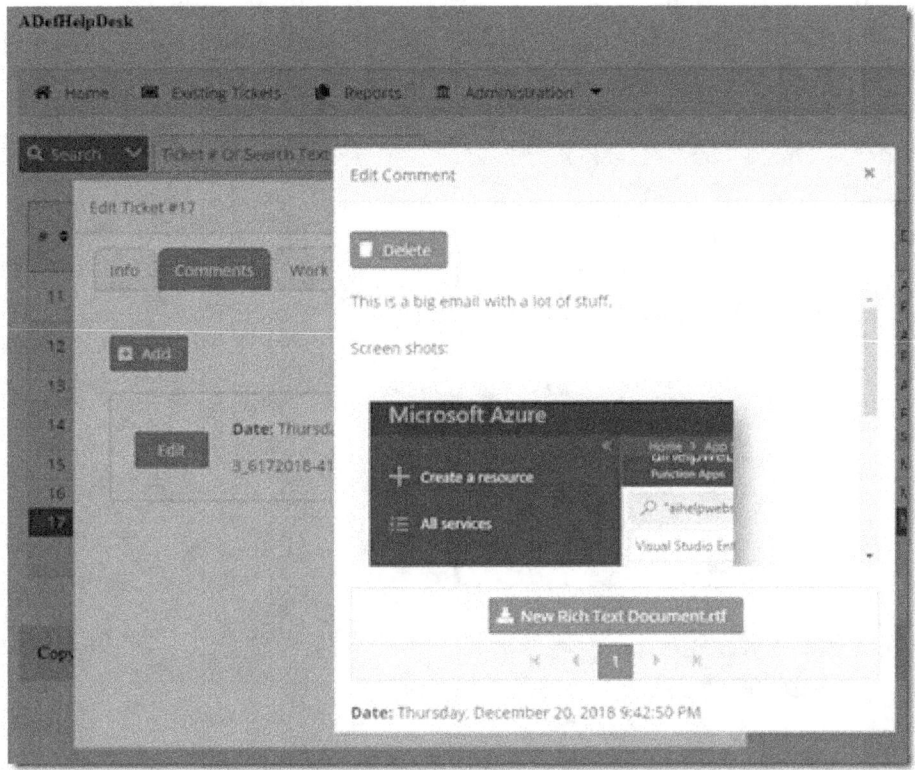

ADefHelpDesk has an **API** that provides the following features that we will explore:

- Requires callers to first obtain a **JSON Web Token (JWT)** (also called a *Bearer Token*) using a combination of a **UserName**, **Password**, and **Application GUID**. The token is then passed in the header of the subsequent requests to the other methods to authenticate the requests.
- Allows an external caller to create **Help Desk Tickets** (and perform all other functionality). We will create a **Microsoft Azure Function** that will retrieve the **Pop3** emails and call the **ADefHelpDesk API** to create the **Help Desk Tickets**.
- As part of creating **Help Desk Tickets**, the **ADefHelpDesk API** allows the external caller to upload files. We will use this **API** function to upload the original email. If the **Email** is in the proper **MIME** format, **ADefHelpDesk**

will display the email and any attachments to the email in its online web interface. Otherwise, it will display a link for the original email to be downloaded.

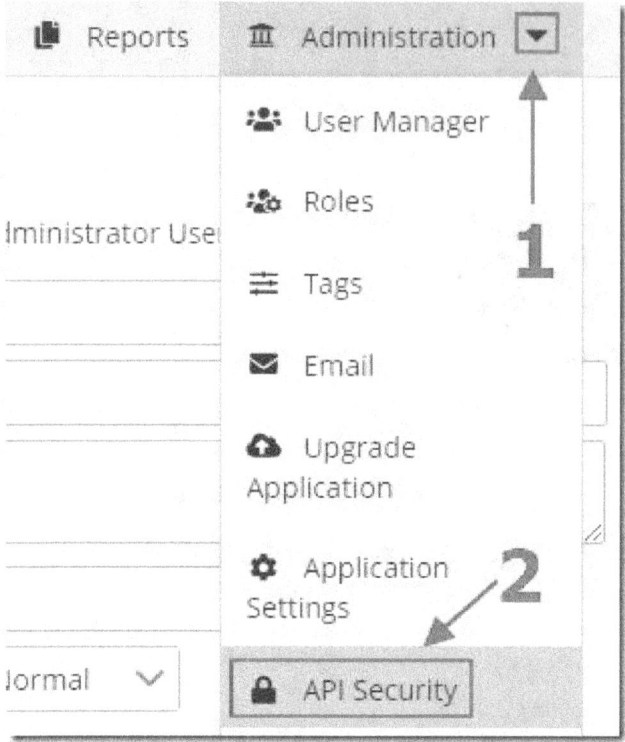

In **ADefHelpDesk**, follow the directions in the **API Security (Swagger Rest API)** section in **Chapter 5: Administration Settings** to create an account that can call the **API**.

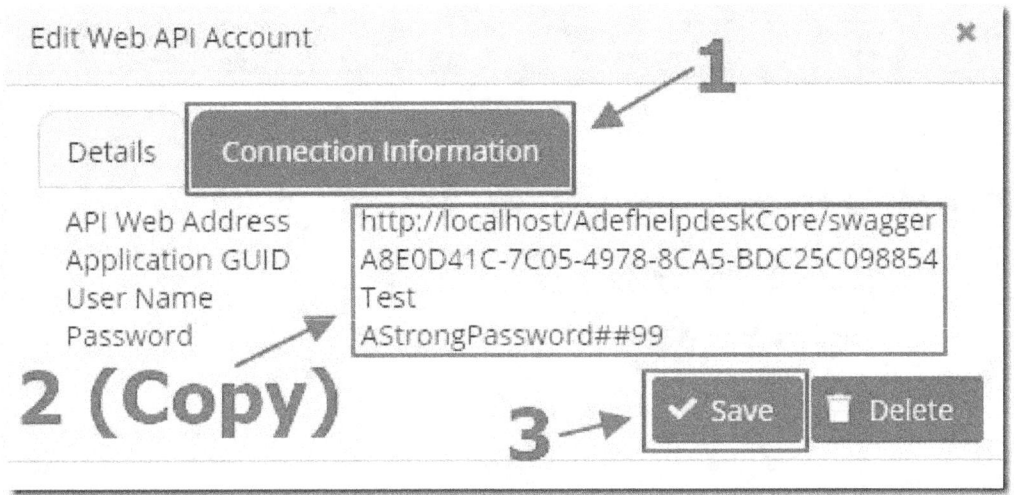

You will need to copy the information on the **Connection Information** tab to use later.

ADefHelpDesk 4

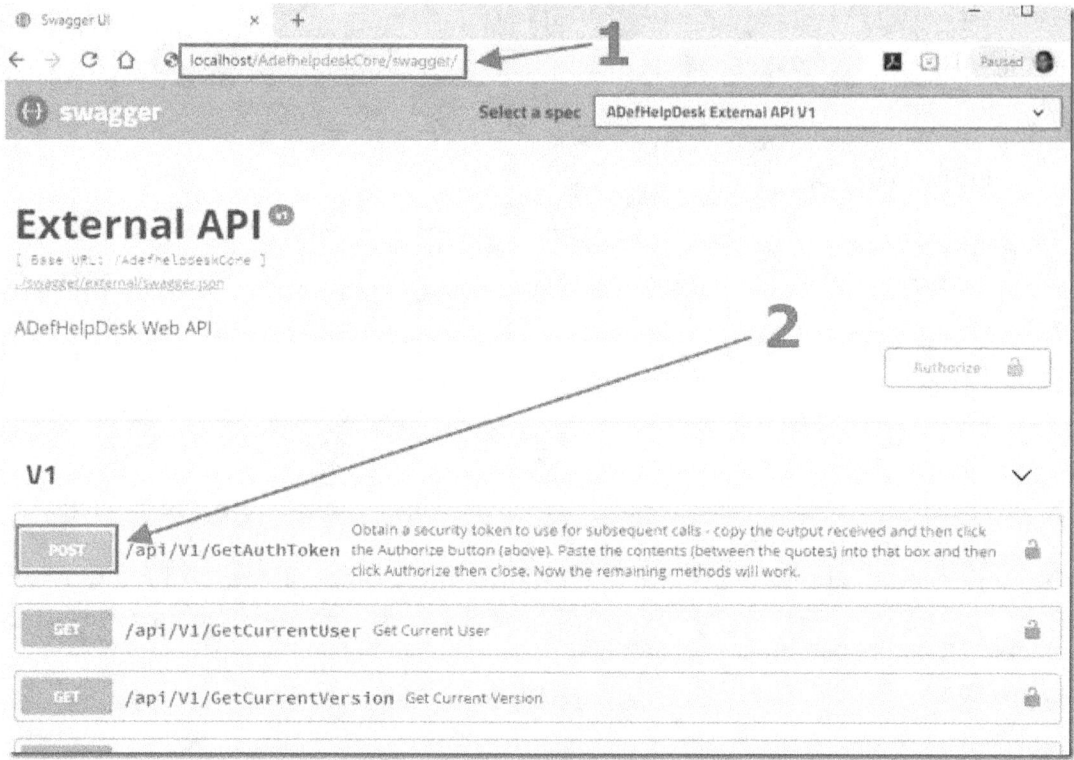

In the **ADefHelpDesk** site, there is a **Swagger page** (see: https://swagger.io/) that documents the *REST based API* endpoints at: ***http://{your default web address}/swagger/*** (for example: http://adefhelpdesk.azurewebsites.net/swagger/).

Create The Application

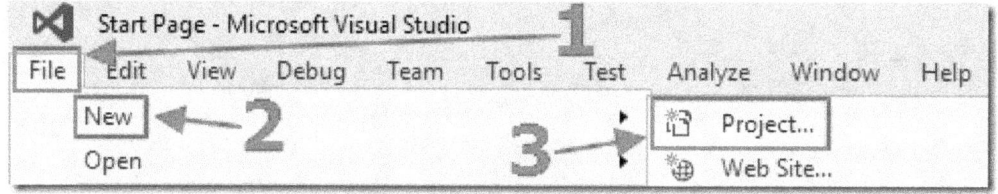

Open **Visual Studio** (Note: You can download the **Community Edition** free from https://www.visualstudio.com/vs/).

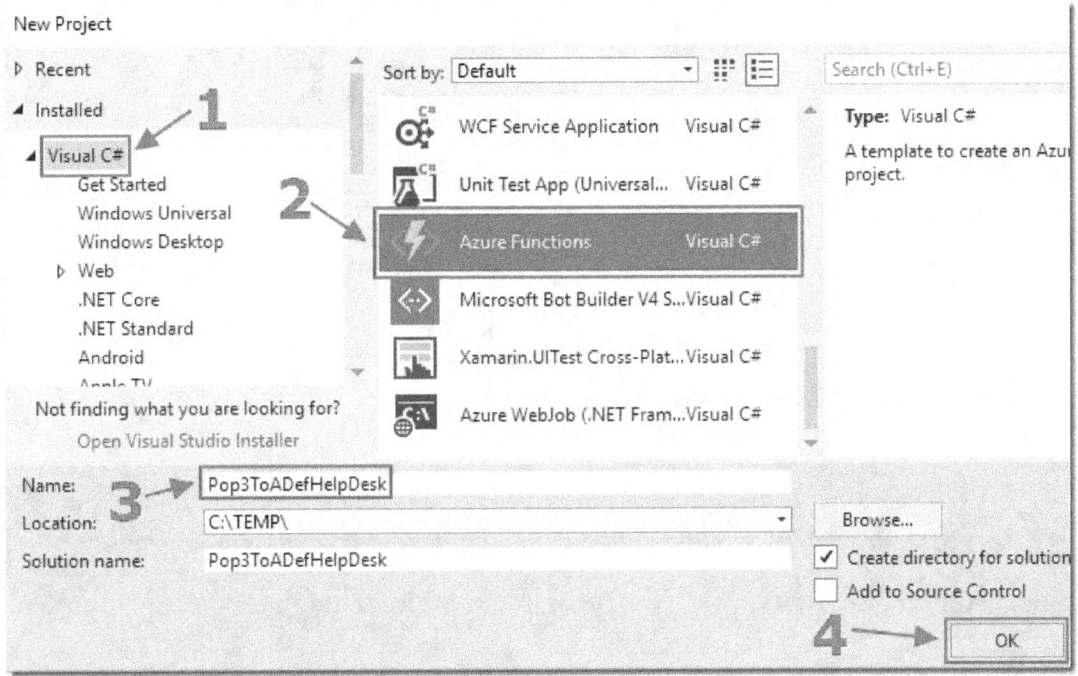

Create an **Azure Function** project.

*Note: Azure Functions Tools is included in the **Azure development workload** of Visual Studio 2017 version 15.4 or a later version. Make sure you include the* **Azure development** *workload in your **Visual Studio 2017** installation.*

ADefHelpDesk 4

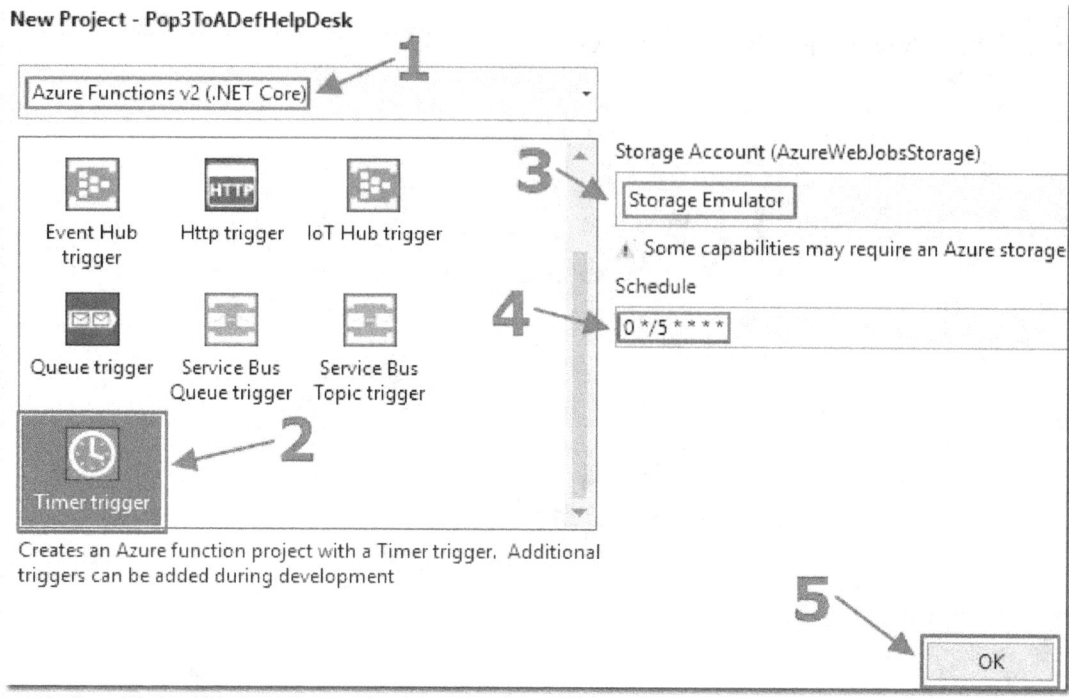

Select **Azure Functions V2 (.Net Core)** and the **Timer trigger**.

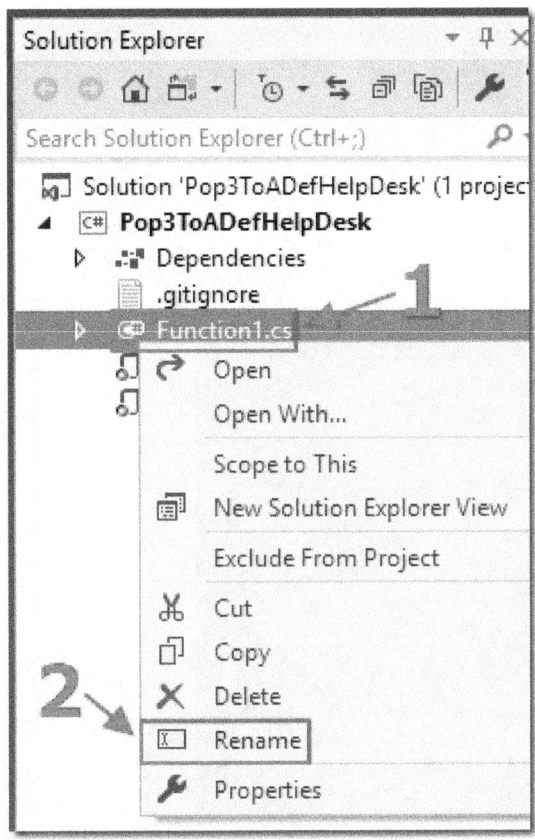

The project will be created.

Rename the **Function1.cs** file to **Pop3ADefHelpDeskEmails.cs**.

ADefHelpDesk 4

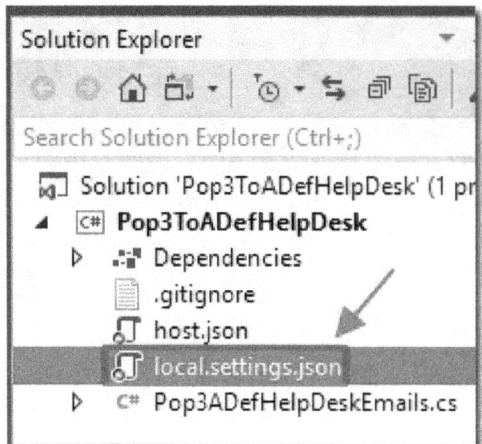

Open **local.settings.json**.

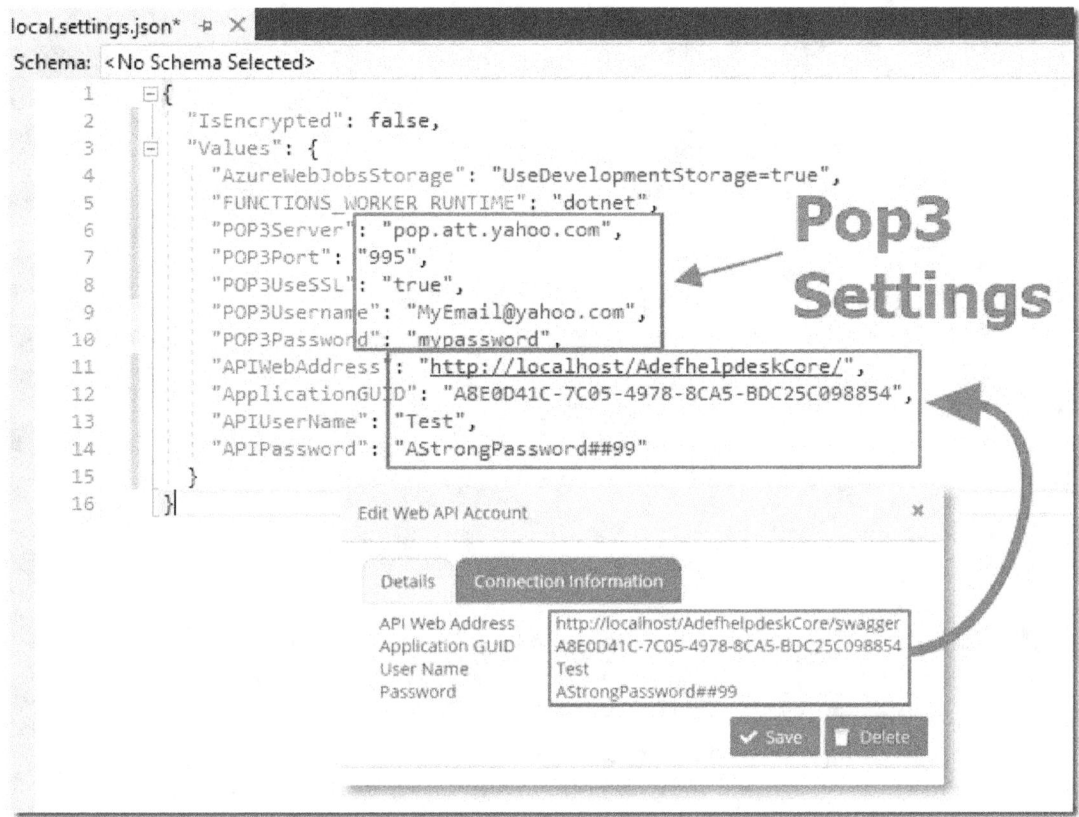

Replace the contents with the following (replacing ** Your Setting ** with your own values gathered earlier):

ADefHelpDesk 4

```json
{
  "IsEncrypted": false,
  "Values": {
    "AzureWebJobsStorage": "UseDevelopmentStorage=true",
    "FUNCTIONS_WORKER_RUNTIME": "dotnet",
    "POP3Server": "** Your Setting **",
    "POP3Port": "** Your Setting **",
    "POP3UseSSL": "** Your Setting **",
    "POP3Username": "** Your Setting **",
    "POP3Password": "** Your Setting **",
    "APIWebAddress": "** Your Setting **",
    "ApplicationGUID": "** Your Setting **",
    "APIUserName": "** Your Setting **",
    "APIPassword": "** Your Setting **"
  }
}
```

Also, add keys and values to log into your **Pop3** email server.

You can get the settings for popular services here: https://domar.com/smtp_pop3_server (also a list here: https://support.microsoft.com/en-us/help/2758902/how-to-set-up-an-internet-email-account-in-outlook-2013-or-2016).

Save and close the file.

Add MailKit

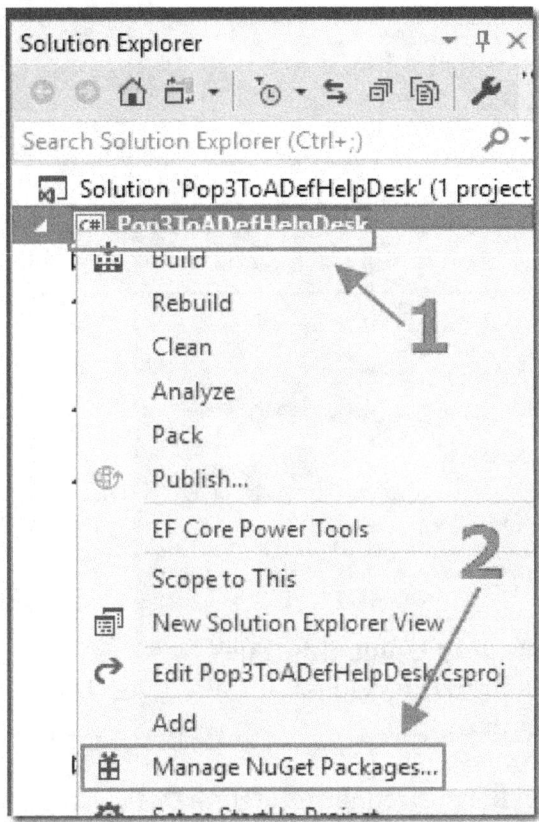

To add **MailKit**, the open source library that will allow us to retrieve emails, we need to *right-click* on the **Project** node in the **Solution Explorer** and select **Manage NuGet Packages…**

ADefHelpDesk 4

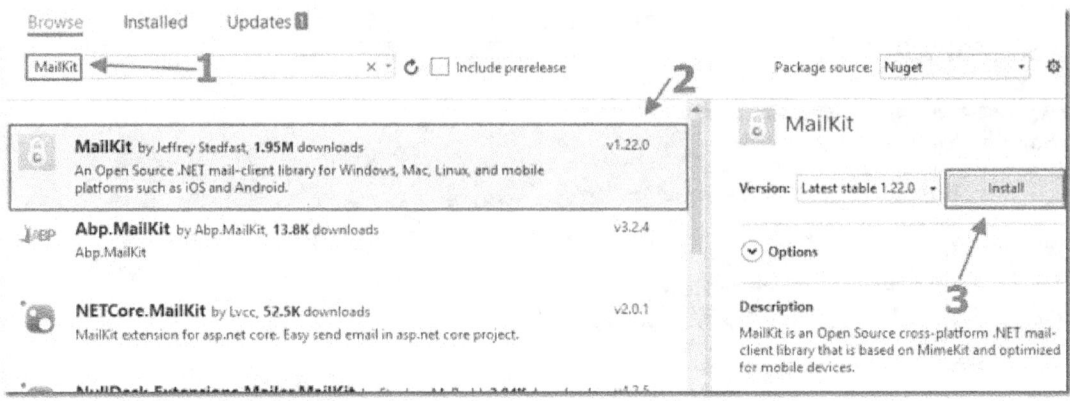

Search for **MailKit**, **select** it, and **install** it.

Add The Model Code

We will copy a lot of the code from the article:

Calling a REST API from .Net Core Including Uploading Files
(http://lightswitchhelpwebsite.com/Blog/tabid/61/EntryId/4320/Calling-a-REST-API-from-Net-Core-Including-Uploading-Files.aspx).

That article goes into depth on how a **Ticket** is created in **ADefHelpDesk** using the **API**, and how to use the **Swagger** page in **ADefHelpDesk** to determine what the properties are that the classes should have.

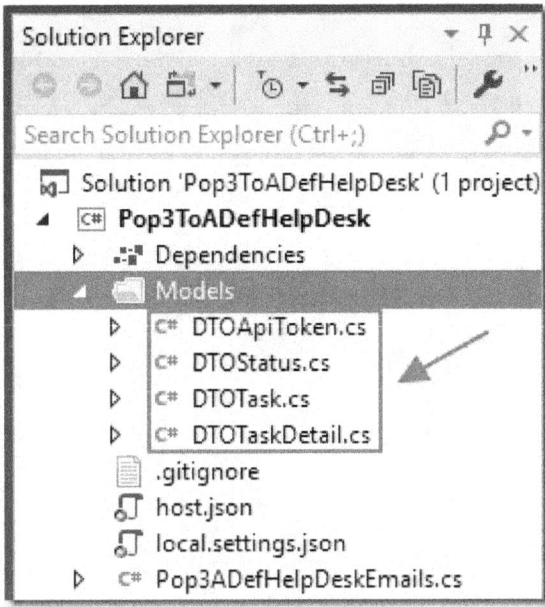

Add a folder called **Models**.

Add the following class files to the **Models** folder using the following code:

DTOApiToken

```
namespace Pop3ToADefHelpDesk
{
    public class DTOApiToken
    {
        public string userName { get; set; }
        public string password { get; set; }
        public string applicationGUID { get; set; }
    }
}
```

DTOStatus

```csharp
namespace Pop3ToADefHelpDesk
{
    public class DTOStatus
    {
        public string StatusMessage { get; set; }
        public bool Success { get; set; }
    }
}
```

DTOTask

```csharp
using System.Collections.Generic;
namespace Pop3ToADefHelpDesk
{
    public class DTOTask
    {
        public int? taskId { get; set; }
        public int? portalId { get; set; }
        public string description { get; set; }
        public string status { get; set; }
        public string priority { get; set; }
        public string createdDate { get; set; }
        public string estimatedStart { get; set; }
        public string estimatedCompletion { get; set; }
        public string dueDate { get; set; }
        public int? assignedRoleId { get; set; }
        public string assignedRoleName { get; set; }
        public string ticketPassword { get; set; }
        public int? requesterUserId { get; set; }
        public string requesterName { get; set; }
        public string requesterEmail { get; set; }
        public string requesterPhone { get; set; }
        public int? estimatedHours { get; set; }
        public bool? sendEmails { get; set; }
        public List<int> selectedTreeNodes { get; set; }
        public List<DTOTaskDetail> colDTOTaskDetail { get; set; }
    }
}
```

DTOTaskDetail

```csharp
using System.Collections.Generic;
namespace Pop3ToADefHelpDesk
{
    public class DTOTaskDetail
    {
        public string taskDetailDescription { get; set; }
        public int detailId { get; set; }
        public string detailType { get; set; }
        public string contentType { get; set; }
        public string insertDate { get; set; }
        public int userId { get; set; }
        public string userName { get; set; }
        public string emailDescription { get; set; }
        public string startTime { get; set; }
        public string stopTime { get; set; }
        public bool? sendEmails { get; set; }
    }
}
```

Add The Extension Code

An extension method will be required to concatenate all the parameter values into a single string when calling the **ADefHelpDesk API**.

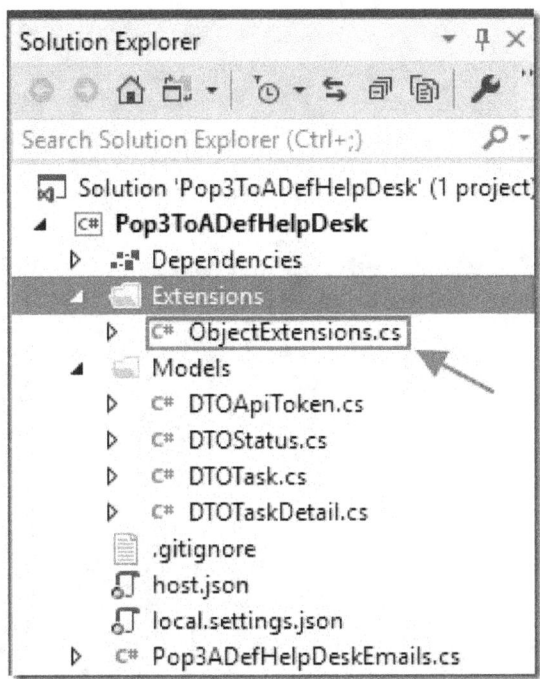

To facilitate this, create a folder called **Extensions** and add a class file called **ObjectExtensions.cs** using the following code:

ADefHelpDesk 4

```csharp
using Newtonsoft.Json.Linq;
using System.Collections.Generic;
using System.Globalization;
using System.Linq;
namespace Pop3ToADefHelpDesk
{
    public static class ObjectExtensions
    {
        // From: https://bit.ly/2A5R70I
        public static IDictionary<string, string> ToKeyValue(this object metaToken)
        {
            if (metaToken == null)
            {
                return null;
            }
            JToken token = metaToken as JToken;
            if (token == null)
            {
                return ToKeyValue(JObject.FromObject(metaToken));
            }
            if (token.HasValues)
            {
                var contentData = new Dictionary<string, string>();
                foreach (var child in token.Children().ToList())
                {
                    var childContent = child.ToKeyValue();
                    if (childContent != null)
                    {
                        contentData = contentData.Concat(childContent)
                            .ToDictionary(k => k.Key, v => v.Value);
                    }
                }
                return contentData;
            }
            var jValue = token as JValue;
            if (jValue?.Value == null)
            {
                return null;
            }
            var value = jValue?.Type == JTokenType.Date ?
                jValue?.ToString("o", CultureInfo.InvariantCulture) :
                jValue?.ToString(CultureInfo.InvariantCulture);
            return new Dictionary<string, string> { { token.Path, value } };
        }
    }
}
```

Get The Authentication Token

The **ADefHelpDesk API** requires that you use the **UserName** and **Password** (the values are stored in the **local.settings.json** file as **APIUserName** and **APIPassword**) to call the **/api/V1/GetAuthToken API** method to obtain a **JSON Web Token (JWT)** to use as authentication for subsequent calls to the other **API** methods.

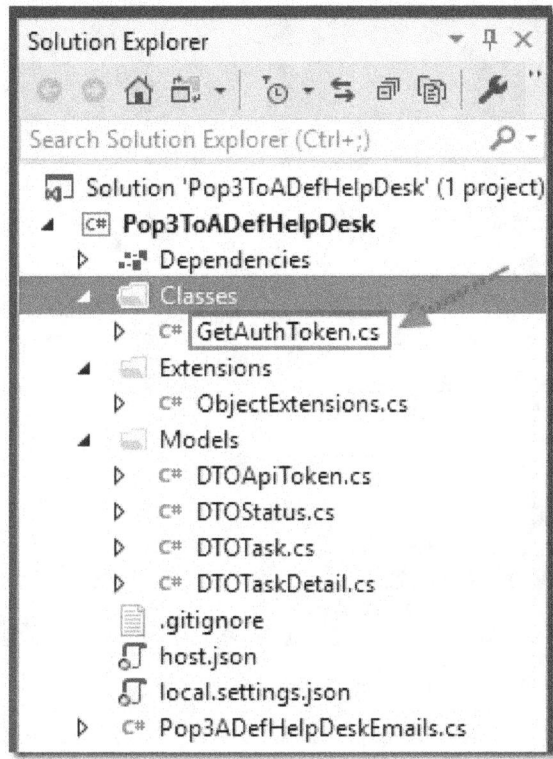

To facilitate this, create a folder called **Classes** and add a class file called **GetAuthToken.cs** using the following code:

ADefHelpDesk 4

```csharp
using Newtonsoft.Json;
using System;
using System.Net.Http;
using System.Text;
using System.Threading.Tasks;
namespace Pop3ToADefHelpDesk
{
    public class GetAuthToken
    {
        public static async Task<string> GetAuthTokenFromADefHelpDesk(
            string APIWebAddress,
            DTOApiToken paramApiToken)
        {
            // Store the final result
            string strResult = "";
            HttpClient client = new HttpClient();
            // Use the HttpClient
            using (client)
            {
                // Create a new REST request
                using (var request = new HttpRequestMessage())
                {
                    // The Swagger page indicates this must be a "Post"
                    request.Method = HttpMethod.Post;
                    // Set the destination to the method indicated
                    // on the Swagger page
                    // to: api/V1/GetAuthToken
                    request.RequestUri =
                        new Uri($"{APIWebAddress}api/V1/GetAuthToken");
                    // Convert the parameters to
                    // JavaScript Object Notation (JSON) format
                    var json = JsonConvert.SerializeObject(paramApiToken);
                    request.Content =
                        new StringContent(json, Encoding.UTF8, "application/json");
                    // Make the request to the API endpoint on the ADefHelpDesk site
                    var response = client.SendAsync(request).Result;
                    // Receive the response
                    var JsonDataResponse =
                        await response.Content.ReadAsStringAsync();
                    // Convert the response (the JWT (Auth Token)) to a String value
                    strResult =
                        JsonConvert.DeserializeObject<string>(JsonDataResponse);
                    // Strip the word Bearer from the token
                    strResult = strResult.Replace("Bearer ", " ").Trim();
                }
            }
            // Return the JWT
            return strResult;
        }
    }
}
```

This code will be called by the main code created in the final step.

Create The Help Desk Ticket

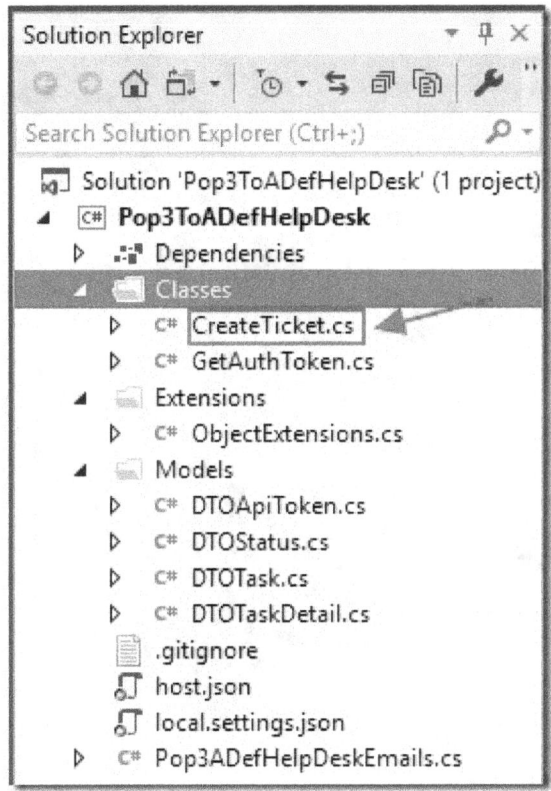

Now, add the code that will call the **ADefHelpDesk API** to create the **Help Desk Ticket** and attach a file that contains the contents of the email.

Create a class file called **CreateTicket.cs** using the following code:

ADefHelpDesk 4

```csharp
using Microsoft.AspNetCore.WebUtilities;
using MimeKit;
using Newtonsoft.Json;
using System;
using System.Collections.Generic;
using System.IO;
using System.Net.Http;
using System.Net.Http.Headers;
using System.Text;
using System.Threading.Tasks;
namespace Pop3ToADefHelpDesk
{
    public class CreateTicket
    {
        public static async Task<DTOStatus> CreateADefHelpDeskTicket(
            DTOTask paramDTOTask,
            DTOTaskDetail paramDTOTaskDetail,
            MimeMessage paramMimeMessage,
            string APIWebAddress,
            string paramBearerToken)
        {
            // Final response
            HttpResponseMessage response;
            // The contents of the file will be stored in the MemoryStream
            MemoryStream stream = new MemoryStream();
            // Initialize classes and variables
            DTOStatus Result = new DTOStatus();
            HttpClient client = new HttpClient();
            string strFileName = "";
            using (client)
            {
                using (var request = new HttpRequestMessage())
                {
                    client.DefaultRequestHeaders.Authorization =
                        new AuthenticationHeaderValue("Bearer", paramBearerToken);
                    // Add Task parameters
                    // Call the ToKeyValue extension method
                    // to concatonate all the values into a single string
                    var TaskParameters = paramDTOTask.ToKeyValue();
                    // If there are Task Details add them
                    if (paramDTOTaskDetail != null)
                    {
                        // Call the ToKeyValue extension method
                        var TaskDetailParameters = paramDTOTaskDetail.ToKeyValue();
                        foreach (var item in TaskDetailParameters)
                        {
                            // the TaskDetail parameters
                            TaskParameters.Add(item);
                        }
                    }
```

```csharp
// The destination is the CreateTask API method
request.RequestUri =
    new Uri(QueryHelpers.AddQueryString(
        $"{APIWebAddress}api/V1/CreateTask"
        , TaskParameters));
// The API method requires the 'verb'
// or 'action' to be a 'Post'
request.Method = HttpMethod.Post;
// Determine the Email type
if (paramMimeMessage.Body.ContentType.MimeType == "text/html")
{
    // This is a "text/html" file
    // Get Email contents
    var EmailContent =
        ((MimeKit.TextPart)paramMimeMessage.Body).Text;
    // Save the Message to a stream
    byte[] encodedText = Encoding.Unicode.GetBytes(EmailContent);
    stream.Write(encodedText, 0, encodedText.Length);
    stream.Position = 0;
    strFileName = "Attachment.html";
}
else
{
    // If the email is not of type "text/html"
    // Save the entire email as a .EML file
    // ADefHelpDesk has the ability to view a EML file
    // and any attachments
    // Save the .EML Message to a stream
    paramMimeMessage.WriteTo(stream);
    stream.Position = 0;
    strFileName = "Attachment.EML";
}
using (stream)
{
    MultipartFormDataContent _multiPartContent =
        new MultipartFormDataContent();
    // Serialize Request
    StreamContent _fileData =
        new StreamContent(stream);
    _fileData.Headers.ContentType =
        new MediaTypeHeaderValue("application/octet-stream");
    ContentDispositionHeaderValue _contentDispositionHeaderValue =
        new ContentDispositionHeaderValue("form-data");
    _contentDispositionHeaderValue.Name =
        "objFile";
    _contentDispositionHeaderValue.FileName =
        strFileName;
    _fileData.Headers.ContentDisposition =
        _contentDispositionHeaderValue;
    _multiPartContent.Add(_fileData, "objFile");
```

ADefHelpDesk 4

```csharp
                    // Set content
                    request.Content = _multiPartContent;
                    // Send request
                    response = client.SendAsync(request).Result;
                }
                // If the Bearer token is expired
                if (response.StatusCode == System.Net.HttpStatusCode.Unauthorized)
                {
                    Result.Success = false;
                    Result.StatusMessage = "Unauthorized";
                    return Result;
                }
                // ADefHelpDesk will respond with JSON
                var JsonDataResponse =
                    await response.Content.ReadAsStringAsync();
                // The final result is the Deserialized response
                Result =
                    JsonConvert.DeserializeObject<DTOStatus>(JsonDataResponse);
            }
        }
        return Result;
    }
}
```

This code will be called by the main code created in the next step.

The Main Code

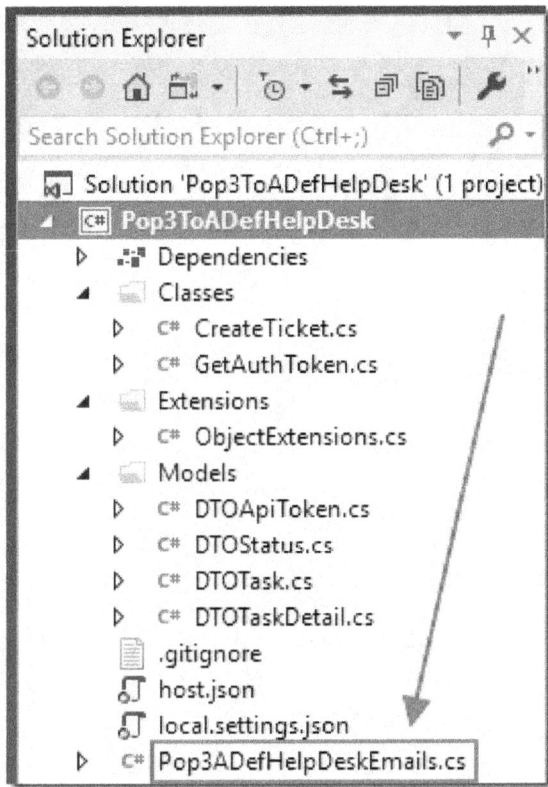

The main code will connect to the mail server and retrieve the emails.

It will then contact the **ADefHelpDesk API** to obtain an authentication token (also known as a **Bearer token** or a **JWT**)). It will use that token to call the **ADefHelpDesk API** to create a **Help Desk Ticket**.

Replace all the code in the **Pop3ADefHelpDeskEmails.cs** file with the following code:

ADefHelpDesk 4

```csharp
using MailKit.Net.Pop3;
using Microsoft.AspNetCore.Http;
using Microsoft.Azure.WebJobs;
using Microsoft.Azure.WebJobs.Extensions.Http;
using Microsoft.Extensions.Logging;
using System;
using System.Linq;
namespace Pop3ToADefHelpDesk
{
    public static class Pop3ADefHelpDeskEmails
    {
        // "0 */5 * * * *" to run once every 5 minutes
        // "0 */1 * * * *" to run once a minute
        [FunctionName("Pop3ADefHelpDeskEmails")]
        public static void Run(
            [TimerTrigger("0 */5 * * * *")]TimerInfo myTimer,
            ILogger log)
        {
            log.LogInformation("function processed a request.");
            string _POP3Server =
                Environment.GetEnvironmentVariable("POP3Server");
            int _POP3Port =
                Convert.ToInt32(Environment.GetEnvironmentVariable("POP3Port"));
            bool _POP3UseSSL =
                Convert.ToBoolean(Environment.GetEnvironmentVariable("POP3UseSSL"));
            string _POP3Username =
                Environment.GetEnvironmentVariable("POP3Username");
            string _POP3Password =
                Environment.GetEnvironmentVariable("POP3Password");
            string _APIWebAddress =
                Environment.GetEnvironmentVariable("APIWebAddress");
            // ********* GET AuthToken from ADefHelpDesk
            // (needed to send the emails to ADefHelpDesk)
            DTOApiToken paramApiToken = new DTOApiToken();
            paramApiToken.userName =
                Environment.GetEnvironmentVariable("APIUserName");
            paramApiToken.password =
                Environment.GetEnvironmentVariable("APIPassword");
            paramApiToken.applicationGUID =
                Environment.GetEnvironmentVariable("ApplicationGUID");
            // Call the GetAuthToken method and retreive the
            // BearerToken (JWT - Auth Token)
            // (required to make the calls to ADefHelpDesk to save the messages)
            string BearerToken =
                GetAuthToken.GetAuthTokenFromADefHelpDesk(
                    _APIWebAddress, paramApiToken).Result;
```

```csharp
using (var client = new Pop3Client())
{
    // ********** GET EMAILS
    // Configure connection to Email Server
    // For demo-purposes, accept all SSL certificates
    // (in case the server supports STARTTLS)
    client.ServerCertificateValidationCallback = (s, c, h, e) => true;
    // Email Server settings
    client.Connect(_POP3Server, _POP3Port, _POP3UseSSL);
    // Note: since we don't have an OAuth2 token, disable
    // the XOAUTH2 authentication mechanism.
    client.AuthenticationMechanisms.Remove("XOAUTH2");
    // Pass username and password to email server
    client.Authenticate(_POP3Username, _POP3Password);
    // Loop through each email
    for (int i = 0; i < client.Count; i++)
    {
        // message contains the entire contents of the email
        // including any attachments
        var message = client.GetMessage(i);
        log.LogInformation(
            $"Got Message: {message.Subject} - {message.MessageId}");
        // ********** Save Email To ADefHelpDesk
        // We need to create a Task and a TaskDetail
        DTOTask objDTOTask = new DTOTask();
        DTOTaskDetail objDTOTaskDetail = new DTOTaskDetail();
        // Create a Task
        objDTOTask.description = message.Subject;
        objDTOTask.priority = "Normal";
        objDTOTask.requesterEmail =
            message.From.Mailboxes.FirstOrDefault().Address;
        objDTOTask.requesterName =
            message.From.Mailboxes.FirstOrDefault().Name;
        objDTOTask.createdDate = DateTime.Now.ToShortDateString();
        objDTOTask.requesterUserId = -1;
        objDTOTask.status = "New";
        objDTOTask.sendEmails = true;
        // Create a Task Detail
        objDTOTaskDetail.taskDetailDescription
            = $"From {objDTOTask.requesterName} [{objDTOTask.requesterEmail}] ";
        // Send the message to ADefHelpDesk
        var response = CreateTicket.CreateADefHelpDeskTicket(
            objDTOTask,
            objDTOTaskDetail,
            message,
            _APIWebAddress,
            BearerToken);
```

ADefHelpDesk 4

```
                // Check the result
                if (response.Result.Success)
                {
                    log.LogInformation(
                        $"Message Saved: {message.Subject} - {message.MessageId}");
                    // [OPTIONAL] Mark the message for deletion
                    // client.DeleteMessage(i);
                }
                else
                {
                    // There was an error
                    log.LogInformation(
                        $"Error saving message: {response.Result.StatusMessage}");
                }
            }
            log.LogInformation("client.Disconnect");
            client.Disconnect(true);
        }
    }
}
```

Run The Project

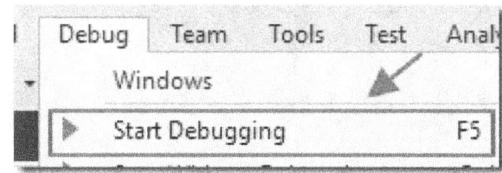

Hit **F5** to run the project.

```
[12/25/2018 2:03:41 AM] WorkerRuntime: dotnet. Will shutdown other standby channels
[12/25/2018 2:03:41 AM] Generating 1 job function(s)
[12/25/2018 2:03:41 AM] Found the following functions:
[12/25/2018 2:03:41 AM] Pop3ToADefHelpDesk.Pop3ADefHelpDeskEmails.Run
[12/25/2018 2:03:41 AM]
[12/25/2018 2:03:41 AM] Host initialized (754ms)
[12/25/2018 2:03:43 AM] The next 5 occurrences of the 'Pop3ToADefHelpDesk.Pop3AD
efHelpDeskEmails.Run' schedule will be:
[12/25/2018 2:03:43 AM] 12/24/2018 6:04:00 PM
[12/25/2018 2:03:43 AM] 12/24/2018 6:05:00 PM
[12/25/2018 2:03:43 AM] 12/24/2018 6:06:00 PM
[12/25/2018 2:03:43 AM] 12/24/2018 6:07:00 PM
[12/25/2018 2:03:43 AM] 12/24/2018 6:08:00 PM
[12/25/2018 2:03:43 AM]
[12/25/2018 2:03:43 AM] Host started (2953ms)
[12/25/2018 2:03:43 AM] Job host started
Hosting environment: Production
Content root path: C:\TEMP\Pop3ToADefHelpDesk\Pop3ToADefHelpDesk\bin\Debug\netco
reapp2.1
Now listening on: http://0.0.0.0:7071
Application started. Press Ctrl+C to shut down.
[12/25/2018 2:03:48 AM] Host lock lease acquired by instance ID '0000000000000000
0000000000E609FCD'.
```

The **Azure CLI** will run.

```
Hosting environment: Production
Content root path: C:\TEMP\Pop3ToADefHelpDesk\Pop3ToADefHelpDesk\bin\Debug\netcoreapp2.1
Now listening on: http://0.0.0.0:7071
Application started. Press Ctrl+C to shut down.
[12/25/2018 2:03:48 AM] Host lock lease acquired by instance ID '00000000000000000000000000E609FCD'.
[12/25/2018 2:04:00 AM] Executing 'Pop3ADefHelpDeskEmails' (Reason='Timer fired at 2018-12-24T18:04:00.0326516-08
:00', Id=7455128d-abbb-43f2-aea5-54a6e70ae00e)
[12/25/2018 2:04:18 AM] function processed a request.
[12/25/2018 2:04:22 AM] Got Message: Top Stories from the World Cup - 100722665.1299665@fantasysports.communicati
ons.yahoo.com
[12/25/2018 2:04:25 AM] Message Saved: Top Stories from the World Cup - 100722665.1299665@fantasysports.communica
tions.yahoo.com
[12/25/2018 2:04:29 AM] Got Message: A Test Message - 002d01d49b26$37bcce50$a7366af0$@ADefWebserver.com
[12/25/2018 2:04:31 AM] Message Saved: A Test Message - 002d01d49b26$37bcce50$a7366af0$@ADefWebserver.com
[12/25/2018 2:04:31 AM] client.Disconnect
[12/25/2018 2:04:32 AM] Executed 'Pop3ADefHelpDeskEmails' (Succeeded, Id=7455128d-abbb-43f2-aea5-54a6e70ae00e)
```

As long as the project is running, it will check for emails every 5 minutes (unless you change the timer setting – see the comments in the code on how to do this).

ADefHelpDesk 4

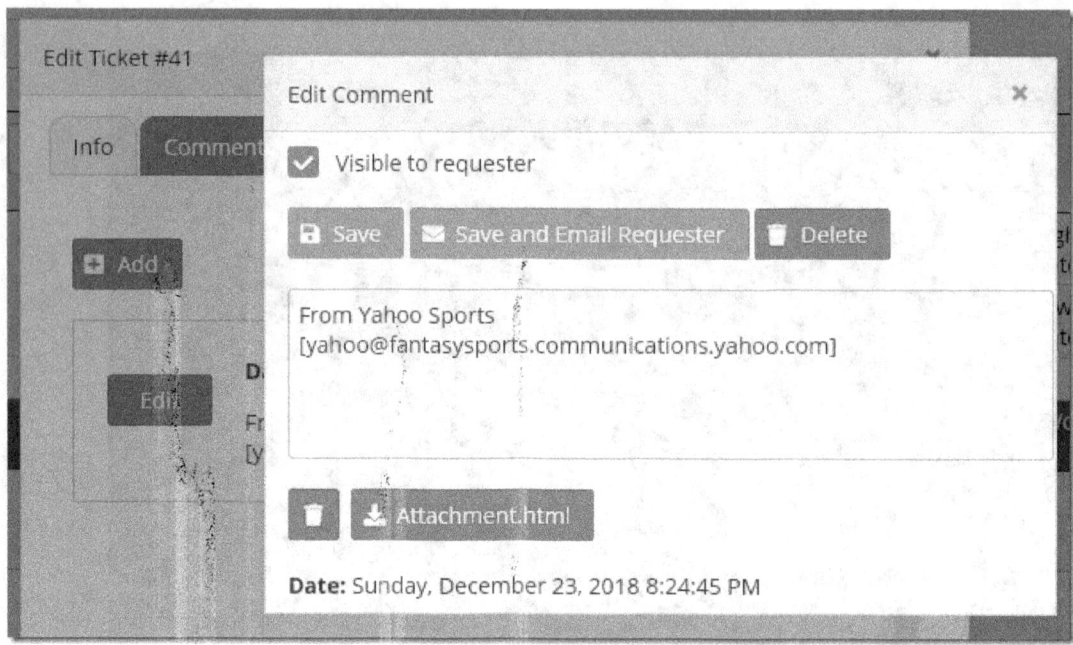

If the email MIME type is "**text/html**" the contents will be attached to the **Help Desk Ticket** as a **.html** file. That file will display a download link on the **Ticket** details in **ADefHelpDesk**.

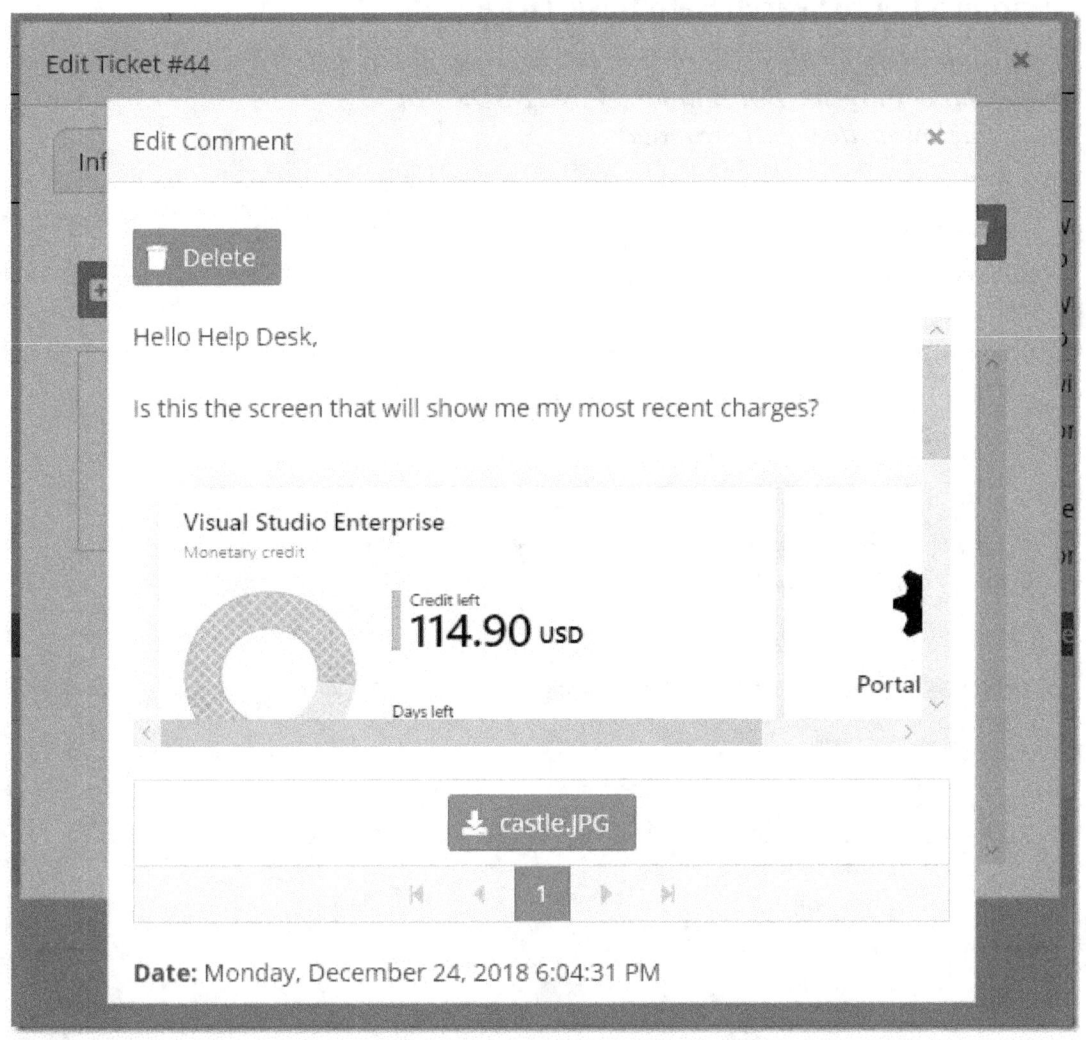

Otherwise the contents of the email will be saved to the **Help Desk Ticket** as an **.EML file**. You can see its contents displayed in **ADefHelpDesk**, and any attachments in the **.EML** file will have download links.

ADefHelpDesk 4

Creating a Bot to Search Help Desk Tickets

The sample code for this section can be obtained at the link "Creating A Bot Using ChoiceFlow for Bot Builder v4 .NET SDK" at http://aihelpwebsite.com/Downloads

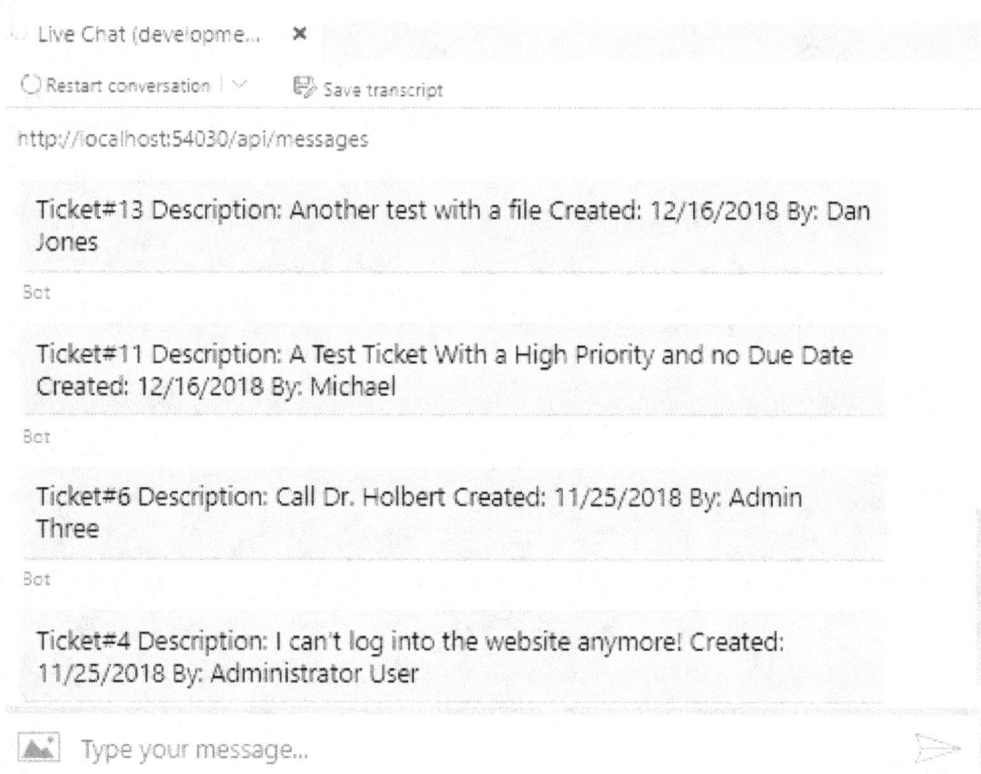

ChoiceFlow is part of the **Bot Builder Community Extensions** (https://github.com/garypretty/botbuilder-community) project, which contains various pieces of *middleware, recognizers,* and other components for use with the **Bot Builder .NET SDK v4** (https://github.com/Microsoft/botbuilder-dotnet).

This *middleware* component allows you to provide the user with a series of *guided choice prompts*, (defined in a **JSON** file, or as a collection of

ChoiceFlowItem objects), similar to calling a telephone line with a series of automated options.

To demonstrate this, we will create a **Bot**, that uses the **ChoiceFlow** component, that will search **Help Desk Tickets** in **ADefHelpDesk**.

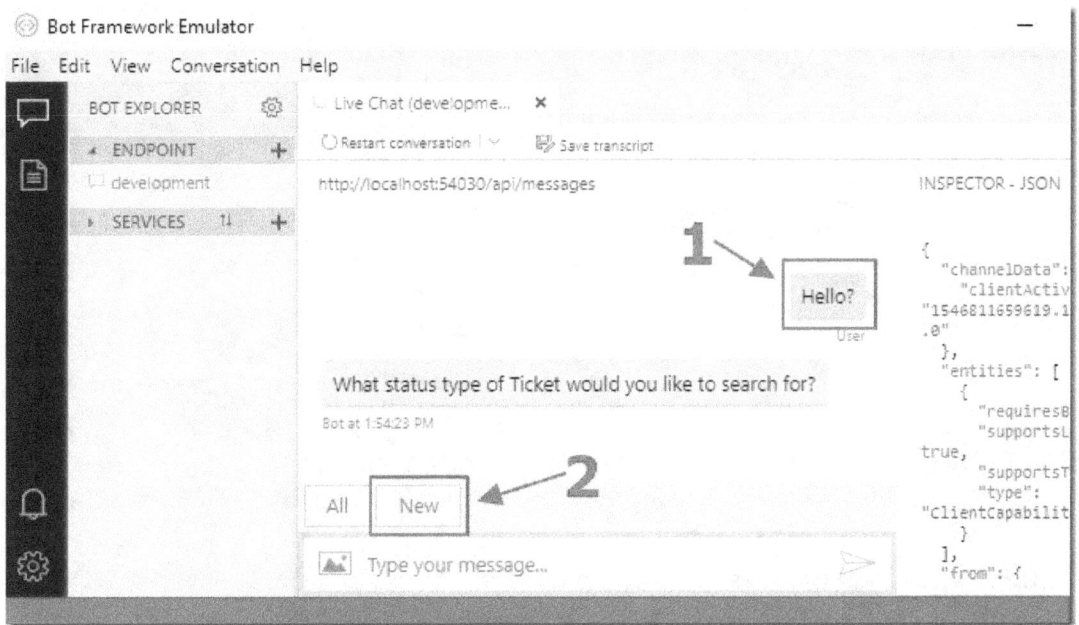

When a user interacts with the **Bot**, they will be presented with questions, and depending on the method they are using to interact with the **Bot**, a series of *cards* will display the acceptable choices. Selecting a *card*, or entering the value in the *chat input*, will make the selection and move through the guided prompts.

ADefHelpDesk 4

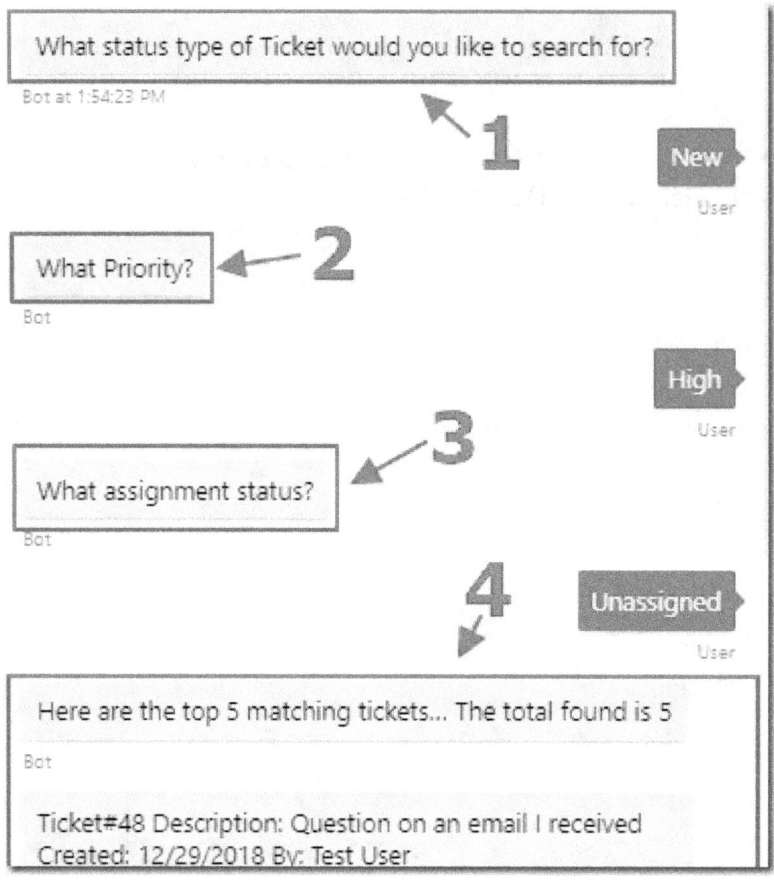

The user will provide a response for the **Ticket** *type*, *priority*, and *status* to search for.

They will then be presented with the *top 5* matching **Tickets** to their search.

Requirements

- **Visual Studio 2017** (or higher) with the following workloads:

- o ASP.NET and web development
- o Azure development
- o .NET Core cross-platform development
- **Bot Builder V4 SDK Template for Visual Studio** (https://marketplace.visualstudio.com/items?itemName=BotBuilder.botbuilderv4)
- Bot Framework Emulator (https://emulator.botframework.com/)

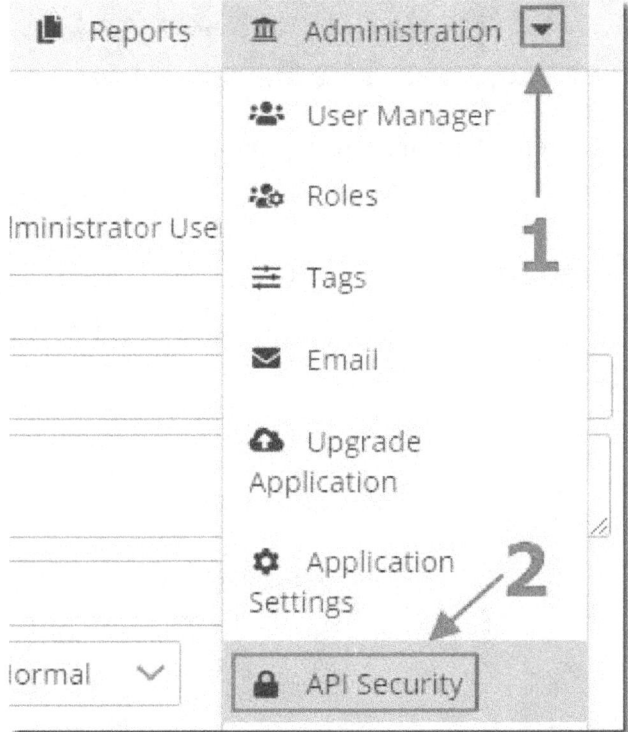

In **ADefHelpDesk**, follow the directions in the **API Security (Swagger Rest API)** section in **Chapter 5: Administration Settings** to create an account that can call the **API**.

ADefHelpDesk 4

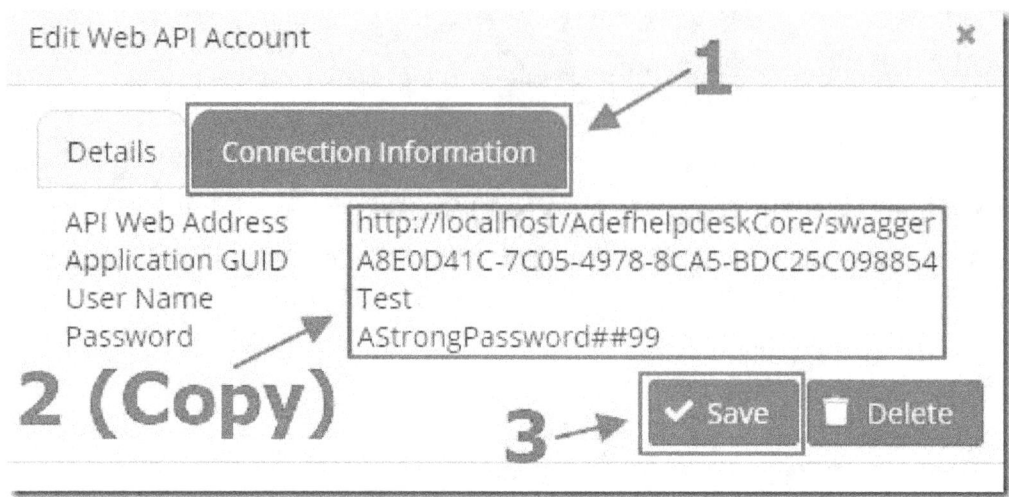

You will need to copy the information on the **Connection Information** tab for the **API** account, to use later.

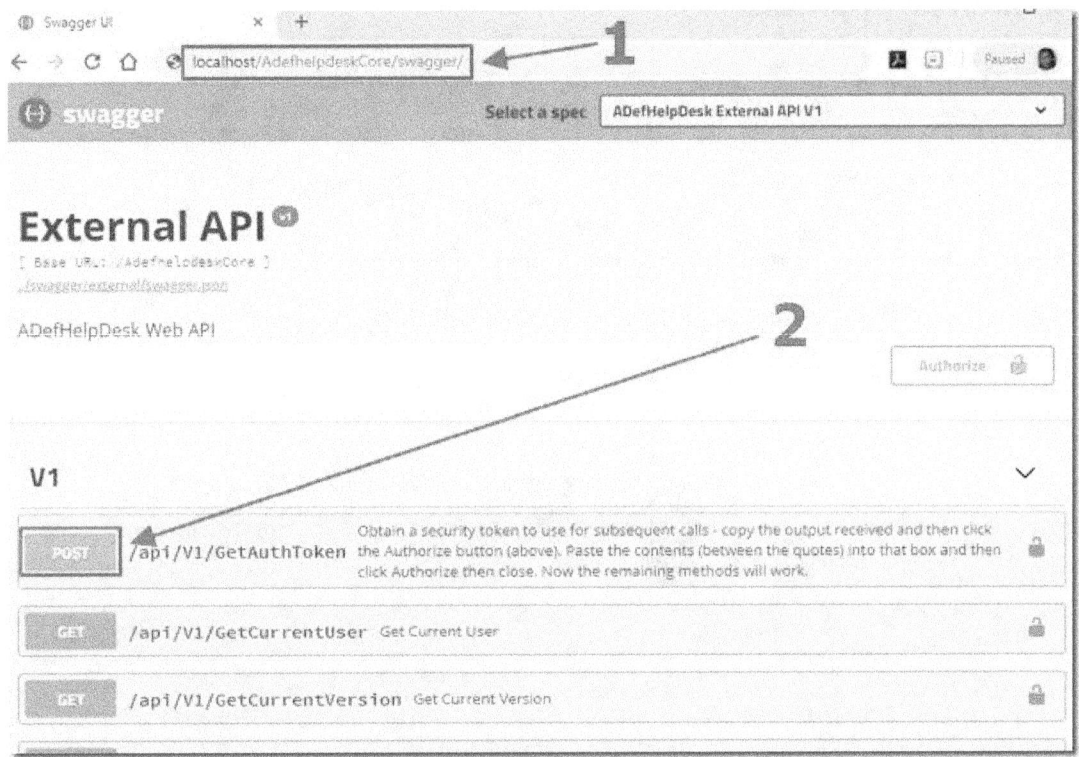

The **ADefHelpDesk** site has a **Swagger page** (see: https://swagger.io/) that documents the *REST based API* endpoints at: ***http://{your default web address}/swagger/*** (for example: http://adefhelpdesk.azurewebsites.net/swagger/).

You will also want to create a few **Help Desk Tickets** of various **Statuses** and **Assignments** so that you have something to search for.

Create The Application

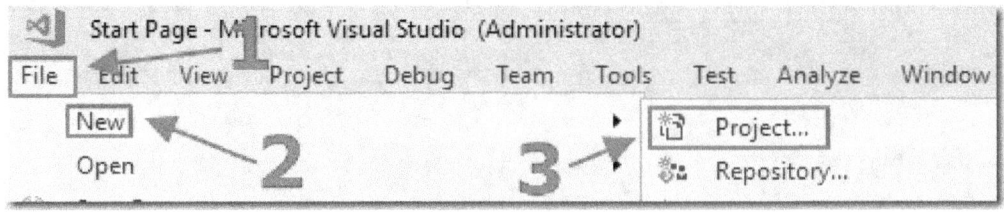

Open **Visual Studio** and select **File**, then **New**, then **Project**.

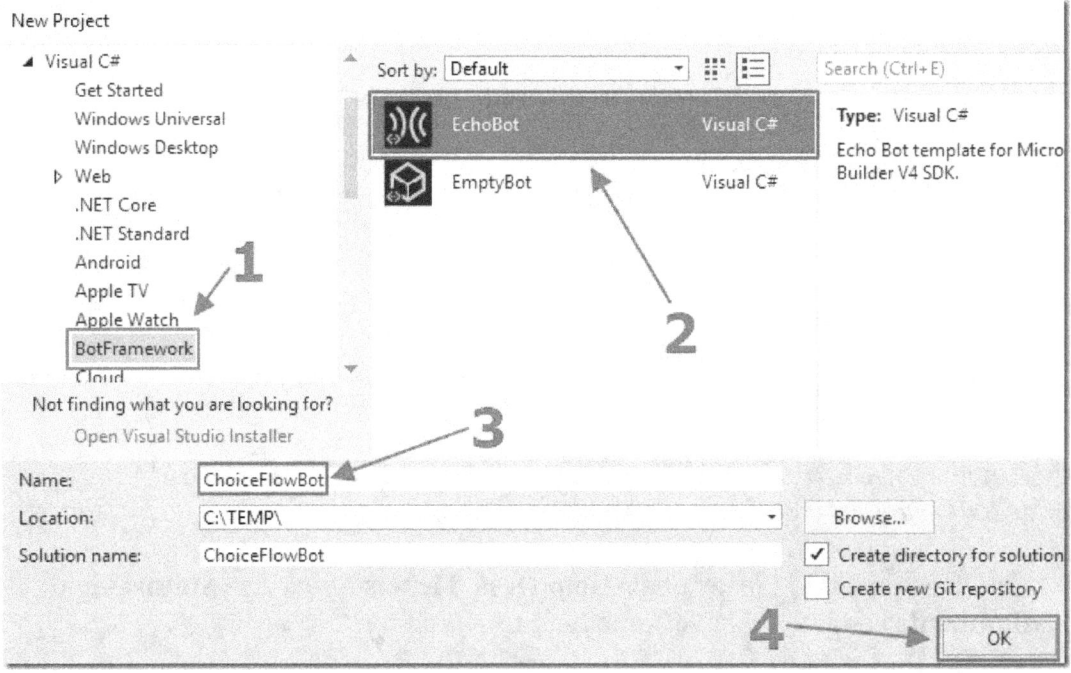

In the **New Project** dialog, select the **Bot Builder Template**, name the project **ChoiceFlowBot,** and click **OK**.

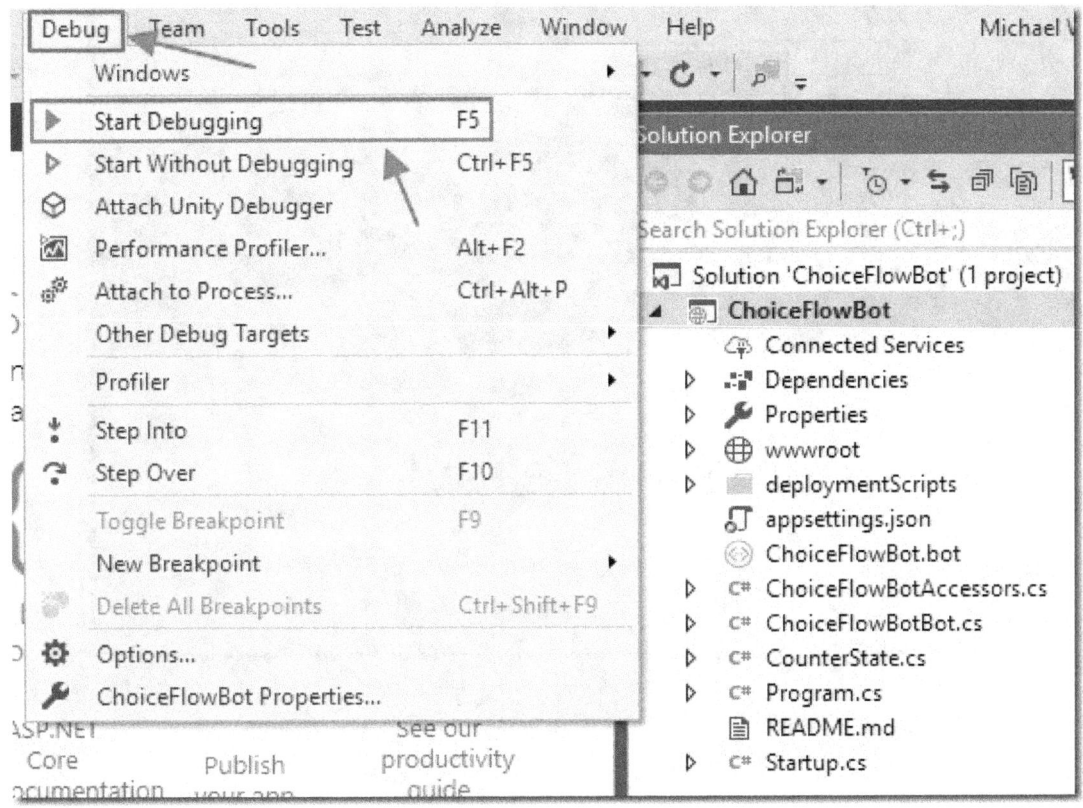

The project will be created.

Hit **F5** to run the project.

ADefHelpDesk 4

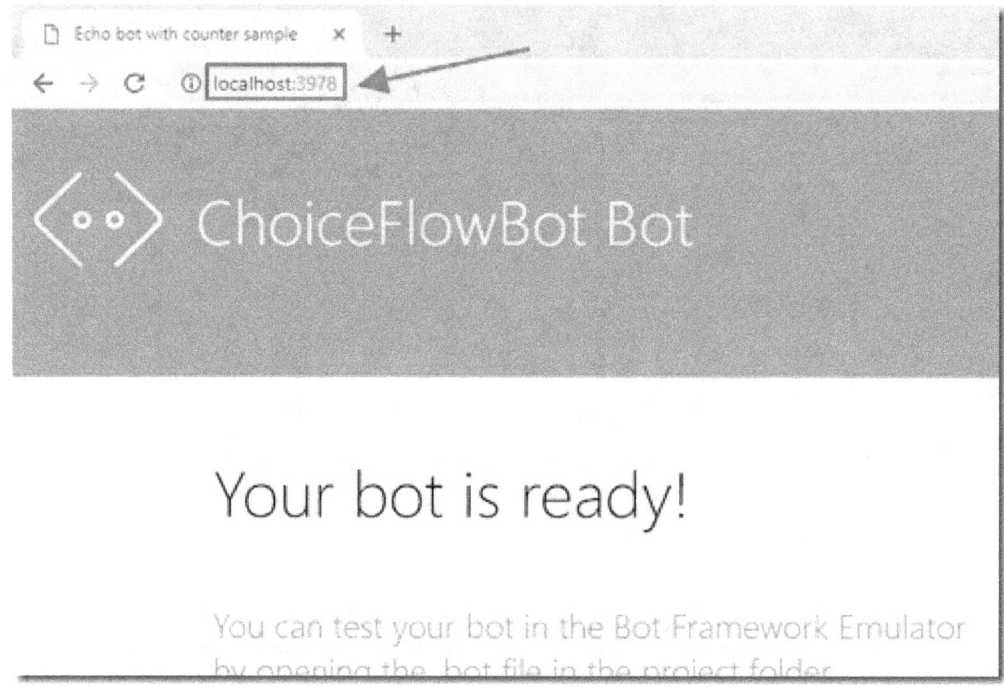

The web browser will open.

Connect Using The Bot Framework Emulator

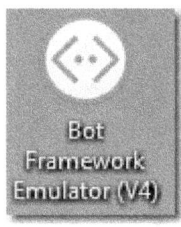

Open the **Bot Framework Emulator**.

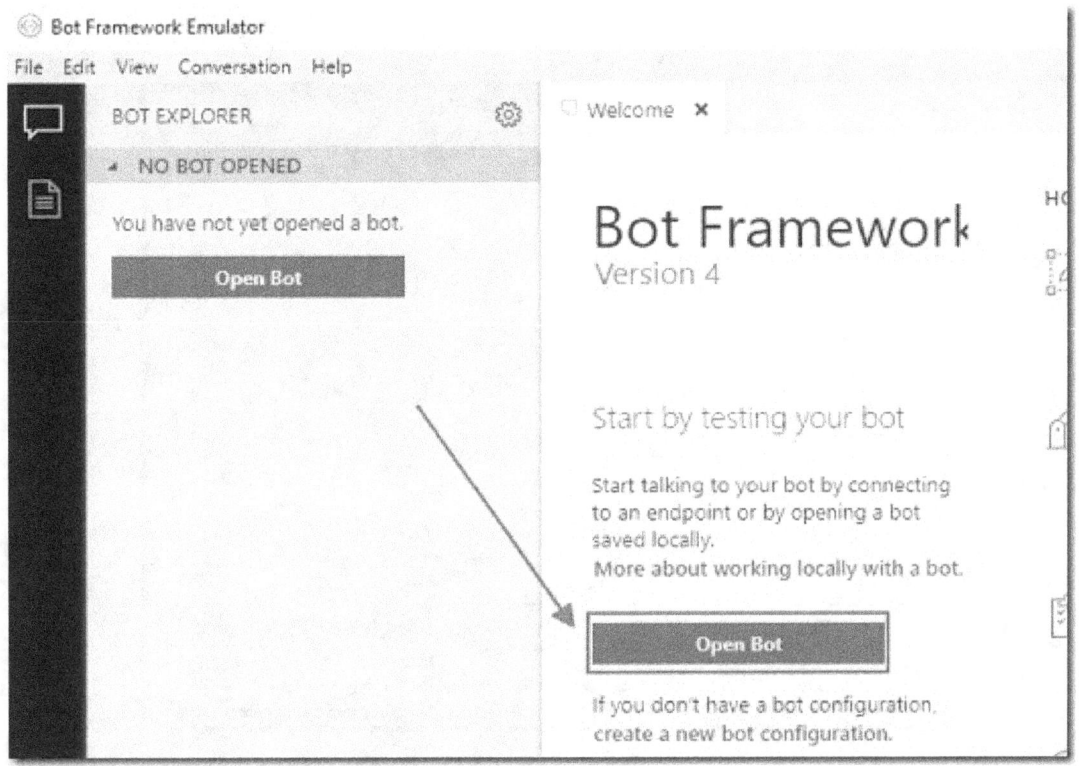

Select **Open Bot**.

ADefHelpDesk 4

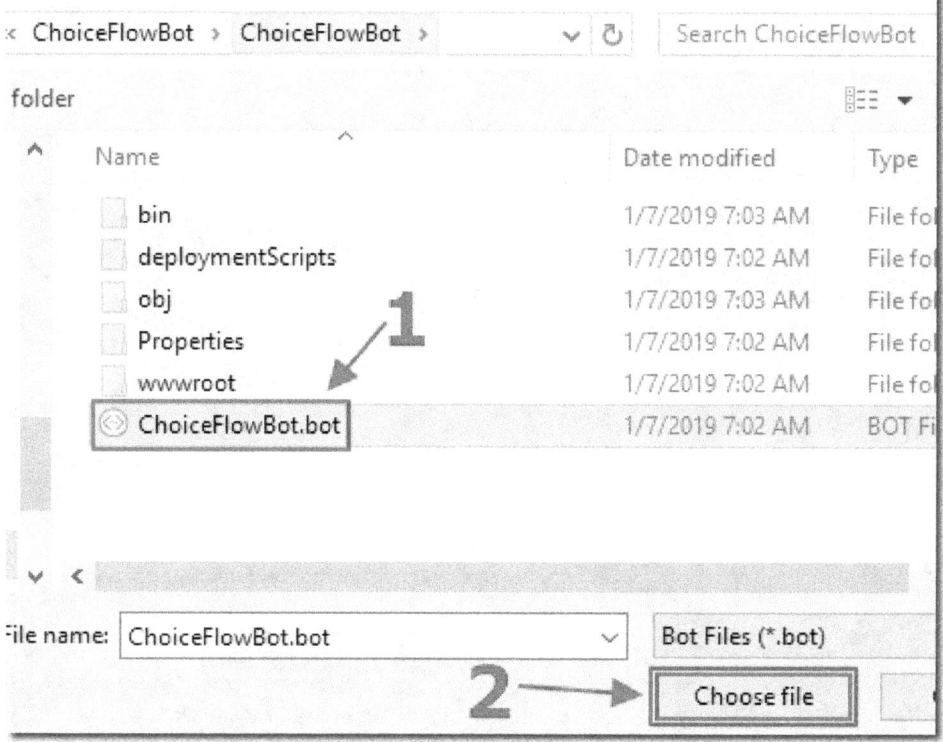

Select the **.Bot** file that is in the root directory of the project.

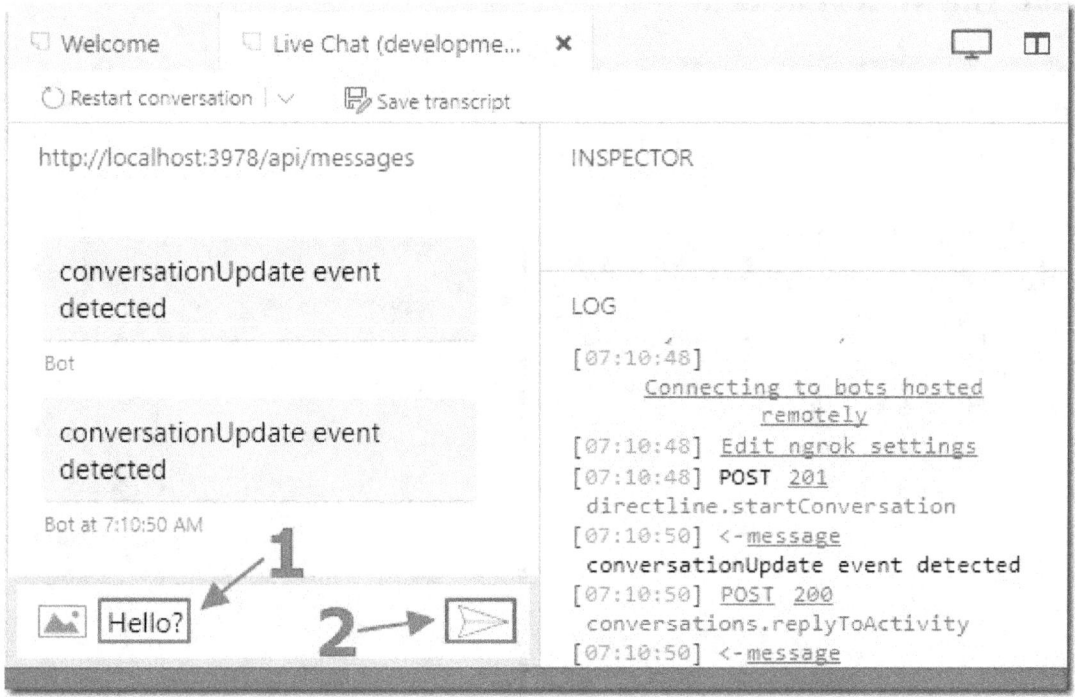

You can now chat with the **Bot**.

Return to **Visual Studio** and stop debugging.

ADefHelpDesk 4

Add The NuGet Package

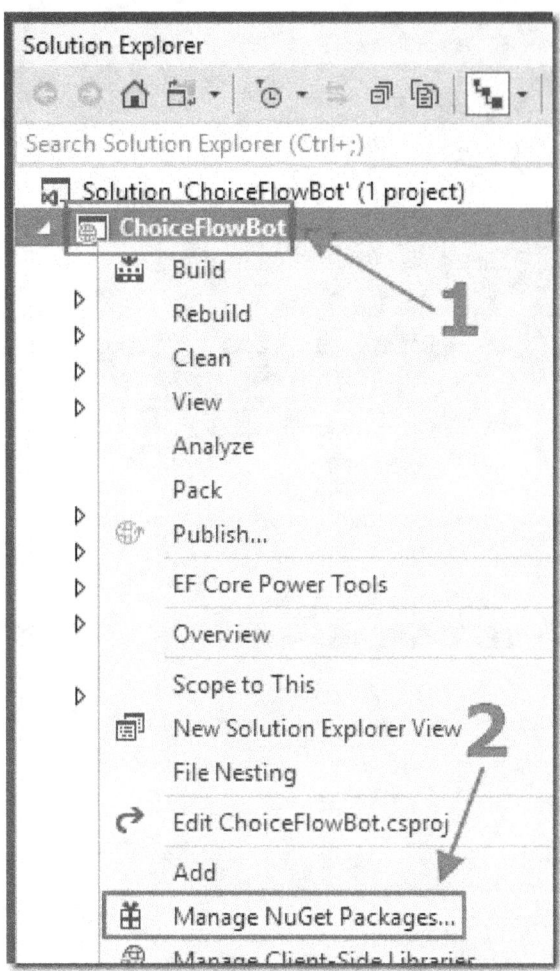

The first step is to add the **Bot.Builder.Community.Dialogs.ChoiceFlow NuGet** package
(https://www.nuget.org/packages/Bot.Builder.Community.Dialogs.ChoiceFlow/).

Right-click on the project in the **Solution Explorer** and select **Manage NuGet Packages**.

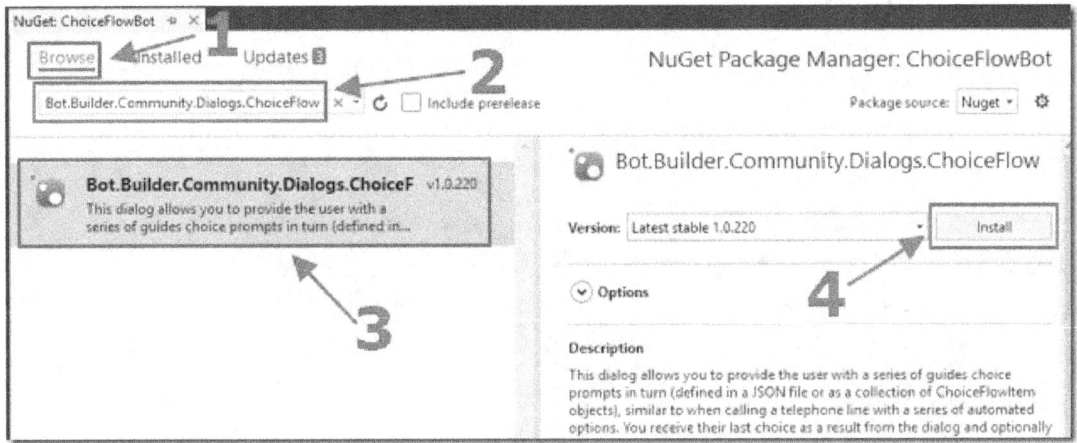

Search for **Bot.Builder.Community.Dialogs.ChoiceFlow** and install the latest version.

ADefHelpDesk 4

Add The Models

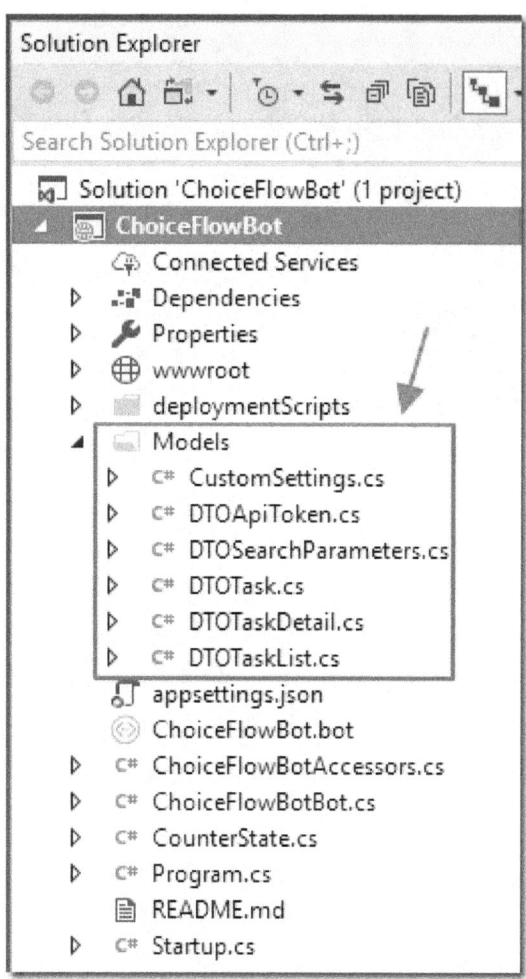

Create a **Models** folder and add the following code files:

CustomSettings.cs

```
namespace ChoiceFlowBot
{
    // This allows us to retrieve custom settings
    // from appsettings.json
    public class CustomSettings
    {
        public string APIWebAddress { get; set; }
        public string ApplicationGUID { get; set; }
        public string UserName { get; set; }
        public string Password { get; set; }
    }
}
```

DTOApiToken.cs

```
namespace ChoiceFlowBot
{
    public class DTOApiToken
    {
        public string userName { get; set; }
        public string password { get; set; }
        public string applicationGUID { get; set; }
    }
}
```

DTOSearchParameters.cs

```csharp
using System.Collections.Generic;
namespace ChoiceFlowBot
{
    public class DTOSearchParameters
    {
        public string searchText { get; set; }
        public string status { get; set; }
        public string priority { get; set; }
        public string createdDate { get; set; }
        public string dueDate { get; set; }
        public string assignedRoleId { get; set; }
        public List<int> selectedTreeNodes { get; set; }
        public string sortOrder { get; set; }
        public string sortField { get; set; }
        public int rowsPerPage { get; set; }
        public int pageNumber { get; set; }
    }
}
```

DTOTask.cs

```csharp
using System.Collections.Generic;
namespace ChoiceFlowBot
{
    public class DTOTask
    {
        public int? taskId { get; set; }
        public int? portalId { get; set; }
        public string description { get; set; }
        public string status { get; set; }
        public string priority { get; set; }
        public string createdDate { get; set; }
        public string estimatedStart { get; set; }
        public string estimatedCompletion { get; set; }
        public string dueDate { get; set; }
        public int? assignedRoleId { get; set; }
        public string assignedRoleName { get; set; }
        public string ticketPassword { get; set; }
        public int? requesterUserId { get; set; }
        public string requesterName { get; set; }
        public string requesterEmail { get; set; }
        public string requesterPhone { get; set; }
        public int? estimatedHours { get; set; }
        public bool? sendEmails { get; set; }
        public List<int> selectedTreeNodes { get; set; }
        public List<DTOTaskDetail> colDTOTaskDetail { get; set; }
    }
}
```

DTOTaskDetail.cs

```csharp
using System.Collections.Generic;
namespace ChoiceFlowBot
{
    public class DTOTaskDetail
    {
        public string taskDetailDescription { get; set; }
        public int detailId { get; set; }
        public string detailType { get; set; }
        public string contentType { get; set; }
        public string insertDate { get; set; }
        public int userId { get; set; }
        public string userName { get; set; }
        public string emailDescription { get; set; }
        public string startTime { get; set; }
        public string stopTime { get; set; }
        public bool? sendEmails { get; set; }
    }
}
```

DTOTaskList.cs

```csharp
using System.Collections.Generic;
namespace ChoiceFlowBot
{
    public class DTOTaskList
    {
        public List<DTOTask> taskList { get; set; }
        public int totalRows { get; set; }
        public string errorMessage { get; set; }
    }
}
```

Add and Load Settings

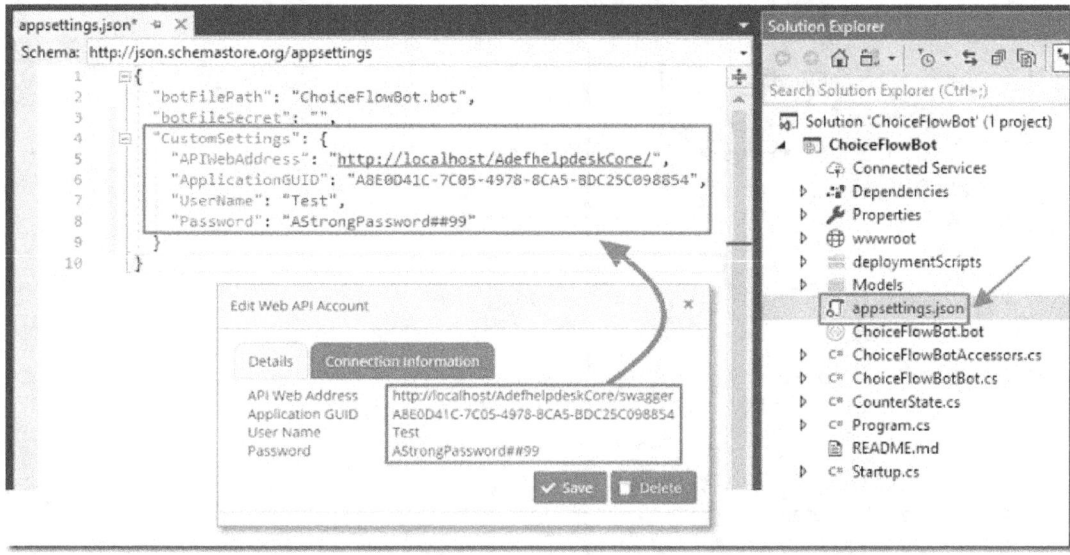

Open **appsettings.json** and change it to the following (replacing **** Your Setting **** with your own values gathered earlier):

```
{
  "botFilePath": "ChoiceFlowBot.bot",
  "botFileSecret": "",
  "CustomSettings": {
    "APIWebAddress": "** Your Setting **",
    "ApplicationGUID": "** Your Setting **",
    "UserName": "** Your Setting **",
    "Password": "** Your Setting **"
  }
}
```

Note: For the **APIWebAddress**, remove the **/swagger** part at the end.

ADefHelpDesk 4

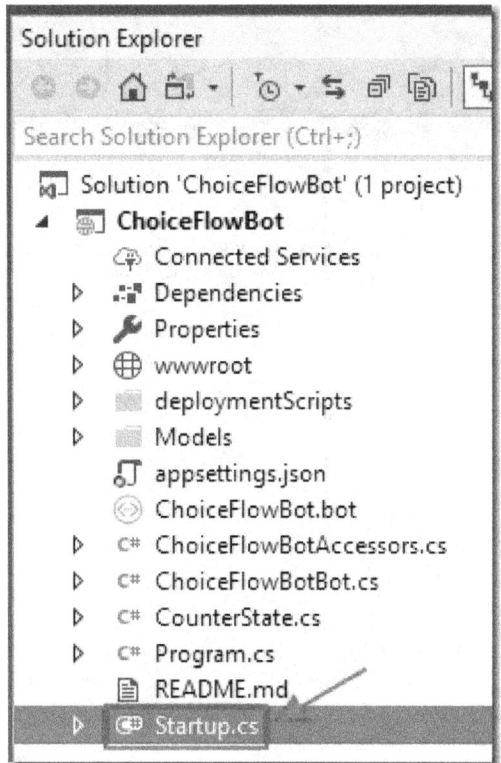

Open the **Starup.cs** file change all the code in the **public void ConfigureServices(IServiceCollection services)** method to:

```csharp
// Get the CustomSettings from appsettings.json
// allow them to be passed to any class using dependency injection
services.Configure<CustomSettings>(Configuration.GetSection("CustomSettings"));
IStorage dataStore = new MemoryStorage();
var conversationState = new ConversationState(dataStore);
services.AddSingleton(dataStore);
services.AddSingleton(conversationState);
services.AddSingleton(new BotStateSet(conversationState));
services.AddBot<ChoiceFlowBotBot>(options =>
{
    var secretKey = Configuration.GetSection("botFileSecret")?.Value;
    var botFilePath = Configuration.GetSection("botFilePath")?.Value;
    var botConfig = BotConfiguration.Load(
        botFilePath ?? @".\BotConfiguration.bot", secretKey);
    services.AddSingleton(
        sp => botConfig ?? throw new InvalidOperationException(
            $"The .bot config file could not be loaded. ({botConfig})"));
    var environment = _isProduction ? "production" : "development";
    var service = botConfig.Services.Where(
        s => s.Type == "endpoint" && s.Name == environment).FirstOrDefault();
    if (!(service is EndpointService endpointService))
    {
        throw new InvalidOperationException(
            $"The .bot file does not contain an endpoint with name '{environment}'.");
    }
    options.CredentialProvider =
    new SimpleCredentialProvider(endpointService.AppId, endpointService.AppPassword);
    options.Middleware.Add(new AutoSaveStateMiddleware(conversationState));
    ILogger logger = _loggerFactory.CreateLogger<ChoiceFlowBotBot>();
    options.OnTurnError = async (context, exception) =>
    {
        logger.LogError($"Exception caught : {exception}");
        await context.SendActivityAsync("Sorry, it looks like something went wrong.");
    };
});
```

ADefHelpDesk 4

Create The Bot Flow

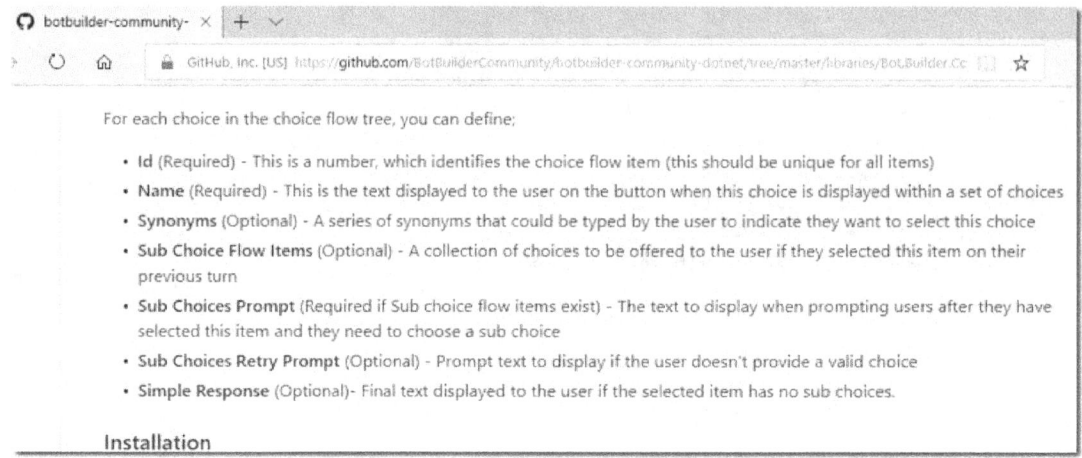

The **ChoiceFlow** component uses a **.json** file to define the *conversation flow*.

The **GitHub page** (https://github.com/BotBuilderCommunity/botbuilder-community-dotnet/tree/master/libraries/Bot.Builder.Community.Dialogs.ChoiceFlow) describes the format for the **.json** file that you use to define the **Bot**.

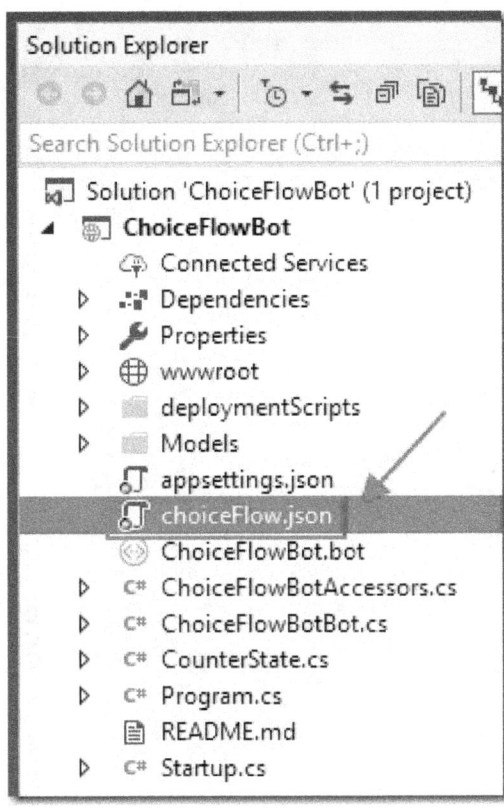

Create a file called **choiceFlow.json** using the following code:

```json
[
  {
    "name": "Top",
    "prompt": "What status type of Ticket would you like to search for?",
    "reprompt": "Choose a type from All or New",
    "id": 0,
    "choices": [
      {
        "id": 1,
        "name": "All",
        "prompt": "What Priority?",
        "choices": [
          {
            "id": 2,
            "name": "All",
            "prompt": "What assignment status?",
            "choices": [
              {
                "id": 3,
                "name": "All",
                "choices": []
              },
              {
                "id": 4,
                "name": "Unassigned",
                "choices": []
              }
            ]
          },
          {
            "id": 5,
            "name": "High",
            "prompt": "What assignment status?",
            "choices": [
              {
                "id": 6,
                "name": "All",
                "choices": []
              },
              {
                "id": 7,
                "name": "Unassigned",
                "choices": []
              }
            ]
          }
        ]
      },
```

```json
[
  {
    "id": 8,
    "name": "New",
    "prompt": "What Priority?",
    "choices": [
      {
        "id": 9,
        "name": "All",
        "prompt": "What assignment status?",
        "choices": [
          {
            "id": 10,
            "name": "All",
            "choices": []
          },
          {
            "id": 11,
            "name": "Unassigned",
            "choices": []
          }
        ]
      },
      {
        "id": 12,
        "name": "High",
        "prompt": "What assignment status?",
        "choices": [
          {
            "id": 13,
            "name": "All",
            "choices": []
          },
          {
            "id": 14,
            "name": "Unassigned",
            "choices": []
          }
        ]
      }
    ]
  }
]
```

ADefHelpDesk 4

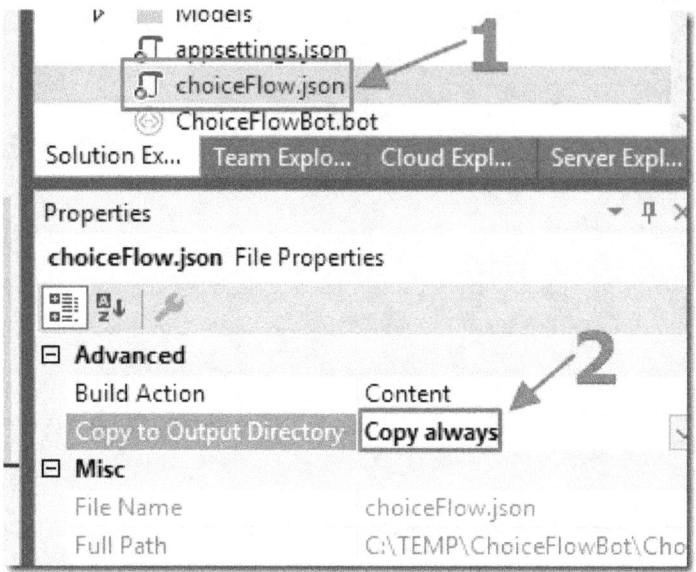

After saving the file, *click* on it, and in the **Properties**, set **Copy to Output Directory** to **Copy always**.

Create The Bot Code

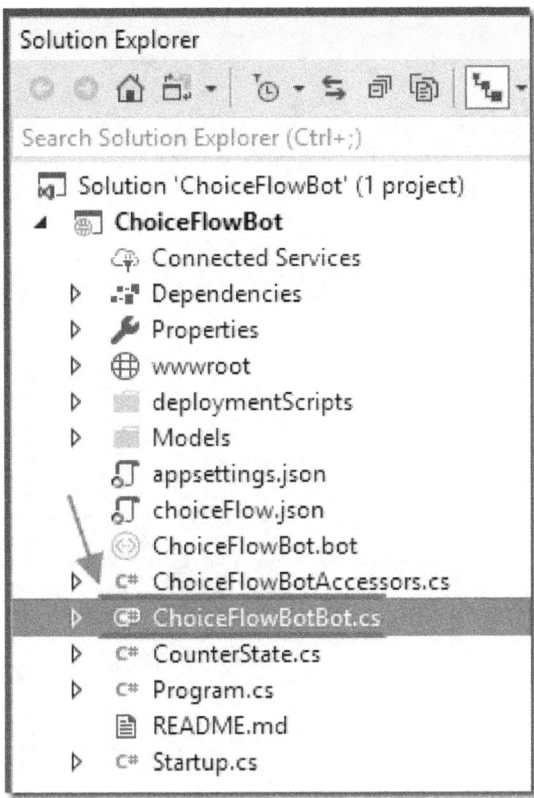

Open the **ChoiceFlowBotBot.cs** file and replace <u>all</u> the code with the following:

```csharp
using System;
using System.Collections.Generic;
using System.IO;
using System.Net.Http;
using System.Net.Http.Headers;
using System.Reflection;
using System.Text;
using System.Threading;
using System.Threading.Tasks;
using Newtonsoft.Json;
using Microsoft.Bot.Builder;
using Microsoft.Bot.Builder.Dialogs;
using Microsoft.Bot.Schema;
using Microsoft.Extensions.Logging;
using Microsoft.Extensions.Options;
using Bot.Builder.Community.Dialogs.ChoiceFlow;
namespace ChoiceFlowBot
{
    public class ChoiceFlowBotBot : IBot
    {
        // Used to make REST calls
        public static HttpClient client;
        // To store the settings from the appsettings.json file
        private CustomSettings _CustomSettings;
        // Tracks Conversation State
        private ConversationState _conversationState;
        // Holds the collection of Dialogs
        private DialogSet Dialogs { get; set; }
        public ChoiceFlowBotBot(
            ConversationState conversationState,
            IOptions<CustomSettings> CustomSettings)
        {
            // Get the custom settings using dependency injection
            _CustomSettings = CustomSettings.Value;
            // The conversation will be tracked in _conversationState
            _conversationState = conversationState ??
                throw new ArgumentNullException(nameof(conversationState));
            // Initialize the Dialogs collection
            Dialogs =
                new DialogSet(_conversationState.CreateProperty<DialogState>(nameof(ChoiceFlowBotBot)));
            // Get the path to the choiceFlow.json file that contains the flow for the Bot
            var pathToChoiceFlowJson =
                Path.Combine(Path.GetDirectoryName(Assembly.GetExecutingAssembly().Location),
                "choiceFlow.json");
            // Use the the choiceFlow.json to create the dialogs
            Dialogs.Add(new ChoiceFlowDialog(pathToChoiceFlowJson));
        }
```

```csharp
// This method is called each time the user interacts with the Bot
public async Task OnTurnAsync(
    ITurnContext turnContext,
    CancellationToken cancellationToken = default(CancellationToken))
{
    // Get the Dialogs from the current context
    // This will contain a 'stack' of Dialogs as the
    // conversation progresses
    var dc = await Dialogs.CreateContextAsync(turnContext);
    switch (turnContext.Activity.Type)
    {
        case ActivityTypes.Message:
            // If we are in the middle of a dialog continue it
            var dialogResult = await dc.ContinueDialogAsync();
            if (!dc.Context.Responded)
            {
                switch (dialogResult.Status)
                {
                    case DialogTurnStatus.Empty:
                        // If we are not in the middle of a Dialog
                        // start one
                        await dc.BeginDialogAsync("MainDialog");
                        break;
                    case DialogTurnStatus.Waiting:
                        break;
                    case DialogTurnStatus.Complete:
                        await dc.EndDialogAsync();
                        break;
                    default:
                        await dc.CancelAllDialogsAsync();
                        break;
                }
            }
            break;
    }
}
```

This sets up the *shell* of the code.

ADefHelpDesk 4

Essentially, the code initializes all the objects that will be needed such as the *dialogs* and the *conversation state*. It also loads the **choiceFlow.json** file and creates a collection of *waterfall dialog steps* from it.

(**Note:** For more information on **Dialogs**, see: **Using Dialogs (MS Bot Framework V4 Edition**: http://aihelpwebsite.com/Blog/EntryId/1032/Using-Dialogs-MS-Bot-Framework-V4-Preview-Edition).)

The code also implements the *OnTurnAsync* method that will be called each time the user interacts with the **Bot** in a conversation.

The *OnTurnAsync* will continue a conversation, by traversing the set of **Dialogs**. If it is not already in a conversation, it will start with the **MainDialog**.

We will create the code that will define the **MainDialog** in the final step.

Add The ADefHelpDesk Methods

The **Bot** will need to contact **ADefHelpDesk** to search for **Tickets**.

Before it can retrieve the **Tickets**, it needs to obtain an *authorization token* (also called a *JSON Web Token (JWT) or Bearer Token*) using the settings entered into the **appsettings.json** file and injected into the class using *dependency injection*.

To facilitate this, add the following method to the class:

```csharp
private static async Task<string> GetAuthTokenAsync(
    string APIWebAddress,
    DTOApiToken paramApiToken)
{
    // Store the final result
    string strResult = "";
    // Use the HttpClient
    using (client)
    {
        // Initialize the HttpClient
        client = new HttpClient();
        // Create a new REST request
        using (var request = new HttpRequestMessage())
        {
            // The Swagger page indicates this must be a "Post"
            request.Method = HttpMethod.Post;
            // Set the destination to the method indicated on the Swagger page
            // to: api/V1/GetAuthToken
            request.RequestUri = new Uri($"{APIWebAddress}api/V1/GetAuthToken");
            // Convert the parameters to JavaScript Object Notation (JSON) format
            var json = JsonConvert.SerializeObject(paramApiToken);
            request.Content = new StringContent(json, Encoding.UTF8, "application/json");
            // Make the request to the API endpoint on the ADefHelpDesk site
            var response = client.SendAsync(request).Result;
            // Receive the response
            var JsonDataResponse =
                await response.Content.ReadAsStringAsync();
            // Convert the response (the JWT (Auth Token)) to a String value
            strResult =
                JsonConvert.DeserializeObject<string>(JsonDataResponse);
            // Strip the word Bearer from the token
            strResult = strResult.Replace("Bearer ", " ");
        }
    }
    // Return the JWT
    return strResult;
}
```

ADefHelpDesk 4

Now, we need to add a method to the class that will use the *authentication token* to search for **Help Desk Tickets**:

```csharp
private static async Task<DTOTaskList> SearchTasksAsync(
    string APIWebAddress,
    string paramBearerToken,
    DTOSearchParameters paramDTOSearchParameters)
{
    // Store the final result
    DTOTaskList strResult = new DTOTaskList();
    // Use the HttpClient
    using (client)
    {
        // Initialize the HttpClient
        client = new HttpClient();
        // Create a new REST request
        using (var request = new HttpRequestMessage())
        {
            // The Swagger page indicates this must be a "Post"
            request.Method = HttpMethod.Post;
            // Set the destination to the method indicated on the Swagger page
            // to: api/V1/SearchTasks
            request.RequestUri = new Uri($"{APIWebAddress}api/V1/SearchTasks");
            // Pass the JWT in the 'header' of the request with the word "Bearer" in front
            client.DefaultRequestHeaders.Authorization =
                new AuthenticationHeaderValue("Bearer", paramBearerToken);
            // Convert the parameters to JavaScript Object Notation (JSON) format
            var json = JsonConvert.SerializeObject(paramDTOSearchParameters);
            request.Content = new StringContent(json, Encoding.UTF8, "application/json");
            // Make the request to the API endpoint on the ADefHelpDesk site
            var response = client.SendAsync(request).Result;
            // Handle if the JWT is expired
            if (response.StatusCode == System.Net.HttpStatusCode.Unauthorized)
            {
                strResult.errorMessage = "Unauthorized";
                return strResult;
            }
            // Receive the response
            var JsonDataResponse =
                await response.Content.ReadAsStringAsync();
            // Convert the response to a String value
            strResult =
                JsonConvert.DeserializeObject<DTOTaskList>(JsonDataResponse);
        }
    }
    // Return the response
    return strResult;
}
```

Create the MainDialog

As the final step, we will create the code that will define the **MainDialog**.

This defines the *starting point* and the *ending point* of the conversation.

At the end of the conversation, the code will call the *GetAuthTokenAsync* and *SearchTasksAsync* methods to search for **Help Desk Tickets**.

Add the following code to the end of the *ChoiceFlowBotBot* constructor method:

```csharp
Dialogs.Add(new WaterfallDialog("MainDialog", new WaterfallStep[]
{
    async (dc, cancellationToken) =>
    {
        // Start the ChoiceFlowDialog that was loaded earlier
        // This will take the conversation through the
        // 'waterfall' steps defined in the choiceFlow.json file
        return await dc.BeginDialogAsync(ChoiceFlowDialog.DefaultDialogId);
    },
    async (dc, cancellationToken) =>
    {
        // This is called after the final step
        // This is called because we have run out of 'waterfall' steps
        // that were created when we loaded the choiceFlow.json file
        if (dc.Result is ChoiceFlowItem returnedItem)
        {
            // *******
            // Get a BearerToken (JWT - Auth Token)
            // Instantiate the DTOApiToken class and set the parameters
            // using the values from CustomSettings
            DTOApiToken paramApiToken = new DTOApiToken();
            paramApiToken.userName = _CustomSettings.UserName;
            paramApiToken.password = _CustomSettings.Password;
            paramApiToken.applicationGUID = _CustomSettings.ApplicationGUID;
            // Call the GetAuthToken method and retreive the BearerToken (JWT - Auth Token)
            string BearerToken = await GetAuthTokenAsync(_CustomSettings.APIWebAddress, paramApiToken);
            // *******
            // Use the BearerToken to search the Tickets
            DTOSearchParameters objDTOSearchParameters = new DTOSearchParameters();
            objDTOSearchParameters.pageNumber = 1;
            objDTOSearchParameters.rowsPerPage = 5;
            objDTOSearchParameters.sortField = "createdDate";
            objDTOSearchParameters.sortOrder = "desc";
            objDTOSearchParameters.createdDate = "";
            objDTOSearchParameters.dueDate = "";
            objDTOSearchParameters.searchText = "";
            objDTOSearchParameters.selectedTreeNodes = new List<int>();
            // Determine what the final dialog Id is
            int intFinalDialogId = returnedItem.Id;
            // Use this chart to determine what parameters to use:
            // (Status/Priority/Assignment Status)
            // 03 - All/All/All
            // 04 - All/All/Unassigned
            // 06 - All/High/All
            // 07 - All/High/Unassigned
            // 10 - New/All/All
            // 11 - New/All/Unassigned
            // 13 - New/High/All
            // 14 - New/High/Unassigned
```

```csharp
switch (intFinalDialogId)
{
    case 3:
        objDTOSearchParameters.status = "All";
        objDTOSearchParameters.priority = "All";
        objDTOSearchParameters.assignedRoleId = "";
        break;
    case 4:
        objDTOSearchParameters.status = "All";
        objDTOSearchParameters.priority = "All";
        objDTOSearchParameters.assignedRoleId = "-1";
        break;
    case 6:
        objDTOSearchParameters.status = "All";
        objDTOSearchParameters.priority = "High";
        objDTOSearchParameters.assignedRoleId = "";
        break;
    case 7:
        objDTOSearchParameters.status = "All";
        objDTOSearchParameters.priority = "High";
        objDTOSearchParameters.assignedRoleId = "-1";
        break;
    case 10:
        objDTOSearchParameters.status = "New";
        objDTOSearchParameters.priority = "All";
        objDTOSearchParameters.assignedRoleId = "";
        break;
    case 11:
        objDTOSearchParameters.status = "New";
        objDTOSearchParameters.priority = "All";
        objDTOSearchParameters.assignedRoleId = "-1";
        break;
    case 13:
        objDTOSearchParameters.status = "New";
        objDTOSearchParameters.priority = "High";
        objDTOSearchParameters.assignedRoleId = "";
        break;
    case 14:
        objDTOSearchParameters.status = "New";
        objDTOSearchParameters.priority = "High";
        objDTOSearchParameters.assignedRoleId = "-1";
        break;
    default:
        break;
}
```

```
            // Call
            var result = await SearchTasksAsync(
                _CustomSettings.APIWebAddress,
                BearerToken,
                objDTOSearchParameters);
            int intTopMatchingCount =
            (result.totalRows > 5) ? 5 : result.totalRows;
            await dc.Context.SendActivityAsync(
                $"Here are the top {intTopMatchingCount} matching tickets... " +
                $"The total found is {result.totalRows}");
            foreach (var ticket in result.taskList)
            {
                await dc.Context.SendActivityAsync(
                    $"Ticket#{ticket.taskId} Description: {ticket.description} " +
                    $"Created: {ticket.createdDate} By: {ticket.requesterName}");
            }
        }
        return await dc.EndDialogAsync();
    }
}));
```

ADefHelpDesk 4

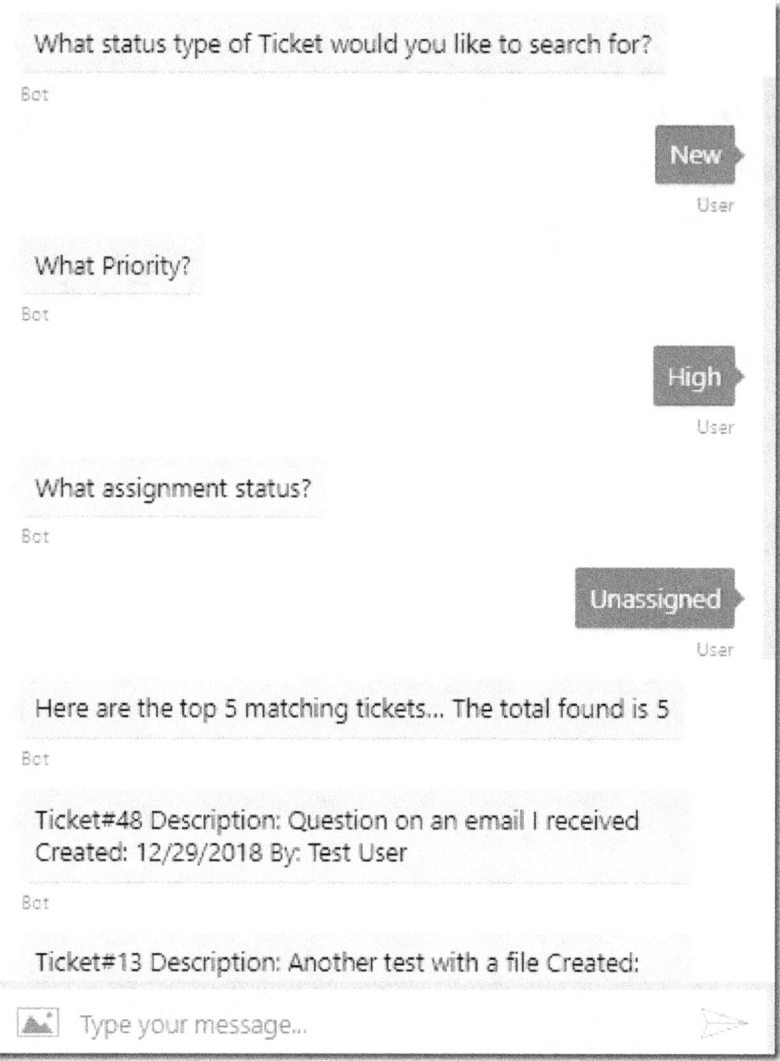

Hit **F5** to run the project.

You can now converse with the **Bot** to search **Help Desk Tickets** on **ADefHelpDesk**.

Chapter 7: Technical

Class Diagram

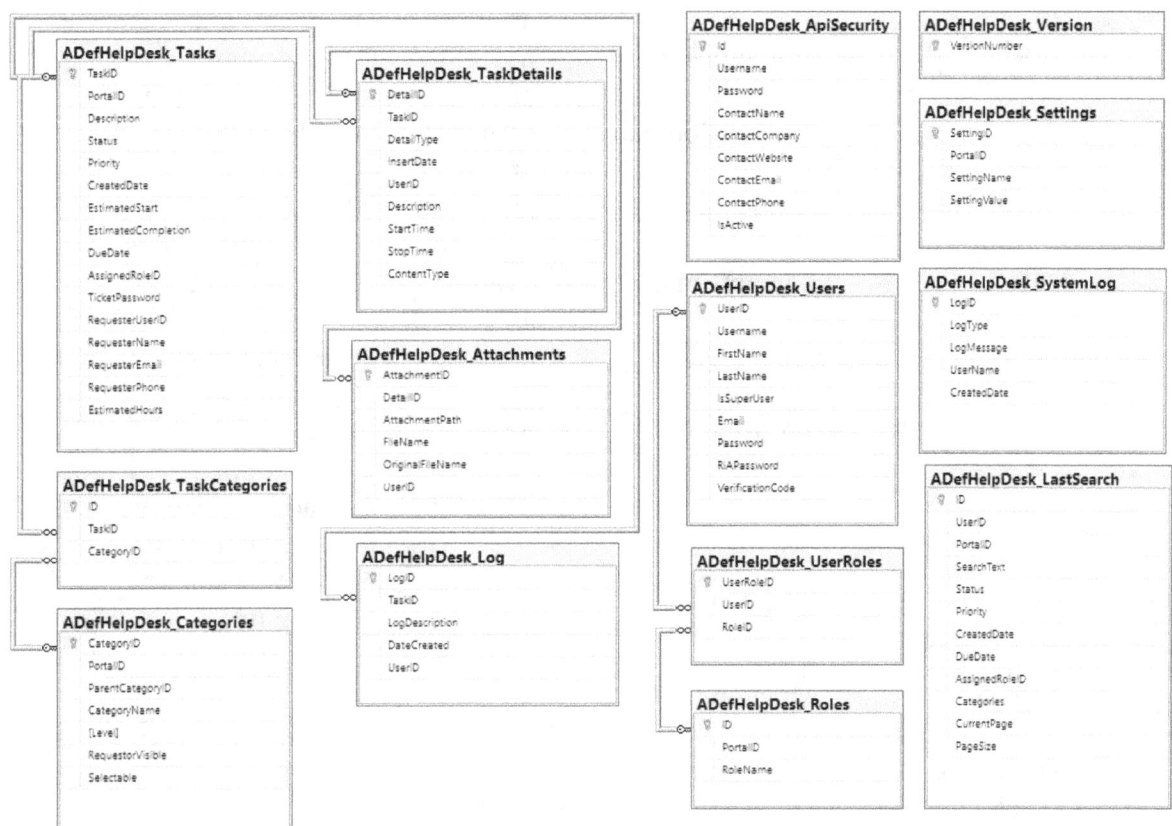

Data Dictionary

Table Name	Column Name	Data Type	Size	Description
ApiSecurity Holds the user	Id	int	4	

ADefHelpDesk 4

accounts that can access the API				
	Username	nvarchar	800	Account user name
	Password	nvarchar	800	Account password
	ContactName	nvarchar	800	Account contact name
	ContactCompany	nvarchar	800	Account company name
	ContactWebsite	nvarchar	800	Account website address
	ContactEmail	nvarchar	800	Account email address
	ContactPhone	nvarchar	800	Account phone number
	IsActive	bit	1	Indicates if account is active. Inactive accounts will not be able to log in
Attachments Tracks the attachments associated to a TaskDetails record	AttachmentID	int	4	
	DetailID	int	4	Foreign key to the TaskDetails table
	AttachmentPath	nvarchar	800	The path on the

				ar	0	file system of the attachment
		FileName	nvarchar	8000		The file name of the attachment when it is stored on the file system. This is programmatically created to be unique and avoid any file name collisions
		OriginalFileName	nvarchar	8000		The file name of the attachment that was originally uploaded. When the file is downloaded, this will be the file name that is used
		UserID	int	4		Foreign key to Users table
Categories All the possible Tags that can be associated with a Tasks record	CategoryID	int	4			
		PortalID	int	4		(future feature) Supports multiple

ADefHelpDesk 4

				instances of ADefHelpDesk
	ParentCategoryID	int	4	References CategoryID and allows nesting of Tags
	CategoryName	nvarchar	8000	Name of Tag
	Level	int	4	(deprecated) The nesting level of the Tag
	RequestorVisible	bit	1	Indicates if non-administrators can see the Tag
	Selectable	bit	1	Indicates if the Tag can be selectable. Otherwise it is a non-selectable label
LastSearch Stores the last filter settings each User Account has used on the Existing Tickets screen	ID	int	4	
	UserID	int	4	Foreign key to Users table
	PortalID	int	4	(future feature) Supports multiple

				instances of ADefHelpDesk
	SearchText	nvarchar	8000	The search text last selected in the search filter
	Status	nvarchar	8000	The status last selected in the search filter
	Priority	nvarchar	8000	The priority last selected in the search filter
	CreatedDate	datetime	8	The created date last selected in the search filter
	DueDate	datetime	8	The due date last selected in the search filter
	AssignedRoleID	int	4	Foreign key to Roles table
	Categories	nvarchar	8000	List of foreign keys to the Categories table last selected in the search filter
	CurrentPage	int	4	The page number last selected in the search filter
	PageSize	int	4	The page size last selected in the search filter
Log	LogID	int	4	

ADefHelpDesk 4

Stores activity related to a Tasks record				
	TaskID	int	4	Foreign key to the Tasks table
	LogDescription	nvarchar	8000	The log entry contents
	DateCreated	datetime	8	The date the record was created
	UserID	int	4	Foreign key to Users table
RIAUsers (deprecated) Allows users to access ADefHelpDesk from outside systems. Use ApiSecurity instead (however, do not give an individual user direct access. Use ApiSecurity to allow an outside application access and have it manage individual user access)	UserID	int	4	

	RIAPassword	nvarchar	8000	(deprecated) The password for the user
	IPAddress	nvarchar	8000	(deprecated) The IP address of the user
	CreatedDate	datetime	8	(deprecated) The date the record was created
Roles Stores all possible Roles	ID	int	4	
	PortalID	int	4	(future feature) Supports multiple instances of ADefHelpDesk
	RoleName	nvarchar	8000	Name of the Role
Settings Stores settings such as email server and upload file path	SettingID	int	4	
	PortalID	int	4	(future feature) Supports multiple instances of ADefHelpDesk
	SettingName	nvarchar	8000	Name of the

ADefHelpDesk 4

		ar	0	Setting
	SettingValue	nvarchar	8000	Value of the Setting
SystemLog Logs activity related to the entire application	LogID	int	4	
	LogType	nvarchar	8000	The type of log entry
	LogMessage	nvarchar	8000	The content of the log entry
	UserName	nvarchar	8000	The user name from the Users table
	CreatedDate	datetime	8	The date and time the log entry was created
TaskAssociations (future feature) Allows Tasks records to be related to each other	TaskRelationID	int	4	
	TaskID	int	4	(future feature) Foreign key to Tasks table
	AssociatedID	int	4	(future feature) Foreign key to Tasks table

TaskCategories Allows a Categories record to be associated with a Tasks record	ID	int	4	
	TaskID	int	4	Foreign key to Tasks table
	CategoryID	int	4	Foreign key to the Categories table
TaskDetails Stores the detail records associated with a Tasks record	DetailID	int	4	
	TaskID	int	4	Foreign key to Tasks table
	DetailType	nvarchar	800	Type of the detail record
	InsertDate	datetime	8	The date and time the detail record was created
	UserID	int	4	Foreign key to Users table
	Description	nvarchar	800	The description of the task detail record
	StartTime	datetime	8	To indicate the date and time

ADefHelpDesk 4

				the task started
	StopTime	datetime	8	To indicate the date and time the task ended
	ContentType	nvarchar	8000	If this is set to EML the contents of the EML file attachment will be displayed when the task detail record is viewed
Tasks The key record that tracks a Help Desk Ticket	TaskID	int	4	
	PortalID	int	4	(future feature) Sßupports multiple instances of ADefHelpDesk
	Description	nvarchar	8000	The description of the task record
	Status	nvarchar	8000	The status of the task record
	Priority	nvarchar	8000	The priority of the task record
	CreatedDate	datetime	8	The date and time the task record was created

	EstimatedStart	datetime	8	To indicate the date and time the task should start
	EstimatedCompletion	datetime	8	To indicate the date and time the task will end
	DueDate	datetime	8	To indicate the date and time the task is due to be completed
	AssignedRoleID	int	4	Foreign key to Role table. Will have -1 if the Ticket is not assigned to a role
	TicketPassword	nvarchar	8000	Used when the task is being accessed by a user who does not have a User Account
	RequesterUserID	int	4	Foreign key to the User table
	RequesterName	nvarchar	8000	To indicate the name of the requester when the RequesterUserID is not set
	RequesterEmail	nvarchar	8000	To indicate the email address of the requester when the

ADefHelpDesk 4

				RequesterUserID is not set
	RequesterPhone	nvarchar	800	To indicate the phone number of the requester when the RequesterUserID is not set
	EstimatedHours	int	4	To indicate the estimated hours the task will take to be completed
UserRoles Allows a Roles record to be associated with a Tasks record	UserRoleID	int	4	
	UserID	int	4	Foreign key to Users table
	RoleID	int	4	Foreign key to Role table
Users Stores the User Accounts	UserID	int	4	
	Username	nvarchar	800	Account user name
	FirstName	nvarchar	800	Account first name
	LastName	nvarchar	800	Account last name
	IsSuperUser	bit	1	Indicates if the

				User Account is the highest level of Administrator
	Email	nvarchar	800	Account email address
	Password	nvarchar	800	(deprecated) Stores password for account (ADefHelpDesk stores passwords in the AspNetUsers table)
	RIAPassword	nvarchar	800	(deprecated) Stores password for external access for the User Account
	VerificationCode	nvarchar	800	Used to store the verification code when verified registration is enabled
Version Stores the currently installed version of ADefHelpDesk	VersionNumber	varchar	800	

ADefHelpDesk 4

(used for the upgrade process)				

Creating An Install or Upgrade Package

If you build the source code of **ADefHelpDesk**, you will need to create an *installation* or an *Upgrade package* to deploy it to your production server. After creating this installation package, you can *deploy* and *install* the code according to the normal installation or upgrade instructions.

The following steps are required to create an *installation* or an *upgrade package* for your version that you will, for example, set as 04.10.00:

- Add new script to AdefHelpDesk\AdefHelpDesk\SQLScripts\
    - /** Update Version **/
      DELETE FROM ADefHelpDesk_Version
      INSERT INTO ADefHelpDesk_Version(VersionNumber) VALUES (N'04.10.00')
- In ADefHelpDeskApp\Controllers\WebApi\InstallWizardController.cs:
    - Update string TargetDatabaseVersion = "04.10.00";
    - Add an entry for the new script to UpdateScripts()
- In Visual Studio, "Publish" AdefHelpDeskBase
- Put the results in its own folder (like C:\Temp\ADefHelpDesk_04.10.00)
- Open appsettings.json and set:
    - "DefaultConnection": "data source=(local);initial catalog=ADefHelpDesk;uid=DatabaseUser;pwd=password"
- Rename Pages\IndexModelRuntime.cshtml to Pages\Index.cshtml

- Copy contents of ClientApp\dist\index.html to Pages\Index.cshtml (only update the sections marked **Update**)
- Remove the ClientApp\dist\index.html page
- Zip up and label it the Install Package

To Make an "Upgrade" Package:

Remove all the other files and directories, so you only have the contents of the following directories:

- ADefHelpDeskApp
- ClientApp
- Pages
- SQLScripts
- SystemFiles

Add a **manifest.json** file to the root directory

```
{
ManifestLowestVersion:"04.00.00",
ManifestHighestVersion:"04.00.00",
ManifestSuccess:"04.10.00 version loaded. Refresh your web browser.",
ManifestFailure:"04.00.00 is the highest version that can be upgraded with this package. This install is being cancelled."
}
```

Zip up and label it the **Upgrade Package**

About the Author

Michael Washington is an ASP.NET C# programmer. He has extensive knowledge in process improvement, billing systems, and student information systems. He is a Microsoft Reconnect MVP. He has a son, Zachary, and resides in Los Angeles with his wife, Valerie.

He is the author of the following books:

- **Azure Machine Learning Studio for The Non-Data Scientist** (AiHelpWebsite.com)
- **An Introduction to the Microsoft Bot Framework** (AiHelpWebsite.com)
- **Creating HTML 5 Websites and Cloud Business Apps Using LightSwitch In Visual Studio 2013-2015** (LightSwitchHelpWebsite.com)
- **Creating Web Pages Using the LightSwitch HTML Client In Visual Studio 2012** (LightSwitchHelpWebsite.com)
- **OData And Visual Studio LightSwitch** (LightSwitchHelpWebsite.com)
- **Creating Visual Studio LightSwitch Custom Controls (Beginner to Intermediate)** (LightSwitchHelpWebsite.com)
- **Building Websites with VB.NET and DotNetNuke 4** (Packt Publishing)
- **Building Websites with DotNetNuke 5** (Packt Publishing)

www.ingramcontent.com/pod-product-compliance
Lightning Source LLC
Chambersburg PA
CBHW080905170526
45158CB00008B/2000